THROUGH THE
RUSSIAN REVOLUTION

By
ALBERT RHYS WILLIAMS

With a Biographical Sketch of the Author
By
JOSHUA KUNITZ

*Illustrated with Russian Posters in Color
and Photographs*

MONTHLY REVIEW PRESS
New York and London

First published 1921 in New York

Reprinted 1967 by Monthly Review Press
116 West 14th Street, New York, New York 10011

Original copyright 1921 by Albert Rhys Williams
Biographical sketch copyright © 1967
by Monthly Review Press

Library of Congress Catalog Card Number 67-19257 .
Manufactured in the U.S.A.

To

THE WORKERS AND PEASANTS OF RUSSIA
WHO FELL IN DEFENSE OF THE REVOLUTION

"Against riches, power and knowledge for the few you began a
war, and with glory you died in
order that riches, power and knowledge should become universal."

CONTENTS

v

PART III

THE OUTREACH OF THE REVOLUTION

ACROSS SIBERIA ON THE EXPRESS

PART IV.

THE TRIUMPH OF THE REVOLUTION

THE SOVIETS AGAINST THE CAPITALIST WORLD

PHOTOGRAPHS AND POSTERS

ALBERT RHYS WILLIAMS

A BIOGRAPHICAL SKETCH

BY JOSHUA KUNITZ

I

In the middle of June, 1917, a little over three months after the hungry, war-weary Russian masses overthrew the ancient tsarist tyranny, Albert Rhys Williams, a thirty-three-year-old Congregationalist minister from Boston, Mass., a handsome, blue-eyed giant, crossed the Finnish border and plunged headlong into the whirlpool of revolutionary Petrograd. A few days later, he jotted down in his notebook:

Socialism is in the air! Socialism is on every tongue! You can scarcely have a talk with a Russian without socialism being mentioned in one way or another. Their socialist erudition is astounding and their devotion thrilling.

Petrograd was then in the grip of a crisis. Tension between the Provisional Government and the most radical elements of the population was nearing explosion. Workers were parading in the streets crying the Bolshevik slogan, "All Power to the Soviets!" challenging not only the Provisional Government but the other potential locus of political authority—the Soviet—as well: for the Menshevik and Socialist Revolutionist majority in the latter were quite unwilling to assume the responsibility of state power. The Bolsheviks were aggressive, their opponents in the Soviet in a state of paralysis, while Kerensky and his ministerial colleagues tried to hide their impotence by resounding speeches and promises of a great victorious offensive against the Germans.

Having just arrived, Williams was unable to evaluate the merits of the various brands of Russian socialism. But it apparently took him no time to decide that as between the two foci of power crystallized by the Revolution—the Provisional Government and the deputies of the Soviet of Workers, Peasants, and Soldiers—he definitely preferred the latter.

A couple of weeks after his arrival, we see him on the rostrum of the All-Russian Congress of Soviets, hailing the Revolution, extolling its promise to translate into reality "the beautiful words Equality, Brotherhood, Democracy," urging an immediate advance "from political to economic tasks," declaring that henceforth the workers of the world will look for inspiration and guidance "no longer to the West, but to the East, toward great Russia, to the Field of Mars here in Petrograd, where lie the first martyrs of your Revolution," and concluding with the ringing slogans: "Long Live Free Russia! Long Live the Revolution! Long Live Peace in the World!"

Quite a debut for a Christian minister from capitalist, imperialist America—and a fitting start for the great adventure that lay ahead of him.

It is unnecessary to dwell on the details of the

adventure, for they are adequately recorded in the text of this volume. A brief outline will do.

Williams spent the months of July and August studying the language, poring over the controversies in the press, interviewing representatives of various parties, cultivating friendships among English-speaking Russians, accompanying them to homes, factories, military barracks, joining them on trips to Moscow, the Ukraine, villages along the Volga— and always, without cease, seeking to capture the mood and the thoughts of the war-ravaged, hungry, sullen masses.

By the middle of September he was ready to assert to his friends among the American newsmen that the Bolsheviks were the only ones who made sense and that they enjoyed the overwhelming support of the Russian people. Except for Bolshevik-oriented John Reed, who had just come to Russia, and for Bessie Beatty, who had high regard for Williams' talents as an observer, the American correspondents thought him mad. Williams dismissed as nonsensical their charges that the Bolsheviks were financed by the Kaiser and that Lenin was a spy and a traitor; he reaffirmed his belief that the Bolsheviks were articulating the will of the masses, the will for peace, and bread, and Soviet rule. A visit to the front and to the Baltic Fleet strengthened this belief.

When the Bolsheviks seized power and stirred the Russian masses into a world-shaking upheaval, an upheaval whose reverberations are still being felt on every continent on this globe and even in outer space, virtually all the Americans in Petrograd were filled with disgust and dismay. A few were jubilant, and foremost amongst them John Reed and Williams.

All through the October days prior, during, and immediately after the Bolshevik seizure of power, Williams seemed to be everywhere, to see everything. He was at the Winter Palace when it fell to the Bolsheviks. He was at the Second Congress of Soviets when the Bolsheviks officially assumed power, and there heard Lenin deliver his famous Decree on Peace. Several days later he was at the telephone station where the forces of reaction made their first spectacular attempt to wrest power back from the Bolsheviks, and where he played a dramatic part in the rescue of the military cadets from the enraged crowd. He appeared at factory meetings and addressed vast gatherings all over the revolutionary capital. And all the time he kept a diary in which he recorded not only the events, but his feelings and actions.

One note jotted down a few days after the great event expressed his feelings beautifully:

I am dismayed by the utter inability of my fellow Americans here, with the exception of John Reed, Louise Bryant, Bessie Beatty, and Raymond Robins, to rightly assess the phenomenon with which they—diplomats, correspondents, armymen, scholars, businessmen—are supposed to deal: the magnitude and significance of what is passing before them, the strength and urgency of the

demands and aspirations of the Russian masses. They have a ring-
side seat at a most colossal drama, but they are totally unaware of
what is really happening. They are in the presence of a magnificent
sunrise, the sky is shot through with riotous colors, but they are
blind with prejudice and bigotry.

The note was more than a passing emotional outburst. It was, we now recognize, a prevision of unhappy American-Soviet relations for decades to
come. It was also, we can now see, a personal com-
mitment to aid, protect, and defend the October
Revolution, and to do everything in his power to
make the world and particularly his own country
conscious of its magnitude and significance.

With each passing day relations between the
United States and the new regime worsened. The
representatives of American official and commercial
life in Petrograd were for the most part bitterly
hostile to Bolshevism and looked disapprovingly at
Williams' conduct. They were quite incensed when
he and Bessie Beatty—after serving at the request
of Colonel Raymond Robins (head of the American
Red Cross mission in Russia) on a committee which
investigated charges that the Bolsheviks were mal-
treating political prisoners in Peter and Paul Fortress—found the charges absolutely false, and signed
a statement to that effect which was published in
Pravda. But Williams, along with Bessie Beatty,
Reed, and Louise Bryant, was undeterred in his
enthusiastic support of the Bolsheviks.

Williams and Reed worked side by side in the Commissariat for Foreign Affairs, preparing insurrectionary anti-war propaganda that was disseminated among the German soldiers at the front. And all the time both were under the constant surveillance of sleuths from the American embassy. Later, when the Germans advanced against Petrograd, Williams (Reed had by then left for the USA), on Lenin's suggestion, helped organize an international brigade to defend the Revolutionary capital.

Williams stayed on in Russia for almost a year, several months longer than Reed, Louise Bryant, and Bessie Beatty. During his trip through Siberia on his way home, he was gratified to find the Soviet regime solidly established along the 4,000-mile route, and the name of Lenin signed on his pass acted as an open sesame wherever he went. Vladivostok, like Petrograd, was ruled by a Soviet. Williams decided to linger in the city for a few weeks.

He was there when the American fleet came into the harbor. He witnessed the fall of the Vladivostok Soviet before the advance of the Allied interventionists. Just before that tragic event, he published in the local paper a remarkably prophetic piece warning the Allies against intervention, pointing to the tremendous popularity of the Bolshevik regime among the masses, and asserting that the venture would ultimately fail and that the result would be needless bloodshed and devastation which would poison Allied-Russian relations for years to come.

He was arrested, his first draft of *Through the Russian Revolution* was confiscated, and he was forced to leave posthaste.

He was not too sorry to go, eager as he was to bring to the people of America the glad tidings of the "magnificent sunrise" he had seen and to warn them against support of the foreign intervention.

Getting back to the States, however, was not a simple matter. Williams had bought passage through Japan, but the Japanese authorities, forewarned of his dangerous connections, stopped him at the Korean frontier. He then decided to return via China. But upon arriving there, he discovered that he did not have enough money for passage. An urgent cable to his friend Upton Sinclair brought no immediate response. He was stuck in Peking for some time. When the money finally arrived he went to Shanghai, where he caught the steamer *Nanking*, which was headed for San Francisco.

On August 28, 1918, the *Nanking* touched Honolulu. Local agents of Naval Intelligence boarded the ship, seized his trunk crammed with Soviet papers and documents which he had managed to salvage upon leaving Vladivostok, and subjected him to gruelling questioning. Their report to the Director of Naval Intelligence in Washington, dated August 29, was crammed with scarifying details:

Conspicuous with the Soviet Government in which he has taken an active part, . . . he has been reported as being strongly anti-American, and has criticized American policies and the President openly . . . has been violently opposed to any Inter-Allied Expedition into Siberia and is especially opposed to Japanese intervention in any form. . . . He has written extensively defending the Soviet form of Government, and his papers taken from him here show his close association with the Bolsheviki. . . . He had been in the process of writing on the steamer an article designed to influence the American people against the Inter-Allied Expedition into Siberia, which was to be published on his arrival in America. . . . There is no question that Williams has worked hard against international intervention in Russia and that he will do all he can to oppose it if allowed liberty in America.

Among the incriminating papers found on him, the report lists some truly horrendous ones: "His Socialist Party membership card; a letter from Morris Hillquit, International Secretary of the Socialist Party of the United States, speaking of Williams' prominence in the Socialist movement; a letter written by Robert Minor, leading Socialist now in Moscow; a card from Comrade Huysmans, Secretary of the Internationalist Socialist Bureau, of the Hague; [and] most important, [an] official authorization, signed by the Provisional Soviet Commissariat for Foreign Affairs, to establish a Bureau of Information" in the United States, and "to employ a staff for this purpose." To this the report adds: "The possible danger of establishing such a bureau is too evident to comment on." In conclusion, the Director of Naval Intelligence is told that all the information has been wirelessed to 12th Naval District in San Francisco, warning it "of his approach."

Actually the authorities in the Navy, the Army, and the State Department, had known about Williams' Bureau assignment almost since the day it was made. It was no deep secret. In the spring of 1918 there was still an American Information Bureau in Moscow, and at that time the Soviet authorities and Williams himself thought that a corresponding Soviet Bureau in Washington would create no difficulties. So everything was open and aboveboard and widely reported in the Soviet papers. The news reached the American military attaché in Stockholm, and he hastened to relay it to Washington, in a message dated May 21, 1918. In the message, the attaché first described most inaccurately Williams' visit to the Baltic Fleet (the visit took place *before* the October Revolution, but the attaché places it *after*) and the "inflammatory" speeches he delivered before the sailors and soldiers in Finland. "Among other things," the report reads, "he was telling them what a terrible country the United States was and that he had come to Finland and Russia in order to learn how they caused their revolution so that he might be instrumental in accomplishing the same thing in the United States." After a few more fabrications and irrelevancies, he comes to the point: "My main object in bringing this matter up now is not to refer to the past but to refer to what is being rumored for the future. It is clear that Williams is about to be, if he has not

already been, sent to America via Vladivostok as
the head of a so-called Russian Information Bureau.
He is proceeding not only with all possible information but also with propaganda films. . . ." This
startling revelation was relayed by Rear Admiral
Roger Welles to A. Bruce Bielaski, of the Bureau of
Investigation in the Department of Justice. So was
the August 29 report from Honolulu.

Everybody was put on guard: the arch Bolshevik
plotter and subversive Reverend Albert Rhys Williams was about to land in San Francisco!

II

When, forty-four years after the events recounted
in the preceding pages, Albert Rhys Williams died,
William Blake, economist, sociologist, novelist, and
all-round literary man, sent the following beautiful
tribute from Surrey, England:

> What a loss! Of all the books about Russia his were the most
> valuable, and the ones that best endure after so much new evidence,
> so many new focuses. He had that rare quality—that of being
> *magisterial* without being pompous. By his name he must have
> been of Welsh origin—he had their magic quality, a sort of chant
> of reason.

The reader must have sensed this magic quality,
this chant of reason, in Williams' hastily scribbled
note quoted earlier; he will find it resounding on

every page in this book. In his unpublished autobiographical writings Williams himself implies that
this quality is Welsh; at least, he puts immense
stress on the Welsh element in his background, experience, and values, and on Welsh conditioning in
his formative years.

Albert Rhys Williams was born in the USA, in
the State of Ohio, in the year 1883. On the paternal
side, he stemmed from a long line of Welsh miners;
on the maternal side, from a long line of Welsh
Congregationalist ministers. Both parents were
born in Wales: his father, David Thomas, came to
the United States in 1863, when he was a boy of
eleven; his mother, Esther Reese or Rhys, came
when she was twenty-four. David Thomas was
fourteen when he joined the other Williamses in the
mines of Youngstown, Ohio, and he was twenty-one
when he decided that he had had enough of the mines
and began to study for the ministry. He worked
his way through prep school and college, receiving
his B.A. degree from Western Reserve University
in 1880. He met and married Esther in June of that
year, a couple of weeks before he entered the theological seminary. In 1883, upon receiving the Divinity degree (Oberlin), David Thomas was called
to assume charge of the Congregational Church in
Greenwich, Ohio. There Albert Rhys, the second
son, was born on September 28 of that year. Later
two more sons were born.

The Williamses did not stay long in Greenwich. A restive family, they moved from one small agricultural or industrial community to another almost every two years, now in Ohio, now in Pennsylvania, now in upper New York. But wherever they moved, they formed a little Welsh enclave, where their proletarian and clerical tradition was kept inviolate, and "where Welsh speech, Welsh songs, Welsh tales, and Welsh memories of 'back home' filled the air with a sweet nostalgia."

In Albert Rhys' own mind most that was good in him and in his brothers originated in this Welsh enclave—"a flair for freedom, independence, rebelliousness, reverence for learning, love for the arts, humor, gentleness, hatred for war and imperial conquest, appreciation for other peoples' traditions and cultures," and above all "service." If he went into the ministry, it was due to the family's Welsh tradition: his three brothers also went into the ministry. If, while still in college, he was drawn to socialism, it was due to the family's Welsh tradition: two of his three brothers also became Socialists while still in their teens. To be sure, he never mentioned the "chant of reason" as a feature of the enclave. But he might have, since the beautiful life and tradition he described do indeed suggest a perpetual chant of reason.

But, of course, his experience was not confined to the enclave, nor was the enclave itself hermetically sealed off from the world outside. There were the streets where Albert played with other children; there were the gardens where in the company of other boys he picked peas and beans in return for "wages"; there were the ponds and the rivers where with gangs of boys he spent whole days fishing, boating, floating rafts, and swimming; there were the fields and forests where they went to pick berries, nuts, and mushrooms; and, above all, there was the little red, one-room schoolhouse where Albert imbibed a love for America, its history, its heroes, and its dream with an eagerness few of the other children could match.

And, finally, far away and as yet vaguely felt, but felt nevertheless, was the impact of the America of great cities, great industries, great banks, great struggles, great scandals, great social unrest, and great movements for reform or radical change. It should be noted that Albert lived his youth in an historic period of momentous upheaval in the United States. The two last decades of the nineteenth century and the early years of the twentieth saw economic crises, financial panics, and political scandals recur with deadly regularity. Violent clashes between capital and labor—strikes, lockouts, pitched battles at factory gates—were the order of the day: between 1883 (when Williams was born) and 1907 (when he completed his academic and professional education) no less than 40,000 strikes occurred.

There was also ominous unrest in the countryside, where mortgage indebtedness was growing, prices for produce were collapsing, and where, in the nineties alone, about 28 percent of the once independent American farmers had sunk to the status of tenants, sharecroppers, peasants. In the cities, dwellers in the rapidly proliferating slums, recent immigrants most of them, were in unhappy ferment.

Among the more thoughtful elements of the population the emergence of the United States as an aggressive imperialist power after the war with Spain generated feelings of fear and foreboding. There was mounting cynicism about the glittering promises of the "American dream." The lofty rhetoric about justice, freedom, equality, and opportunity, about a perfect American social order bringing inspiration and hope to suffering humanity everywhere, began to sound tired and flat to more and more ears. Disillusionment was widespread. Disaffection was rife. Hosts of reformers, radicals, union organizers, muckrakers, social theorists, and liberal churchmen created spiritual and intellectual turmoil and provoked a loud clamor for change.

Campaigns were waged against the concentration and abuse of power in the hands of "malefactors of great wealth," against trusts and monopolies and imperialist adventures, against the unspeakable corruption of politics, against the blight of proliferating slums, against "political bosses," sweatshops, child labor, against every other social evil, including the spoliation of the country's natural resources. Scholars emerged from their cabinets, religious leaders from their sanctums, poets and artists from their ivory towers, to grapple with these social evils.

Intimately connected with this general upheaval was a mighty upsurge in labor organization and in socialist agitation. A few figures should suffice as reminders. In the four years between 1896 and 1900, union membership nearly doubled, reaching a total of 868,000; and in the next four years it more than doubled again, jumping to more than 2,000,000. The Socialist Party ticket, led by Eugene V. Debs, polled 96,878 votes in the national elections of 1900. This number jumped to 420,000—an increase of over 400 percent—in the national elections four years later.

Socialist publications multiplied. Membership in the Socialist Party grew by leaps and bounds. Among the most active recruits were scores of Christian ministers, mostly Protestants, who were zealous to work for a truly humane, truly just society. Most of these ministers came to the Socialist Party via Christian socialism, a movement that was generated within the Church itself.

Back in the small agricultural and industrial communities surrounding the Williams enclave the mode of life and prevailing attitudes still bore the earmarks of an innocence that elsewhere had all but

disappeared. Teachers and preachers still intoned
the faded rhetoric of the American dream which
young Albert accepted as divine truth. But even
so the enclave was not entirely immune to the occasional tremors from the turbulent beyond, and
these did impinge ever more insistently on the growing boy's consciousness. As a child, when many of
the Williams clan still worked in the mines, he often
listened to conversations with visiting kinsmen about
wages, strikes, unions, scabs, and violence, and his
heart went out to the relatives who had to bear all
these terrible things. He was very young when he
realized that the family income depended on the
uncertain incomes of the workers and farmers in
his father's parish, and he shared his father's worries
about strikes, unemployment, cuts in wages, bad
crops, falling produce prices, and foreclosed mort-
gages. He heard bitter talk about "the Company"
or "the Trust" and developed a dislike for them and
a corresponding admiration for those who resisted
them. In an autobiographical note, Williams recalls
a strike in a neighboring company town. The
strikers' families were evicted from the company
houses. It was winter. In defiance of the company's wrath, David Thomas threw his church open
to the evicted families. Williams speaks proudly
of the "heroic gesture" and of the devotion with
which his father and mother tended to the unhappy
people during the many days they lived in the

church. To young Albert these and similar episodes seemed only local troubles; he never thought of them as symptoms of a grave national malaise.

Albert was in his last year in high school and going on fifteen when reverberations of two events occurring in the other, the still unknown America, intruded into the periphery of his consciousness.

The first was the appearance, sometime in January, 1898, of Socialist posters on the main street of Hancock, New York—in anticipation of the elections that were to take place ten months later. Socialism had heretofore been unheard of in Hancock and the posters with their alien-sounding appeal to "class struggle" created something of a sensation. Whether inspired by others or on their own initiative, a gang of high school kids went out to tear down those posters. Albert, who did not know what socialism was and who had no feeling about it one way or another, could not resist joining in the fun. "I went at it with verve," he recalls, "in the gay spirit of youthful vandalism." Still, the word "Socialism" stuck in his mind.

The second was the news of the sinking of the USS *Maine* in the Havana harbor and the patriotic fervor that swept the town when the United States declared war on Spain. Fighting began on May 1, 1898, just when Albert was in the midst of his final examinations, and it lasted only twelve weeks. Those were delirious days of parades and marches and flowery orations about American military prowess, democratic ideals, and dedication to justice. Albert was not temperamentally a chauvinist, but being a normal boy he could not withstand the appeal of such martial music as Sousa's "Stars and Stripes Forever" played by the bands and the rag-time march "There'll Be a Hot Time in the Old Town Tonight" that was being banged on every piano in Hancock. Still, he had some instinctive reservations about the glory of war.

Naturally, he saw no connection between the posters he had gleefully destroyed and the stirring beat of Sousa's march; he had no idea that he had been introduced to the two polar extremes of the emerging twentieth century—socialism and modern imperialism.

Williams was fourteen years and nine months old when he was graduated from high school in Hancock at the top of his class. Too young to get the most out of college, he was sent for a year to a prep school. He spent another year working in a general store in Apex, New York. The store was connected with a sawmill and a lumber yard—all owned by one man. It was a hard job, with long hours and little pay, but educationally it was worth years of college.

Recalling his experiences in Apex, Williams wrote:

This was my first intimate contact with a community of workers, Italian, German, Irish, and native American. Primitive, raw, uncouth, at first glance, they turned out to be at base not too much different from other cross sections of society. They weren't commonplace. (There are no commonplace people if you scratch the surface.) There was among these men about the same proportion of strong, outstanding characters as you will find in any group; the same quota of the bizarre, the dreamers, and the depraved.

Williams had just turned seventeen when he entered Marietta College, a Congregationalist school in Marion, Ohio. By then he was much more learned in books and experienced in the ways of the world than most of his contemporaries from the American hinterland. And though he had to work to support himself, this scarcely affected the quality of his academic work. He was always near or at the top of his class. He found time to engage in athletics, and soon became captain of the basketball team. He also found time to write for the college literary magazine and became one of its editors. His favorite subjects were, as they had been in high school, history and literature. But the subjects that really opened new horizons were sociology, economics, and philosophy, and these he pursued with special zeal. This was reflected in the remarkably mature articles he wrote for the college magazine —on new trends in penology, on factory laws and child labor, on woman suffrage. However, according to Williams himself, the two most important things he learned during the four years at Marietta—the fundamentals of socialism, and the problems and methods of labor organization—were learned off campus.

He first heard and thrilled to the socialist message from a street corner orator and from a picturesque German butcher. The butcher, particularly, left an indelible impression, and Williams' description of him is so colorful and affords so vivid a glimpse into the passions of the times that it merits reproduction:

The first deeply disturbing man I met while I was at college was in East Liverpool, famous pottery town, whither I used to go occasionally with my basketball team. And he was a butcher who first gave me *The Appeal to Reason,* the socialist paper.

From under the counter he drew forth pamphlets and papers—and presented them to me in a low confidential voice. All very secret and conspiratorial.

Later I often saw him dilating lustily on the current capitalist villains—Rockefeller, Morgan, Harriman—his meat axe or cleaver poised in the air, then bringing it crashing down with extra vigor on a beef joint or neck of a chicken—doubtlessly serving in lieu of a capitalist, almost guillotining his thumb along with the capitalist who lay on the chopping block.

He was deeply convinced that the condition of the world was of chief and primary concern; that all other problems and concerns were irrelevant so long as this was unsolved; and that all these philosophers, religionists, and mystics served to anodyne [*sic*] the mind or deflect it from the main issue.

He was sincerely agitated over the state of the world and was therefore a good agitator.

He was the first one to mention to me the name of Eugene V. Debs. And he was the first to suggest the antithetical nature of Imperialism and Socialism, when he read to me what Debs had said about our war with Spain and our conquest of the Philippines. The lines he quoted I have used many times since. They were: "We are opposed to war, but if it ever becomes necessary for us to enlist in the murderous business, it will be to wipe out

capitalism, the common enemy of the oppressed and downtrodden of all nations." And—"We are making a market over there in the Orient for the products of half-paid labor in this country; making the market by the force of arms and at the expense of the lives of a people whose only offense has been their love of freedom and self-control."

Up to and including his junior year, Williams worked part time in a local haberdashery, and had the opportunity to observe the inhumanly long hours, including Sundays, that the retail clerks in the town worked, and the miserable pay they got. There was talk of a union under AFL auspices. Williams leapt at the idea. He became one of the organizers and charter members of a local branch of the first retail clerks' union in the country. In his notes he recalls that in 1904 when he left Marion, "carrying the A.B. diploma in my bag and the union membership card in my pocket, I was as proud of the little card as of the august parchment."

Incidentally, his valedictory address at the graduation exercises bore a title characteristic of the period as well as the valedictorian: "Altruism and Egoism in Politics"; it was a plea for political action motivated by a spirit of service, social justice, and concern for the laboring masses.

Williams was exactly twenty-one when, with many misgivings, he entered the Hartford Theological Seminary in the fall of 1904.

III

In accordance with preconceptions shaped by historical, cultural, and ideological conditions, Williams' friends in the Soviet Union never wearied of playing up his "miner" heritage, but uttered scarcely a word about his religious-clerical heritage, and none at all about the fact that prior to his coming to Russia, he had spent almost thirteen years in studying for and working in the Christian ministry. The following, taken from the warmly appreciative introduction to the latest Russian edition of *Through the Russian Revolution*, is typical:

> The offspring of a hereditary miner's family, he was keenly interested in the Russian Revolution, the newly liberated people. The paper he wrote on graduating from college bore the title "Altruism and Egoism in Politics" and was a passionate appeal for political action, full of sympathy for the toiling masses. Later Williams probed a bit into socialist and communist teachings, and was attracted to them. But he still lacked a firm world outlook. Drawn by what was taking place in Russia he dove into the revolutionary maelstrom, and it was the Revolution, which he observed with searching, keen, unprejudiced eyes, that became his political school.

This unfortunate passage belongs to the pen of a renowned Soviet novelist, Boris Polevoy. His simplistic theory of class determinism has led him to evade certain relevant facts. So out went a good part of the Williams story—not only the most dramatic and revealing chapter in his tortuous development as a socialist and a writer, but also a most interesting episode in the history of American radicalism. And instead of the richly representative yet brilliantly unique American phenomenon that was Albert Rhys Williams, the Soviet reader is given a paper cut-out.

It is not true that Williams lacked a "firm world outlook" when he came to Russia. To be sure, he was no Marxist materialist and certainly no Leninist-Communist, but he was a thoroughly convinced socialist internationalist, firm and dedicated. This socialist-internationalist outlook was marked by two characteristic, distinctly personal features in Williams—an all-pervasive populist mystique and an absolute freedom from any trace of dogmatic rigidity or party elitism. This very individual world outlook was an organic part of his personality, a natural outgrowth of his total experience. It was rooted not only in the proletarian, but also in the humanist, libertarian, and deeply religious tradition of his Welsh background; it was enriched by the democratic-egalitarian ideals of the American dream, was strengthened by exposure to the conflicting currents of American reality, was intellectually structured by much delving into books on socialism and related subjects, was tempered by years of frustrating efforts to combat the evils of capitalist America by a dedicated application of the ethics and theology of the Christian faith, was given final shape by the

sight at close range of the savagery unleashed by
capitalism when it plunged humanity into the First
World War. Williams was introduced before the
Congress of Soviets as a socialist internationalist
from America, and that he was with every fiber of
his being. And he observed the revolution not with
"unprejudiced" eyes, but quite definitely with socialist-internationalist eyes. How otherwise could
he have so completely identified with it, so won-
drously recreated it?

Doubtless, as Polevoy says, the Russian Revolution was a school for Williams as for everyone exposed to it. But in that school different people
learned different things, depending on different tem-
peraments, apperceptions, philosophies, and earlier
experiences. Williams came to Russia a non-Marxist
and a non-Communist, he left it a non-Marxist and
non-Communist, and he remained a non-Marxist
and non-Communist for the rest of his life. In 1953,
in an unpublished note found in his files, he wrote:

I never attempted to join and never was a member of the
Communist Party. For one thing Communism is incompatible and
alien to me on philosophical grounds. If I adhere to any school
of thought it is to Humanism and not to Dialectical Materialism.
. . . Plenty of opportunity was afforded me and even pressures
exerted on me to join the C.P. Lenin himself once suggested that
I join a Marxist and Communist study group which he would lead,
but he did not succeed in enticing me into it. And John Reed once
stayed up all night alternately trying to cajole and coerce me
into joining the Party, and he also failed. All other pressures
exerted on me in this direction failed similarly. . . . Besides philo-

sophic objections, there were other cogent reasons for my resistance, one of them being the discovery, at the cost of considerable
pain, that by temperament, nature, and disposition I am not a
joiner.

Throughout the introduction Polevoy links the
names of Williams and Reed as the two great American partisans of the Bolshevik Revolution. This is
just. But nowhere does he note the difference in the
philosophical and organizational principles each drew
from the Revolution. To have noted the difference
would have confronted him with a conundrum:
Reed, the offspring of a prosperous upper-middle-
class family, responded to the lessons of the Revolution with no reservations, avowing Marxism, joining the Party, and remaining a zealous Communist
to the day of his death; while Williams, "the offspring of a hereditary miner's family," responded
no less enthusiastically but, as we have seen, selec-
tively and with some fundamental reservations. To
him, it seems, the Revolution proved primarily to
have been a school in the pragmatic *application* of
concepts and principles he had brought with him
—socialist, internationalist, populist, democratic,
egalitarian—principles and concepts he had discovered and accepted much earlier, in quite different schools, not the least important of which was, of
all places, the Hartford Theological Seminary!

As we have previously indicated, Williams entered
the Seminary with grave misgivings. The years in

college had opened up so many intellectual horizons
he yearned to explore, and had revealed in him such
a variety of talents—oratorical, athletic, literary,
and organizational—he longed to put to immediate
practical use, that another three years of school,
any narrowly professional school, seemed not at all
alluring. Also he had some doubts about the ministry as a profession, sharing to some extent the
opinion of many of his classmates that the ministry
was an escape from the challenge of an active life
and was "not a man's job." On a more fundamental
level, he feared that his religious feeling lacked the
intensity and fervor required of a minister. He was
troubled by the realization that no matter how hard
he tried he had never been able to achieve the "conviction of personal sin," or the sense of "conversion"
and "salvation" which he had heard his father so
often urge upon his flock. Even the figure of Jesus,
so real and appealing when Williams was a little
boy, had soon begun to dim and seem alien, because
of the "strange mysticism," as he later wrote, "in
which Father's orthodoxy enwrapped him, the 'im-
maculate conception,' the 'Resurrection,' the 'Ascen-
sion,' etc." Finally, he had some doubts concerning
the role of the Church, "its passivity to the real pains
of the real world."

In short, he felt he was unfit, and he told that
much to his family. To soften the blow, he agreed
to "take a year in the Seminary—a year of proba-

tion." He wrote to Alfred T. Perry, the President of
Marietta College, telling him of his doubts and his
decision, and asking for advice as to which Seminary
to enter. President Perry urged Albert not to worry
about fitness: "It is not a question of fitness, but of
the Master's will. If you are willing to be guided,
He will guide you." The President also warned
against Union Theological Seminary in New York,
first, because "the spirit of controversy is strong
there," and, second, because of the "radical attitude"
of some of the faculty. He recommended Hartford
Seminary, because of the "warm spiritual life there,"
and because "you will be among my friends—that
will mean much to you, I know." Eager for the
security which being "among my friends" held out,
the young man chose Hartford.

President Perry's hope to shield his protégé
against radicalism and controversy was quite naive.
By 1904 the whole country was convulsed by controversy, and no church or religious school could
remain completely aloof from the challenge of
modern, urban, industrial life. For more than two
decades all kinds of radically-tinged trends and
movements had been springing up within the various
Protestant denominations. Christian socialism,
which had come upon the American scene along with
the Knights of Labor, had been gaining clerical adherents steadily. Everywhere, the social gospel was
offering vigorous competition to the orthodoxy of

individual piety. By and large the churches of America remained, to be sure, as they had long been, middle class in character, business-dominated, smug, self-satisfied, and scarcely disturbed by the alleged alienation of the working classes. On the other hand, in many churches, highly active and vocal minorities were now championing the workingmen— crying for progressive labor legislation, endorsing unions, supporting strikes, urging alleviation of the lot of the disinherited, the slum dwellers, the sweated children, the sharecroppers, the migratory laborers, the night-working women, clamoring for reform in the prisons, public hospitals, orphanages. The impact of this Christian socialist minority on the churches, the divinity schools, and on the religious community at large cannot be overestimated. "Though relatively few in numbers," wrote Charles Beard in *The American Spirit*, "they yet, nonetheless, reached multitudes of people in all parts of the country and impressed their world view indelibly upon thought." To have imagined that an active, socially sensitive, and inquiring mind like Williams' could be protected against this radical influence was absurd, all the more so since it had already been irremediably infected with the labor and socialist virus.

Williams threw himself into his seminary studies with great zeal, determined thus to generate in himself the religious fervor he knew he lacked. Theology, church history, the Bible—he gulped down everything in Gargantuan doses, persuading himself that he liked every bit of it. This lasted a few months. Then his interest in labor unions, socialism, and radical reform began to reassert itself. He started reading the local press, paying special attention to labor items strewn haphazardly through the papers. He conceived the idea of a labor column in which all the labor news could be seen at a glance, and succeeded in selling the idea to the liberal editor of the *Hartford Evening Post*. Not only did he sell the idea, but he got himself hired to edit the column, which began appearing in the paper in January, 1905, and which quite frequently ran pieces, signed and unsigned, by its youthful editor.

In connection with this column, Williams undertook an intensive course of reading in labor history and socialist theory, entering meticulous summaries of every work he read in a special notebook. President Perry would have been shocked to learn that his protégé found all this radical and controversial literature on the well-stocked shelves of the seminary library—a sign of the times!

Perusing Williams' pieces in the column, one is struck by their steady progress from the mild theme of class reconciliation in the first articles to the socialist-tinged militancy of the later ones. This progress reflected, no doubt, the cumulative effect of his reading. In his notebook he recorded resumés of works on the industrial revolution, on the labor movement in England and on the European continents, on various economic theories, factory legislation in England, utopian socialism, Marxism, and, naturally, in most detailed presentation, the origin and development of Christian socialism in England, and the difference between it and the similarly named movements in Germany and France. Some of the points underscored are particularly revealing, as in a long note on St. Simon: "His basic principle —*Let each work according to his capacity and be rewarded according to the service he renders.*" In a note on Proudhon: "*Qu'il est propriété? Propriété c'est vol.*" [What is property? Property is theft.] In a note on Louis Blanc: "*From everyone according to his faculties, to each according to his needs.*"

"With all that reading," Williams wrote six years later, "and with editing the labor column, I began to see more clearly the social structure—a house of many stories. To the dwellers in the lower stories my sympathies went out, and the determination to devote myself to them followed, and to this task I pledged my whole self. With this is connected my deepest spiritual experience."

The deepest—and the most poignant. For the young man's pledge to consecrate "the full measure of my heart's devotion" to the dwellers in the lower stories was in sharp conflict with another pledge he had given himself, the pledge to consecrate his whole being to the attainment of moral perfection, personal salvation, conversion, to the attainment of that mystical communion with God that would render him worthy of being a minister. This conflict in the "embryonic minister's" purposes reflected the conflict within the Church: individualistic otherworldliness versus socialistic this-worldliness; individual salvation versus social salvation. By the time Williams was to be graduated from the seminary the psychological tension produced by this conflict reached great intensity.

A vividly dramatic record of this conflict is contained in a diary Williams kept which encompassed the period of his senior year at the seminary.

In the summer of 1906, the seminary assigned Williams, as part of his practical training, to the Spring Street Presbyterian Chuch in New York. The Church's summer program included two different kinds of activities, some oriented toward individual piety and individual salvation, others toward social issues and social redemption. An important activity in the first category was the running of a so-called Tent, where every evening salvation was offered to the human flotsam and jetsam that drifted in from the nearby tenements and rookeries—drunkards, prostitutes, derelicts, and reprobates of all varieties. Activities in the second category included settlement work, lectures, forums—all designed to demonstrate the Church's desire to build a bridge between itself and the "alienated" toiling masses and the Church's deep concern with such social sins of the day as slums, sweatshops, plutocracy, unfettered exploitation of labor, political corruption, etc.

Williams' diary entries show the conflicting moods

induced in him by the various activities. He starts
with visits to the poor of the neighborhood and is
thrilled with the success he has in "stealing an entrance into the hearts of the people." But in another note he confesses to embarrassment at using
deliberate techniques (taught him in the seminary)
to achieve this success. In several entries he
proudly notes his truimphs as a preacher—"much ap-
proved," "good effect," "great success." But in one
note he refers to his sermons as "drool" and rejoices
in the prospect of not having to preach any more
for the rest of the summer. A number of entries
register delight in his success at the Tent. "The
Tent radiates an influence which cannot be overestimated," he boasts, claiming 150 souls saved.
Indeed, so heady is this triumph that he thinks he
finally has attained that state of religious ecastasy,
that sense of conversion that had always eluded him
in the past:

> I look up at the stars and really think what a great and awe-
> some being God really is, how he is just and must punish us for
> our littleness and our sins, and how if he is loving he must pro-
> vide an escape therefrom. Strange how these simple facts must be
> inwrought into a person's mind before they really mean anything
> to him; how they must pass through his own experience. This
> thing I must do: Make the simple facts plain—that there is a
> God; that there is sin; that sin is punished, etc., etc.

But other entries put into question the enthusiasm
over the Tent by cynical comments about "theat-
ricality," "scaring people into conversion," the "fat

salaries" of some of the evangelists who preach in the Tent, and about his puzzlement "how these men with liquor on their breath assert that they do not drink a drop." Even his perfervid confession of faith just quoted, on re-examination betrays a grain of wishfulness born of uncertainty. The forced rhetoric, the over-emphasis of the word "really," suggest a lack of absolute conviction and remind one of Dostoevsky's tortured outcry: "I believe. I believe. I *wish* to believe." And then there is one entry in which the whole theological postulate upon which the Tent operates is all but negated. The entry pertains to a debate run by the Church on the topic, "Resolved that the Improvement in the Morals and Habits of the Workingmen Would Better Their Material Conditions." Williams reports:

I held to the ground that while of course such improvement was likely to be reflected in the workers having better homes, better food, etc., nevertheless all history shows that it is in great social upheavals that the workingmen have won their rights by wresting them away from the upper classes, and that in England, Germany, and Russia while the morals and habits of the workers were comparatively good, yet as a matter of fact they were oppressed until they had won better conditions by labor unions, strikes, etc. But Mr. Bates, as usual, put the whole thing on a deeply religious basis.

As one dips further into the diary the sharply alternating moods gradually create the impression of a split in the author's personality, of two irreconcilable characters pulling in opposite directions—

one, to the world of man and material reality; the
other, to the realm of God and elusive spirituality.
One is wholesome, dynamic, life-loving, a believer
who dares question and doubt, an activist who revels
in facing problems and contemplating radical solutions. The other is pietistic, self-righteous, fussing
about his own sins and virtues, and quite uncon-
cerned about the real woes of the real world. Each
of these writes his own characteristic entries into
the diary, and each seeks to gain ascendancy over
the other.

Generally, it is the first who seems to have the
upper hand. His entries range from descriptions of
athletic contests in which he participates ("Allen
and I have a little boxing match." "Fierce game of
basketball!" "Coasting party on Prospect Hill.")
to comments on the young ladies he meets (Nellie
Garvin—"amiable, gracious, common-sense sort
of girl." Jennie Roberts—"put on quite a little
refined casuistry.") to criticisms of plays he sees
and books he reads, to impressions of labor and
socialist leaders, and above all to his observations
on the life of the "dwellers in the lower stories." His
interest in this life is insatiable, and the energy he
applies to the gratification of this interest is incredible.

He visits mines, factories, prisons, orphanages,
hospitals, reformatories, saloons, doss-houses, slum
areas, millionaires' estates, building sites; he asks

questions, takes down figures, stimulates discussions, engages in arguments, and enters everything with meticulous care in his diary. He not only sees and records, but he also reacts, keenly, passionately. His hatred for injustice, poverty, and human degradation is all-consuming; his vision of social betterment, social salvation, all-embracing.

Wherever he happens to be, he uncovers evidence of social evil. In Hartford, a Sunday morning stroll takes him from the broad avenues, shady elm trees, and private homes of the wealthy section to the "dirty, half-ripped-up streets and crowded slums where the workers live." Indignant with the city's politicians, he writes: "While they clean the uptown avenues of every particle of dirt and mend every little tear, here they let everything go to wrack and ruin." Upon further investigation, he is outraged to learn that "here where the poor live in slums, one-fourth of the city's population is crammed into only one-thirtieth of the city's total area!"

At West Stafford, walking along the new electric railroad being built, he observes the downtrodden appearance of Italian immigrants at work. After inquiries, he notes in disgust: "Get paltry 65 cents a day; miserably housed in ramshackle buildings and filthy hovels."

On a walking trip through the beautiful Berkshires, he spends a day in the famous Berkshire Textile Mills. He had never seen anything like it before, and his impressions are mixed. A tribute to the "marvelous efficiency of such an industrial plant" and the "fine web spun with lacelike delicacy," is followed by an outburst of incredulity that "amidst these blessed hills and valleys in green verdure clad," that "amidst the beauty and gladness of blooming springing nature" there could exist these "noisome, monotonous, and wearisome factories," these "monstrous machines which were almost like hells." The most depressing sight are the workers: "Toiling ten and a half hours a day, these men, women and children are being devitalized and demoralized to make profit for others. . . . The people are sallow, palefaced, and seemingly half-dead." At the sight of two boys slinking in the corner, "pallid and downcast," the thought passes through his mind that "the man who could live in luxury upon the blood-money coined from these boys is destined some day to be confronted with the results of his hardness of heart." His final comment is that "only radicalism," only "socialism" will "cure the evil in this great plant."

There are dozens of similar entries. Together they provide an unforgettable picture of what America looked like to a socially sensitive young man in the crisis year 1907. Some of these entries are written with such gusto, such relish for detail that one cannot but feel that it is precisely in them that the diarist finds his fulfillment as an aspiring socialist writer. Here in incipient form we already discern those qualities of eye and heart we find in his mature writings of later years. And certainly, here we find the facts observed at first hand which ineluctably propelled the 23-year-old seminarist to seek radical solutions.

These solutions he finds on the library shelves, as he works diligently on a paper for a sociology class, entitled "A General View of Socialism," a solidly erudite essay full of learned references, an impressive bibliography, and not a few brilliantly original ideas which leave little doubt concerning his firm grasp of the socialist philosophy. The pages are speckled with such Marxist phrases as "class struggle," "class interest," "production relations," "surplus value," "iron law of wages," "materialistic conception of history," and so on; also with names famous in the history of socialist thought from Robert Owen down to Marx, Engels, Lafargue, Lassalle, Bebel, Liebknecht, the Fabians. . . .

The essay opens with a polemic against William H. Taft, then Secretary of War, who in a speech before the Yale alumni deplored the rising interest in socialism among university people. The first paragraph sets the tone:

Secretary Taft in a recent address to the Yale alumni bewailed the increase of what he calls the "parlor Socialist," remarking that it showed a lack of balance for a university graduate to take up with such ideas. A man, he said, who had been denied the privileges of life might be excused for expressing his discontent

with the present order and seeking to establish a new one, but
for an educated man to do this betokened some inherent and vital
deficiency. This attitude of Taft's is as common as it is errone-
ous, in that it assumes that Socialism is some sort of mere dream
or desire of discontents or of the lower classes to overturn existing institutions in the hope of gain for themselves and for class
interests. Socialism at times may be accused of being merely this,
but today it presents a philosophy of life and a system of government and laws—above all considered in their practical aspects—
which demand something more than superficial condemnation.

Curiously, in defining the role and function of
the intellectual in the socialist movement, Williams
hits upon a line of thought very close to the one
Lenin had advanced in 1902, in his historic polemic
against the Economists. The parallel in the content
and even the form of the argument is remarkable.
Here is what Williams writes:

Modern Socialism is not primarily the product of the discon-
tented, nor of the uneducated and uncultured; but it represents
the ripest experience and best thought of such men as Robert
Owen, the successful millionaire; Charles Fourier, the brilliant
Frenchman; Ferdinand Lassalle, idolized and deified by the German masses; and Karl Marx, the versatile scholar and bulwark of
Socialism. . . . And yet while the chief exponents of Socialism
have not been men of the working class, it *is* a working class
movement and these men are simply the voice of the submerged
tenth, or more accurately, the nine-tenths. Thanks to their abilities and genius, through their training and education, they express
the longings, hopes, and aspirations of the toilers and so they
have been received as the prophets of the proletariat.

Paralleling Lenin's contention that modern socialism springs from "the main highway of world civilization" and answers "questions propounded by the

world's most advanced thinkers and noblest dreamers," Williams makes a lengthy excursion into the
past, starting with the Judeo-Christian antecedents
and ending with the various trends in socialism in
the early years of this century—the emphasis on
trade-unionism in England, on political socialism in
Germany, and on syndicalism and anarchism "in
the more despotic countries in Europe." Marx and
Marxism are allotted the lion's share of space in the
essay.

The essay concludes with a discussion of the clash
between individualism and socialism.   For those
who have been impressed with Orwell's *1984* and
Zamiatin's *We* and with the dithyrambs to individualism that our American bards of capitalism, free
enterprise, and the cold war have been dinning into
the world's ears, the discussion is amazingly contemporary and relevant.   Here is the essential part
of it:

> Socialism stands opposed to individualism. Socialism can win
> its victory only as it can overthrow the principles upon which
> the present system of industry and life are based—namely the
> principles of individualism. . . .
> Individualism, say its defenders, rests on the principle that a
> man shall be his own master. The basis of popular individualism,
> they claim, lies deep down in the fundamental facts of the universe,
> in the power, the worth, the consciousness of responsibility in the
> individual soul. To have the State interfere with the action of the
> individual weakens character. Paternalism might lull to eternal
> sleep the power of self-choice. In a recent anti-Socialistic novel
> by Parry, *The Scarlet Empire,* this objection is strongly urged;

the Socialistic country he depicts as existing under the sea where men all wear the same garments, are known by numbers, and live a spiritless mechanical existence; and certainly indeed such an existence is repulsive to any man who longs for the free and open battle of the world which in its resistance and obstacles develops manhood.

Socialism replies to this by hurling the charge back in the face of individualism, by saying that only under its regime can man have the fullest and highest degree of individual freedom. The majority of men are driven by iron laws of necessity to do certain things and thus are fastened upon them rigid and unbending laws of competitive life which allow no mercy. Mills says, "The restraints of communism would be freedom in comparison with the present conditions of the majority of the human race."

No one will suggest that this paper, intended to meet the requirements of a study course in sociology, was a contribution to socialist philosophy. But, on the other hand, the reading, research, and pondering which its writing entailed and the bold originality of some of the ideas it contains do attest to the seriousness of the young seminarist's effort and accomplishment in the mastery of socialist thought.

But what, in the meantime, does young Williams' religious-mystical *alter ego* do? He butts in, he nags, he disapproves, he challenges, he parades his own Christian virtues and assails others' transgressions. As the day of graduation and formal consecration into the ministry draws near he grows fearful that he may not be deemed worthy of a diploma and certainly not of the fellowship for study abroad to which his academic standing at the top of the class would entitle him. His entries in the diary show his mood. The reader need not be burdened with too many quotations. Here is a characteristic one:

Jan. 27 [1907]. Walk with Dougherty to Miss Wangle's and Miss Potter's house and read the "Transformation of Miss Phillurd." Am contrasting the feeling I have now and that I had about three years ago. I have come to some sure convictions, my ideals have taken on tangible, visible reality. They are *convictions,* not vague emotions, as they were in Marietta College. My character is 100% better I believe. I have little trouble on the score of purity. I can truly feel the spirit. Christ has come in to drive out these other things. Yet, there is little appeal in the dogmatic theology classroom to any of my experiences.

I do feel the actuality of sin (it has been disturbing me more of late than for some time), but the propitiatory theory seems to have little hold upon me, and yet I feel as though I would want more than the subjective moral theory of atonement. I feel the greatness of Christ the prophet, teacher, guide, supreme moral force, and yet the mystic religionism of the living Christ is a great reality. At moments, in my room, as I hum those simple tunes—"Grace fathomless as the sea," "Glory Song,"—and then those nobler hymns, such as "Our fathers plunged in prisons dark," an irresistible spirituality steals into my nature. It is only when burdened with a great thought or stirred by the sins of society or the sacrifices of a noble man that I can really pray aright. My other prayers amount to 5 minutes or less and mean little to me. I feel an adaptability to society, but need to cultivate a better grace and ease. My voice, my gestures, and my facial expression need marriage between the three, says Professor Meriam. I have a message of individual salvation from my own experience: That Christ can drive sin and evil from our life, but, as far as my work, social salvation will be my best hold.

The final confrontation of the two conflicting egos occurs on April 1, 1907, at the crucial qualifying test for "licensed" preaching. For weeks Williams had strained to get himself into the proper pious mood. He knew from experience as a student-preacher that most of the important professors and church dignitaries, though tolerant, did not especially savor his sermons when he propounded a bit too enthusiastically the workman's cause. So he tried to be cautious. He skirted the subject of socialism altogether, using instead the safer term "social salvation." But this kind of compromise went against his grain, and he began seriously to wonder whether "a genuine friend of Labor and an open foe of Mammon," whether a real avowed Socialist, would be granted the license. He was worried how his distaste for theology might affect his sermon before the examiners and sought during the final weeks to cultivate a taste for it, and had almost succeeded. "This morning I am thinking," reads the February 24 entry, "that all my revolt against theology is beginning to wear away and that these theological terms begin to hold some meaning for me. I am really glad in a way." I say *almost,* because the very next sentence reads: "Yet I see the danger of divorcing myself from the active life and that of the common people." This painful vacillation goes on till four days before the examination, when he sits down and, in defiance of the *alter ego,* writes out a sermon in which he passionately avows his most cherished emotions and thoughts. It is a spontaneous outpouring, and Williams is very pleased and relieved: Whatever comes, comes.

On the appointed day, Williams and several of his classmates went up for the test. Three notoriously orthodox theologians were the examiners. The fellows who preceded Williams delivered their sermons and answered the questions in accordance with strict doctrinal precepts and, it was obvious, "passed with flying colors." The examiners were responsive and looked pleased. Albert's sermon was quite heterodox and revolved around the concept of *social* salvation which he espoused with great warmth. The examiners looked icy. They asked him no questions, and involved him in no discussion. "My voice became husky and quivered," reads the diary entry, "my eyes filled with tears. . . . They were kind enough not to press any questions on me. I had managed to struggle through my sermon. But I felt utterly crushed. . . . I went down to the basement of the church, then through the church, but I could not gain control of myself. . . ."

Actually it all turned out better than Williams dared hope. Not only was he granted the license, but he received the coveted fellowship for a year of foreign study. This happy outcome was due not only to Williams' excellent academic record and his demonstrated ability as preacher and administrator, but also to the spirit of the times. It was the crisis year 1907. The situation of the dwellers in the lower stories was desperate. Many young and socially responsive seminarists all over the country were committing themselves to the social gospel.

And examiners, no matter how orthodox, could scarcely take it upon themselves to penalize an otherwise splendid candidate for expressing deep concern over the woes of the workingman or for preaching active struggle against the social evils of the day.

IV

On Williams, the happy denouement of the protracted psychological drama had a marvelously restorative effect. The whole tone of his diary suddenly changed. No more nagging *alter ego*. No more wrestling with sin. Not one mention of theology or any related subject. The subterfuge term "social salvation" disappears, while the word "socialism" crops up ever more insistently and militantly, as do references to socialist meetings and discussions, and such socialist-favored words and phrases as "proletarian," "smug bourgeois," "bloated capitalist," "bourgeois opportunism," etc. And above all, evaluation of events and individuals in terms not of Christianity and Christian ethics, but of socialism and socialist ethics.

Here and there throughout the diary Williams' socialism bears traces of youthful sentimentality and romanticism. But the outstanding feature of the whole document is its alert realism, a direct product of the young man's intellectual independence, his skeptical, ironical, inconoclastic turn of mind.

He is not easily taken in.

Thus, upon hearing much Christian socialist praise heaped upon "enlightened capitalism," he visits the plant of the National Cash Register Company "to observe such capitalism in action." He is not impressed: "It's true the condition of the workers is a little better than average; but theirs is a company union—they belong body and soul to the Company." His conclusion: "An exhibition of benevolent feudalism!"

If company unions fail to satisfy his socialist standards, so do many of the AFL craft unions. This is recorded in several diary entries. For example, at Spring Street he and Norman Thomas, his colleague and the future Socialist leader, call on the President of the Tile Layers' Union to invite him to represent the Union's viewpoint at a Church-sponsored forum. Though he turns down their invitation, they engage him in conversation. Williams' entry reads:

> Tomkins attacked the Tile Dealers' Association because, he said, it is hard for an independent dealer to get in. We then asked him if it was easy for a man to get into Tomkins' labor union. Tomkins replied: "Yes, dead easy, we take in a man anywhere if he can pass the exam before our walking delegate." "Well," we asked, "how much is the initiation?" Tomkins: "Oh, one hundred dollars." Imagine, a workingman raising one hundred dollars before getting in—practically makes it a trust!

Nor do most of the "big names" in socialism, Christian socialism, and Single Tax meet his socialist standards. A characteristic entry reads:

One very interesting thing is the aristocratic tendencies of our Friends of the Proletariat and champions of the workingmen. Henry George, Jr. made Holmes [John Haynes] wait one and a half hours while he [Henry George] ate his dinner and then sent him a short curt note, on swell City Club of N. Y. stationery, saying "no" to his request for an interview. . . . Josiah Strong has fine offices and hours 9-3. Lovejoy, the great anti-child labor man, evidently considers himself a child laborer and, practicing what he preaches, doesn't work at all, knocking out that much of the child-labor evil. . . . All this is quite in accord with the dainty luncheons of the socialists—Phelps Stokes, Patterson, etc. —up in Connecticut.

Then there is the devastating note on Dr. Parkhurst, minister of the Madison Square Presbyterian Church in New York, a highly publicized sacred cow of the Christian socialist movement. Williams went to see the famous man in trepidation and awe, expecting to meet "a great champion of Christian socialism, a strong, gaunt, fiery battler for social justice," but he found a smooth operator, "an unabashed apologist for the established order," and a foe of labor unions "because they were setting class against class." Williams was as disgusted with the Doctor's resplendent church as he was with the Doctor himself. "I could not help contrasting all that richness and splendor with the numberless dark rooms in New York and all the misery, toil and sorrow; and the wall was emblazoned with gold leaf letters of the Ten Commandments, and I thought how every one of them was violated by the church."

Always on the alert against pretensions and sham, the young radical is very hard on do-gooders and philanthropists, especially those with great liberal reputations. Upon hearing one such do-gooder refer to the "disgusting" behavior of the people in the slums, he gets into a "socialist discussion" with her, following which he comments: "She says she is humanitarian, she bewails the contrast between wealth and poverty, yet she overlooks the contrast between her own nice home and the terrible homes in the slums not too far away. E. B. Bax is right: the bourgeois are impervious to real facts, and their pity for the poor is too often theoretical." And when another such liberal lady describes her domestic help, Negroes, as "shiftless, lazy, and incompetent," and her daughter, an "emery-voiced old maid of 25–27" speaks with horror of a white woman kissing a Negro child whose skin she says feels "like that of a monkey," Williams burns with indignation, characterizing the mother as an "obnoxious bourgeois," and her daughter as "an insipid, vapid, good-for-nothing bourgeois."

The only ones to stir his love and admiration are workingmen and "*principled* socialists," but even workingmen, when not class-conscious or rebellious, drive him to despairing indignation. Once, shocked by the "unimaginable display of wealth" he observed during a day's survey of the millionaire estates in Lexington, Massachusetts, he turned to some workmen he saw around to find out what they thought "of the awful robbery which must be perpetrated to maintain such establishments," and was both revolted by their "resignation and servility," and awed by the amount of agitation and propaganda yet to be done. "The spirit must work hard before it can move such complacency into action!"

A climactic episode in the young man's research into the evils of the capitalist order and their crushing effect on the poor and the jobless is recorded (and distorted) in two July, 1907, issues of the then important morning paper, *The New York Herald*.

The editor of the paper had decided to investigate the impact of the financial crisis on the employment situation among the dwellers in the New York slums. While looking for a qualified young scholar to do the job, he was directed by a mutual friend to young Williams because of the latter's pronounced interest in sociology, labor, and the poor. Williams got the assignment.

On June 29, 1907, almost immediately after receiving the Bachelor of Divinity degree, the fledging minister, dressed in workers' clothes, a shabby cap on his head, a battered old satchel in his hand, and eight crumpled dollar bills in his pocket, stepped off the Hartford-to-New York boat and vanished incognito in the jungles of the big city.

A few days later (July 1) the Herald startled its readers with a half-page story headlined:

PREACHER IN SLUMS TO STUDY POVERTY FOUND
IN 20-CENT ROOM. UNABLE TO GET WORK

The gist of the story was given in the first couple of paragraphs:

Sleeping at night in a twenty-cent room, and tramping the streets by day in search of work, Albert R. Williams, a young preacher who has chosen to live the life of the New York poor this summer . . . has found in the first forty-eight hours of his ordeal that New York City . . . has but few jobs for the boy who comes here without money, references, or technical training to win his bread. . . . His small money supply is dwindling and he has not yet found the means of making any more. . . . Mr. Williams has graduated recently from the Hartford Seminary with high honors and a valuable scholarship abroad. Before assuming the duties of his scholarship, however, he resolved to study the conditions among the poor of the slums at first hand. . . . The young man was reluctant to talk of his experiences. . . . When he finally consented to tell of the things that have befallen him, he uncovered powers of description that argue well for his future work. His eyes are open and he is seeing the world in a light unknown to him when he was in school.

It was, indeed, a corking good story that Williams told, full of vivid details about fruitless searches, wrong leads, and pathetic and comic situations. Reader interest must have been considerable, for three weeks later (July 21) the *Herald* published another story—this time spread over two pages— flamboyantly headlined:

Minister Looking for Work Becomes a Coney Island Barker

Williams was outraged by the two stories. They were travesties on what he had written. The editor had "played false" with him, he had cut out the most devastating facts and comments ("moralisms") and inserted some inane stuff of his own. "The trouble with him," complained Williams in the diary, "is he didn't care a bit about the scientific and economic value of a young fellow's experience in N.Y., but rather wanted a sensational story about a young preacher getting into a number of ridiculous situations." It was capitalism. The scramble for circulation, profits. The truth? The truth be damned!

Still, Williams did not regret his "sociological spree." So far this was the most intimate insight into the workings of capitalism, including capitalist journalism, that he had had. Also, it was the most harrowing first-hand insight into what it meant to be a penniless worker hunting for a job. Altogether it was an immensely enriching experience, one that sharpened his conviction that the only cure for the capitalist abomination was socialism and that the only worth-while work for him would be work in the socialist cause, to help remove the workingman's "servility and resignation," to stir his terrible "complacency" into action.

Small wonder Albert Rhys Williams was thrilled when, ten years later, he beheld the complacency of the once servile and resigned Russian masses moved into action. No wonder he could understand so well their rage when they broke into the Winter Palace and saw the "unimaginable display of wealth" in that monument of awful tsarist robbery, or when they sacked and burned millionaires' residences and landlord estates during the first days of liberation. No wonder he could identify so utterly with the revolutionary masses' hatred for the *bourjouis,* for the servitors of the Church, the bourgeois press, for the wishy-washy liberals, the reformists, the gradualist socialists. These types revolted him in America as far back as 1907, and he sympathized with the Russian revolutionists who rejected them in 1917. He embraced the Russian Revolution because it was, he believed, the socialist revolution he had envisaged in 1907, because its slogans and dreams were the slogans and dreams he had cherished since he first pondered them in the quiet library alcoves of the Hartford Theological Seminary.

This is certain: At the end of his three-year stint at Hartford young Williams' theological education, though good, was not nearly so good as his socialist education. Acquiring the first was a matter of painful self-discipline; acquiring the second was a matter of eager choice. Theology was completely irrelevant to the mood of the times or to the young man's own spiritual and intellectual quest; socialism was supremely relevant. Williams' urge to master socialism stemmed from his own sociological observations, from his own researches in the library, from his own grieving over the widening gap between American ideals and American realities.

At the same time it should be noted that Williams left the seminary bearing not the least trace of animosity. Quite the contrary, he regretted parting with the many good friends he had made, he appreciated the many opportunities to see and to learn which the seminary afforded him, and the freedom he enjoyed to pursue his own intellectual and spiritual interests. "Nobody ever said Nay to me," he reminisced years later. "A student could bring the results of his independent inquiries into the classroom for general discussion without fear of losing his scholastic status." He did not really resent even the time he had spent in the study of theology and church history. Reminiscing on this point, Williams wrote:

While I revolted in Hartford against the preoccupation with the mystical and intangible, the rather murky overloaded theological atmosphere, I nevertheless, in retrospect, can clearly see how I derived from it certain distinct intellectual and spiritual benefits. Indeed, in a rather vague way, I was cognizant of them, even as I revolted.

From studying the history of religion and the church I received some inkling of the ideas and issues that once so wholly absorbed the mind and energies of man. "A man who has no knowledge of the heritage of the past can never be a Communist." (Lenin) The average modernist hasn't the slightest concept of the great realms of thought and feeling which the rest of mankind has had. To this extent he is cut off entirely from any sympathy or understanding of a great and important experience of great numbers of fellowmen. For example, instead of regretting the lost time and energy spent in evangelical service, the learning of rather shoddy and superficial hymns, and instead of envying those Unitarians, for example, who had a more rational religious upbringing—or those outside the church who had no upbringing whatsoever, I rather pity them that they were deprived and shut off from this direct contact with vast areas of ideas and emotion. They have no inkling of the stuff and fabric, the hopes and dreams in the lives of their fellowmen, and to that extent, they are not in a position to understand their viewpoint, to speak the same language and idiom, and are thereby bereft of understanding and sympathy.

Theological training gives one a more philosophical outlook on the world. Some reason for its name "Queen of the Sciences." We fret and revolt against evils, at the slow process of eliminating them from the world, at our inability to overcome them, to put curbs, fetters, restraints on them. To this McKenzie replied "But God likewise can't do everything he wants to do. He too is conditioned!"

That point of view keeps us from needlessly fuming and fretting, from "kicking against the prickles." It teaches us that everything is subject to certain laws, and conditions, and makes us submit to those conditions and laws, keeps us from wasting energy in assailing them instead of working with them—"cooperating with the inevitable." In short, he learns patience and the process of life and of reform is a long, long one.

V

Much of the ten-year interval between his graduation from the seminary and his journey to Russia, Williams spent in travel. From the autumn of 1907 to the autumn of 1908, his fellowship took him to England, France, and Germany. On his return to America, he spent two months covering the length and breadth of the state of New Jersey, campaigning for the presidential candidate of the Socialist Party, Eugene V. Debs. After that he became minister of the Maverick Congregational Church of East Boston in a working-class district. A couple of years later he took temporary leave from the Church in order to accompany, as personal secretary, a very wealthy old cleric aristocrat and his family on a leisurely study trip to the West Coast. In the summer of 1914 he went for a trip to Europe. He was in England when the First World War broke out, and at the request of *The Outlook* magazine, crossed the Channel and followed the German troops during their invasion of Belgium and France. Upon his return to the United States, he crisscrossed the continent, delivering lectures on the Chautauqua Circuit on his experiences at the front.

When he was not traveling, Williams attended to his duties at the Maverick Church. These he found so time-consuming that he soon shifted most of them to his father and mother whom he had persuaded to move to Boston. He himself concentrated on conducting, under Maverick auspices, a Wednesday night Men's Forum, in which he had the most prominent socialist speakers in the country participate. Frequently he would take a few days off, dress himself up in workers' clothes and go out onto the industrial suburbs and towns around Boston on Socialist exploration. And always he took an active part in every labor struggle in the city and its environs, often using his church as the rallying point for strikers and socialist demonstrators. In 1912, during the bitterly-fought textile strike in Lawrence, Massachusetts, he gave most of his energy and oratorical talent to the raising of money in support of the strike and its jailed leaders. As time went on, his leaves from the church grew longer and more frequent. By 1916 he had virtually ceased functioning as minister. While he traveled and lectured, his place as Forum leader was taken over by his assistant, Paul Blanshard, also a socialist.

Through all this period, Williams did an enormous amount of writing—travel impressions, diaries, notes for a contemplated (but never completed) book on "The Church and Labor Unions," outlines of lectures, speeches, sermons, etc. All this was raw material which he, essentially if not always consciously a creative artist, a writer, obviously intended someday to transmute into finished literary works. In 1908, he did utilize some of his English notes in an excellent essay entitled "Socialism in the English Universities," which was published the same year in the important monthly periodical of that time, *The Outlook*. And in 1916 he whipped much of his material for his Chautauqua lectures into a book

entitled *In the Claws of the German Eagle,* which
was published early in 1917. A general heading for
the entire output might be: "1907–1917: A Decade
Through an *American* Socialist's Eyes."

The word American is stressed because the author's ultimate frame of reference, no matter where
he is or what he deals with, is America: her youth,
her essential egalitarianism and democracy, her
haunting perfectionist dream, her relative freedom
from the weight of millennial history. Thus, after
a brief moment of thrill with English historic monuments, traditions, and socialist and labor victories
in the years 1907–1908, his Americanism reasserts
itself ever more insistently.

"A half a day is quite enough to thrill to the
past!" he exclaims after a weary round among the
"towers and spires" of Oxford. And a ramble
through a museum of ancient armor evokes from him
the comment: "No use glorifying the past—the same
knight with his grandiose manner would relentlessly
and remorselessly inflict abuse and insult upon
women not of his courtly caste. The knights of King
Arthur's Court never were." Wandering through
an art museum, he is distressed by the thought that
all "this art, beauty, loveliness" was produced for
the upper classes, the aristocracy, by artists and
artisans "under the sting and goad of poverty, of
unutterable grief and desolation," that most of it
was "built on blood"; and, as if anticipating an

emotion he would much later experience in the Imperial City of St. Petersburg, he cries out: "Thank God, we haven't got so much of this at home. If art and beauty and loveliness must thrive on a foundation of strife, and bitterness, and penury, and hate, then we better smash the whole thing to pieces. . . ." And after a visit to an ancient cathedral: "The people look subdued and downcast—weary and worn by the weight of historicity that presses on their shoulders. . . . When I get back to America I am going to yell with joy over the sense of liberation from this weight, and thank the Lord we are only a few years old!"

He is at first quite impressed by the aristocratic socialists at Oxford, but he soon discerns their class snobbishness, their condescension to the brilliant worker-students at Russell Hall, and his American soul rises in revolt. Personally he feels no social discrimination, nor do the other American students, but Williams is not assuaged. He writes:

This graciousness on their part does not extend to their own countrymen of the lower social strata. They take in all of us Americans because they know that we Americans treat one another on a level of equality. They would not give us the least thought, considering our economic and social positions, if we were Englishmen. *We force our American self-esteem upon them.*

With a group of English and American students he observes a demonstration of unemployed. The gathering takes place in a church, but the speakers,

quite uninhibited, use profane language to express
their revolutionary mood. Some of Williams' com-
panions, even some Americans, are critical. But
Williams invokes the experience of the American
Revolution in the workers' defense:

> Harvey was shocked that such coarse language and threats of
> violence were used within the precincts of the Church. He forgot
> the Boston tea party! Personally I think it is a marvelous dese-
> cration of the church to have a turbulent labor meeting in it.
> Have rights ever been won by anything but force? These self-
> satisfied New Englanders, Harvey and the others, who counsel
> moderation to the aroused workingmen, how did their forefathers
> obtain their rights when they happened to be the wronged class?
> England urged moderation, but that very counsel exasperated them,
> so that not only did they refuse to accept the tea, but in their
> rage they assembled *in the church* and in disguises frantically
> pitched all the tea into the harbor!

But it is regimented, militarized, Prussianized
Germany that administers the greatest jolt to his
American sensibilities. Every diary entry is an outcry of disgust. The journal is filled with instances
of German arrogance, brutality, chauvinism. He
sees it in the streets, in student fraternities, in duelling, in the whole system of rearing and educating
the youth, in the children's war games. He hears
a professor lecture to a group of university students
on the kindness with which criminals and delinquent
youths were treated in the Elmira Reformatory in
the USA, how they were given bright clothes and
brought together in assemblies and served bacon for
breakfast. But instead of being impressed by the
humane American experiment, the students made

loud guffaws at each example of kindness cited by the professor. "They laughed," notes the outraged American, "at such a comical conception of a reformatory where the milk of human kindness was used instead of this ever-present Prussian military force and compulsion." "Brutal, brutal, brutal," he exclaims after watching students cutting each other's faces in duels. "This is a military, regimented government," he says in another note. "He who doesn't fit into the archives must be chopped into shape and put therein, cattle or evangel."

A visit to the Krupp Works inspires a long indignant entry, part of which reads:

On a monument to Krupp—which appear very numerously all over—are the words, "The object of labor shall be the common good." And this is on a cannon monument!!! A wit has said that it really reads, "The object of labor shall be *my good*." And how true. The boy I asked on the street was 14 years old and was earning 80 pfennig a day and going to night school. The common good! God! What a lie. And this pernicious lie about preparing for war being the best preventive of war—where the war spirit is continually nurtured and developed in the people the resistance to it becomes weakened and powerless and the whole people assume the war ideal—it tinges their whole thought, brutalizes them through and through. Essen, which sends its armaments and cannons, was the city which advertised for money for Zeppelin because it was a war machine. Are we going to drive the military spirit into America? Are we going to brutalize our people? You cannot understand how it creeps into the very life of the people, slowly poisoning them.

Hoping to forewarn Americans, Williams compiles horrible examples of the toxic effect of militarism on the German people:

An officer makes recruit do 1800 knee bends while he (the officer) continues to eat his *Abendbrot* (supper). Another sat on his raw recruit on the bend of his leg and tried to straighten his leg meanwhile holding one hand over the mouth and with the other striking him in the face.

The good woman from Baldisch (Baltic?) provinces at pension 16 Maximilian Str. who was speaking how fearfully unthankful (*furchtbar undankbar Volk*) were the native peasants who had been cultivated and cultured by the arrival of the Germans there and now were in revolt against their Lords. However, some had been captured and though they rounded up a bunch they selected every fifth man and killed him as an example. This was justice? The good woman deplored such leniency and showed her superior statecraft with a sigh. "Yes, but you never can tell about these people. The only safe way is to kill them all!" [Oh shade of Hitler!—J.K.]

The only surcease from the horror of Prussianism, is visits with the Social Democrats, who call him Genosse, invite him to picnics, and speak of the changes they will introduce into German life comes the social revolution. And it is due to them that Williams leaves Germany not utterly dejected.

But the enchantment distance lent to America evaporates upon his return to his native American shores. And his American notes and diaries throughout the decade are even more consistently critical than his earlier ones, and, if possible, more militantly socialist.

Read in chronological order, this American material records not only Williams' preoccupation with socialism, but also the consistent broadening and deepening of his socialist education, the shedding of Christian-socialist illusions, the acceptance of revolution (violent if necessary) as the only escape from the capitalist impasse, the growing emphasis on internationalism as the *sine qua non* of socialist policy and ethics, and, after 1914, the impassioned opposition to the evils of militarism, war, and imperialist conquest.

Even the collapse of the Socialist International and the sight of socialists of different nations killing each other failed to shake his faith. In 1916, his letters to friends were always signed with "Yours for the Social Revolution." And in 1917, shortly before the overthrow of tsarism in Russia, he expressed ringing affirmation of his socialist internationalism, in the introduction to *In the Claws of the German Eagle.* He wrote:

> To myself, out of these insights into the Great Calamity there has come reinforcement to my belief in the essential greatness of the human stuff in all nations. Along with it goes a faith that in the New Internationalism mankind will lay low the military Frankenstein that he has created, and realize the triumphant brotherhood of all human souls.

The publication and warm critical reception of *In the Claws* signalized a decisive turn in Williams' life and perspective. For years his attitude to the church and his work in it had been eroded by a mounting sense of ambiguity and tenuousness. The youthful dream of transforming the Christian Church into the leading organ of the social revolution had long since vanished in a fog of doubt and disillusion-

ment. More and more the ministry had ceased to
be a mission, but had become a job, a chore. Even
the pleasures derived from running the Maverick
Forum began to pall—the same audience, the same
speakers, the same empty, eternally reiterated
clichés. Every time the thing became unbearable
he would seek escape in travel, observation, and
writing. And the more frequent these interludes,
the more keen his longing for a permanent departure.
The only avenue that beckoned to him ever more
insistently was writing. He knew he had some talent.
But was it commensurate with his lofty aims? The
laudatory reviews of his book dissipated his last
doubts. He would bid farewell to Maverick, give up
the ministry. He would not officially resign, not yet,
but he would unofficially cease to function as a minister. He was an acknowledged writer at last. All
he needed now was a new socialist theme for a new
book.

VI

Williams had barely set out in search of an appropriate theme when Providence provided him with
one. It was the news of the overthrow of tsarism
in Russia, followed, within a few days, by reports
of the emergence in Petrograd of a uniquely revolutionary parliament called the Soviet of Workers',

Soldiers', and Peasants' Deputies. His imagination fired, Williams resolved forthwith to go to Russia, to observe the unfolding revolution with his own eyes. The resolve was strengthened when the United States, in the wake of tsarism's fall, declared war on Germany and thus found itself an ally of the revolutionary government in Petrograd.

In order to help finance the trip, as well as to facilitate the obtaining of an American passport and the opening of Russian doors, Williams decided to wangle a reportorial assignment from one of the major newspapers in New York. While engaged in exploring the journalistic possibilities, he learned from friends close to the State Department that the United States government was planning to send a goodwill mission to Russia, which mission was to include some socialists and literary figures. He expressed vague interest, and his name was submitted to the Department. Yet he was far from being sold on the idea, apprehensive as he was of the direction United States policy vis-à-vis revolutionary Russia was taking at the time, and fearful of being identified with that policy. Accordingly, he continued with greater intensity than before to seek a journalistic assignment. When he finally obtained it from the *New York Evening Post,* he hastily withdrew his name from consideration for the proposed mission.

Before departing for Russia, Williams spent many days scouring the Russian colony in New York for people who had contacts in their homeland. He interviewed and obtained briefings from representatives of various political parties active in the revolution, solicited letters of introduction (dozens of them) to leaders in the Provisional Government and the Soviet—Miliukov, Rodzianko, Kerensky, Brezhkovskaia, etc. Most important, as it would turn out later, he made close contact with, and obtained letters of recommendation from, the editorial staff of the *Novy Mir,* a Russian socialist paper in New York which at one time or another counted among its editors and contributors such distinguished Bolsheviks as Trotsky and Bukharin.

Williams' projected route to Petrograd lay via the Scandinavian countries. Since Stockholm, a neutral capital, had recently been named as the gathering place for a widely-publicized Socialist Peace Conference (to open sessions on or about May 15), Williams naturally wished to stop there and, if possible, to observe the proceedings. He knew that Morris Hillquit, Victor Berger, and Algernon Lee—the Socialist Party's officially elected delegation to the Conference—had been denied passports by the State Department on the basis of the century-old Logan Act. This circumstance, he thought, made the presence of a socialist observer from America at the Conference all the more desirable. Hillquit, delighted with the idea, handed Williams a letter of such high recommendation as to open, so it was hoped, all socialist doors in Stockholm, in Russia, everywhere.

On May 19th, 1917, armed with credentials from the *Post,* a letter of recommendation from Hillquit, a pack of introductory letters to everybody that was anybody in revolutionary Petrograd, and, of course, his Socialist Party membership card, Williams sailed forth to fulfill his destiny—a free, happy, hopeful man.

When Williams left the United States in the spring of 1917 he could scarcely have foreseen the corrosive effect which our war to make the world safe for democracy would have on our own democracy, nor have anticipated the bitter official hostility he would encounter upon his return home fifteen months later. In Honolulu he received the first intimation of what awaited him. On September 4th, 1918, as the S.S. *Nanking* was about to enter the San Francisco harbor, he was taken off the boat by officers of the Naval Intelligence, taken to Naval Headquarters, searched, grilled, and grilled again, and held under virtual arrest for two days. When it became evident that he had committed no act on which he could be legally held, he was released (September 6th, at 3 P.M.), but on condition that he go forthwith to Washington and report to the Central Office of Naval Intelligence.

Before proceeding to Washington, however, Williams, tagged by the secret service, stopped off at

Upton Sinclair's where he prepared a report on the Russian Revolution. He then went to Washington where, according to subsequent testimony before a Senate investigating committee, he had talks with and presented his report to "certain members of the State Department, to Justice Brandeis, to Colonel House, and through him to the President." And then, on September 18th, he finally made his appearance at the Office of Naval Intelligence, where, after a prolonged interview, Lieutenant Hugh R. Johnstone, provided him with a To-Whom-It-May-Concern document, proclaiming that Mr. Albert Rhys Williams had on such and such dates arrived in San Francisco, "left the office of the Aid for Information, 12th Naval District, and reported to the Office of Naval Intelligence in Washington."

But that did not end his troubles. All his personal documents which had been taken away from him in Honolulu, as well as a big trunk crammed with all kinds of material he had intended to use in his writing, were being withheld from him. This, on top of the fact that the first draft of the book he was working on and most of his notes were destroyed when the interventionists seized Vladivostock, worked havoc with the immediate execution of his literary plans. Persistent inquiries proved of no avail. Finally, on October 21, he was informed by the Director of Naval Intelligence, Rear Admiral Roger Wells, that his trunk and papers had been turned over to the Department of Justice. What the Admiral failed to tell Williams was that in turning over the trunk, he also turned over a recommendation from the State Department, signed by Leland Harrison (October 16), as to what disposition to make of Williams' belongings.

"In my opinion," wrote Harrison, "these documents should not be returned to Williams nor should those contained in the trunk—certainly not at this time and perhaps not after the close of the war." To this Harrison added an account of Williams' misdeeds while in Russia, and concluded: "I believe that Williams is extremely dangerous and his activities should be very closely watched. It may well be that if his suspicions are not aroused he will shortly say or do something which will make it possible for the Department of Justice to prosecute him." Needless to say the documents and the papers were not immediately returned, which could not but arouse Williams' suspicions.

Unsuccessful in his efforts to influence Washington's Russian policies, unable for the moment to work on his book because of the unavailability of his notebooks, Williams went to New York resolved to appeal to the American people directly. When he dropped in to see Reed in the offices of the *Liberator* (alias for the recently suppressed *Masses*) a spontaneously organized discussion with the staff and a few invited guests took place, and was recorded and published in the December, 1918, issue of the magazine, under the title "Recent Impressions of Russia: Verbatim Report of a Conversation with Albert Rhys Williams." The questions propounded at the *Liberator* were identical with the questions Williams heard in Washington and elsewhere. This, plus the readers' warm response to the question-answer format of the article, suggested the idea of a pamphlet along the same lines: "76 Questions and Answers on the Bolsheviks and the Soviets."

Published and sold at ten cents a copy by the Rand School, a socialist institution of considerable influence in those days, and republished by many other organizations, the pamphlet created something of a sensation, attaining, it is estimated, a sale of almost 2,000,000 copies. Overnight, the name of Albert Rhys Williams became a byword in radical circles throughout the land. Requests for personal appearances and lectures came pouring in from all sides. Eager to spread his message, Williams accepted every invitation, spoke everywhere, and drew ever increasing crowds. He, John Reed and Louise Bryant formed a small band, spreading "the truth about Russia" wherever they could.

It took courage those days to write what they wrote and say what they said. The country was in the throes of a savagely anti-Bolshevik, anti-Soviet, anti-Red convulsion. Official propaganda, the capitalist press, tsarist emigrés, and vociferous anti-

Bolsheviks on the Left (pro-war socialists, supporters of the Mensheviks, Right Socialist-Revolutionaries, the Anarchists in Russia, etc.) filled the air with blood-chilling tales about Bolshevik tyrannies, villainies, robberies, and bloodbaths; lurid tales about Bolshevik licentiousness, godlessness, and contempt for civilized values; fantastic stories about the stupidity, incompetence, or demonic cleverness of the Bolshevik leaders. Passions ran high: there were attacks on Socialists and pacifists, raids, arrests, deportations; mobs of misguided patriots rioted at the doors of every meeting suspected of Bolshevik leanings. Those who dared say anything favorable about the Bolshevik revolution or its leaders were violently denounced as anti-Americans, Bolshevik agents, propagandists bought with "Moscow gold."

Of the little band of truth tellers, Williams was the most effective. This "ex-minister of the Gospel" with a "faint aroma of the left-wing pulpit" was, according to the not unbiased recollections of William Henry Chamberlain (*Confessions of an Individualist*, 1940) "the leading lion in New York pro-Bolshevik circles in 1919." His speeches drew vast and enthusiastic audiences and his pamphlet "was a sort of ABC of popular Communist information, and one could hear genuine or garbled excerpts from it being cited with all the authority of Holy Writ at discussions among radicals."

Williams' unique effectiveness as orator and writer

is also attested to by two editorials which the venerable *New York Times* felt impelled to devote to his activities. The first editorial (Feb. 17, 1919), written in an ironic vein, starts out by expressing incredulity with respect to reports of victories won by the recently formed Red Army—the Bolshevik destroyers could not create anything, let alone an efficient army—and concludes with a jab at Williams: "No, we still think that the greatest creation of Bolshevism is not Trotsky's army, but Albert Rhys Williams and the singular audiences that applaud him." The second editorial (March 14, 1919), written in a solemn vein, took up the matter of Williams' pamphlet, denouncing it on moral and educational grounds. The title of the editorial was "Education in Robbery."

In 1919, Williams was officially still a Christian minister, and was regarded as such by his audiences. Indeed, this, added to the fact that, unlike Reed, he had not joined the Communist party, imbued him with a very special distinction on the Left. He was a free spirit, a man of conscience, committed to no political party or rigid doctrine, addicted to no dogmas and mouthing no clichés, and his speeches carried all the more conviction because they pulsated with the rhythms of the Bible, the vision of the prophets. He spoke, and those who heard him believed. To many, the very fact that a Christian minister testified in favor of the revolution and the Bolsheviks made them both respectable and acceptable. That the minister was tall, handsome, charming, and blessed with a sense of humor and poetry only added to the credibility of what he said.

Jessica Smith, who has devoted her entire life to the fostering of American-Soviet understanding and friendship, parallels this writer's own recollection of Williams' tremendous impact on the young socialists of those days. She writes:

The glowing sun that was Williams rose over my horizon when he had just returned from Russia. . . . I was blessed to be among those on whom his golden words fell as he went around the country telling the story of Lenin and the Revolution, of the dawn of socialism. . . . American to the core, steeped in our history and democratic traditions, he identified himself with the socialist aims of the Russian people as an extension of the American dream of human equality, of the inalienable rights of all men to life, liberty, and the pursuit of happiness. . . . His words were full of the colors and sounds and texture of life. . . . He had about him an aura of romance and adventure—the high adventure of pioneering the way to a new society. . . . He never glossed over the terrible difficulties. . . . Urging patience with the mistakes of the Soviets, he asked that the terrible years of Tsarist oppression be remembered, the losses of millions in the War, the unimaginable devastation; and how, despite all obstacles, despite having to defend themselves on four fronts, the Soviets were restoring industry and agriculture and meeting the deep hunger of the people for knowledge. He pointed out that little violence accompanied the Revolution, until armed intervention from the outside caused bloody civil war. He did not conceal Soviet blunders. He told the whole truth. But in all he said and wrote, the splendor of the goals for which the revolution was made, the glory of the people's struggle to achieve them, came through. . . .

Such was Williams as he appeared to those "singular audiences" that read, heard, and applauded him. A relatively small, if ardent, group, to be sure. But.

as the Russian proverb says, *U strakha glaza veliki,*
fear has big eyes; and the anti-Sovieteers were truly
alarmed. One fairly well-known Right-wing socialist described by Chamberlain as "an apoplectically
indignant anti-Bolshevik," rushed out a question-
answer pamphlet under the cumbersome title:

THE BOLSHEVIKS AND THE SOVIETS
Questions
which
Albert Rhys Williams
Failed to Answer
and
The Answers
By
HENRY L. SLOBODIN

A rather clever if not always ingenuous exposé
of various points in Williams' hasty answers, the
pamphlet concluded with a venomous attack on
Williams personally, a psychological explanation of
how this minister of the gospel became a "Bolshevik
propagandist." The opening couple of paragraphs
set the tone of the whole chapter:

> Mr. Albert Rhys Williams visited Bolshevik Russia armed with
> a sympathetic heart, enormous gullibility, an absolute innocence
> of any knowledge of Bolshevism, Socialism, Russian language,
> history, conditions, or anything at all that would help him to ap-
> praise critically and to form a correct judgment of people and
> events in Russia. The Russian environment reacted on Mr. Wil-
> liams' emotions in a peculiar way. Evidently, Mr. Williams landed

right in the midst of indescribable commotion and noise—people were running to and fro, gesticulating, yelling, Mr. Williams didn't know what; everywhere speakers were exhorting crowds, Mr. Williams did not know what about, everywhere some people were shooting other people, Mr. Williams did not know what for.

The well-known mass psychology, or as some call it, mob spirit, seized upon Williams' very receptive emotions. He cast aside the old Williams. A new Williams was born. He ran with others to and fro; he gesticulated and yelled as others did, only he did it in English; he exhorted as others did, only nobody understood him, and finally he, *no doubt, shot and killed some people as others did, only he still did not know why.* [Emphasis added.]

Another anti-Bolshevik "expert" to join in the campaign to demolish Williams was A. J. Sack, Director of the Russian Information Bureau in the United States, a semi-official agency of the Provisional Government overthrown by the Bolsheviks. Politically suspended somewhere between the Kadets and the Right Socialist-Revolutionists, Sack felt especially aggrieved because it was he, in the weeks when Williams was preparing for his trip to Russia, who had supplied the young American minister with many letters of introduction and given him a thorough briefing on his version of the social and political forces in the revolution. He felt betrayed. "There are still people," wept Sack in a long and heavily documented chapter, "who, notwithstanding all the facts, consider the Bolshevik regime in Russia as a sort of paradise on earth and who believe that the many crimes of which the Bolshevist rulers are accused were never committed. The point of

view of these people on the Bolshevist regime is
probably best expressed in a pamphlet entitled 'The
Bolsheviks and the Soviets,' by Albert Rhys Williams." But, argued Sack, what did Mr. Williams
really know? He had "spent only about a year in
Russia, hardly speaks Russian, and his affiliation
with the Bolshevist government naturally made him
see Russia through Bolshevist eyeglasses." Then,
taking Williams' pamphlet apart, point by point, he
proceeded to "establish" the author's blindness,
ignorance, credulity, and naiveté.

The most concentrated newspaper attack on Williams and his band of truth tellers occurred as a
result of a spectacularly successful meeting they
addressed on February 2, 1919, in Washington, D.C.
The auditorium of the Poli Theater was crowded; in
the audience one could see some rather distinguished
people, including some Congressmen, a couple of
Senators, and several men in army uniform; the
speakers (Williams and Louise Bryant) were tumult-
uously applauded, especially Williams. The press
was outraged by the impudence of the group. *The
New York Times* led the pack with a long piece
signed BY ONE WHO WAS PRESENT (we now know
that the anonymous scribe was Herman Bernstein, a
gentleman who was among the first to inform Naval
Intelligence of Williams' Bolshevik sins in Russia,
who remained a violent red-baiter in subsequent
years, and who was finally honored for his service

by an ambassadorship to Turkey). The account struck the tocsin, by denouncing the speakers as follows:

> The outpost of the Bolshevik propaganda army, whose cunning strategy is even better than that of the German propaganda army, with which it was sometimes connected, had, indeed, made a quick movement on the national capital, camped in Poli's Theater, near the treasury [*sic*] and got away with it.

A few days later, still using the Washington meeting as the pretext, the *Times* came back to the subject of Williams, Reed, and Louise Bryant with the already mentioned editorial about the great Bolshevik achievement of having won the support of a man like Williams and, on the same page, with a two-column piece by the highly publicized millionaire-philanthropist and pro-war Socialist, J. G. Phelps Stokes. Among Stokes' numerous charges, the most serious, one not made heretofore by anyone in print, was that "until recently" Williams had served as "Commissar in Charge of the Whole Bureau of International Revolutionary Propaganda in the Ministry of Foreign Affairs of the Soviet Government" and that the Bureau "had as its immediate object promotion of the revolutionary overthrow of all non-Bolshevik governments, that of the United States included," and that "very immense sums of money were placed at the disposal of Williams and his associates in the furtherance of that object."

While all this was going on in the press, Congress

took decisive action on this grave threat to national
security. The Congressmen who had ventured into
the meeting at the Poli Theater were subjected to
severe criticism from the floor. At the same time,
the Senate, by special resolution, empowered an
already existing subcommittee (created during the
war to investigate German propaganda in the USA)
"to inquire concerning any efforts being made to
propagate in this country the principles of any party
exercising or claiming to exercise authority in Russia, whether such efforts originate in this country
or are initiated or financed from abroad." An inquiry
was launched.

But this is a story in itself.

VII

For more than two weeks the Overman Subcommittee hearing resounded with the testimony of a
long line of police investigators, professional spies
and red-baiters, anti-Sovieteers and anti-Bolsheviks,
who had given the Senators a horrendous picture of
the Bolsheviks, the Soviets, and the Dictatorship of
the Proletariat, and blood-curdling details of the
all-pervasiveness and demonic cleverness of Bolshevik propaganda in America and throughout the world.
Over and over again, the names of Albert Rhys Williams and John Reed were brought up.   The con-

sensus was that the two men were agents of Bolsheviks, supplied with fabulous amounts of Moscow gold to be used in subverting the American people to paths of violence, revolution, and destruction.

Williams was to be the first witness before the Committee with a pro-Soviet point of view. But on February 21, the papers throughout the country came out with a sensational story suggesting the strange disappearance of the man. Even the non-sensationalist *New York Times* joined the cry when it reported:

> Albert Rhys Williams, formerly of the Bolshevist propaganda bureau in Petrograd, was to have been the first witness, but he was not at hand. He is under subpoena, and left Washington ten days ago after assuring the Committee that he would return whenever summoned. The telegram sent to him in New York yesterday was returned to the Committee marked "Undelivered." It was reported that he was in Chicago. In the absence of Williams, the Committee called as its first witness Mrs. John Reed, who writes under the name of Louise Bryant. . . . She made a valiant effort to defend Bolshevism.

While Louise Bryant was on the witness stand, Senator Overman evinced a special interest in Williams.

> *Senator Overman:* Did this man Albert Rhys Williams come to this country after being in the employ of the Bolsheviki?
> *Miss Bryant:* Yes, he came here to open a bureau of information for the Soviets, I think.
> *Senator Overman:* Is he in this country as an employe of the Bolshevist government?

Miss Bryant: I don't think so.
Senator Overman: What salary did he get in Petrograd?
Miss Bryant: They all got $50 a month.

Louise Bryant completed her testimony, but Williams had not made his appearance, so John Reed was called. And again there was questioning about "that man" Williams.

In the meantime, "that man" Williams, who had previously offered to testify only in *open* session, learned from the papers in Chicago, where he was on a lecture assignment, that he was wanted. He telegraphed the Committee that he would be on hand the following day. He testified throughout Saturday, February 22 and Monday, February 24.

Major Hume, the secretary of the Committee, who conducted the questioning, started out with raising the question of Williams' relation to the Church. Was the witness a minister? Was he affiliated with the Church? If not, when did he formally resign from the Church and withdraw from the ministry? The intent of this line of inquiry was clear—to embarrass the witness, to suggest renegacy and apostasy and thus to prejudice the devout Senators and the Christian people of America. But the witness refused to be fazed. Yes, he was a minister. He never formally severed relations with the Church or resigned from the ministry. He had not felt the need to; he simply drifted away, drawn by other interests and pursuits. "Formally," he said, "I am still a member of the Church, and I suppose still a member of the ministerial association." The feeling he unmistakably conveyed was not that of animosity to the Church, nor of rejection, but simply of a temperamental and intellectual preference for ideas and concerns he came upon outside its confines. No, his very candor and absence of bitterness made it impossible to pin the label of renegade on him, and Hume quickly dropped this line of inquiry.

At another point Williams happened to remark that he had spoken to Trotsky in German. German? The alert Major pricked up his ears. He had heard all about Lenin and Lenin's trip through Germany, and the Sisson papers which proved the ties between the Bolsheviks and the German General Staff, and now Williams was admitting that he spoke German to the arch-Bolshevik plotter Trotsky. The sinister implications were inescapable, and the Major made the most of them. "German? You lived a long time in Germany? You speak German well?" But, again, Williams shrugged off the insinuations with a maddening frank casualness. Yes, he had been on a student fellowship in Europe in 1908, six months in England and about six months in Germany. This line of inquiry, too, was abandoned as abruptly as it was taken up.

But it was Williams' ties with the Bolshevik propaganda machine and the Moscow gold he reputedly had at his disposal that lay at the core of the inquiry.

Here the charges were specific and the evidence formidable. All kinds of incriminating particulars had appeared in the press. Stokes was not the only one to have levelled such charges. Enough could be culled from Reed's and Williams' own articles and speeches to make the accusations plausible. Furthermore, one of the Subcommittee's star witnesses, a Mr. Simmons, only the day before, "revealed" that Williams had been officially appointed representative of the Soviet Government to the United States. Simmons said that he could not disclose in open hearings the name of the man who told him about it, but that he would be glad to give the name in secret at closed hearings, because this man would most likely be killed if his name were divulged in public. Williams had anticipated stiff questioning on this point, and he prepared a written statement with respect to it to be presented to the Subcommittee.

Accordingly, when, after some preliminary queries leading up to the point, Senator Overman asked bluntly: "Who employed you, Trotsky or Lenin, or how were you employed?" Williams offered to the Committee the prepared statement which, he promised, "will cover the whole case exactly." With the permission of the Chairman he read it into the record.

Since the statement contains a great deal of biographical material not heretofore presented in these pages, it is reproduced in full:

After the signing of the armistice* in November, 1917, the commissar of foreign affairs of the Soviet government, Leon Trotsky, addressed an appeal to the toiling masses of Germany to rise in revolution.

The president of the American Red Cross mission in Russia, Raymond Robins, stated that he would give 100,000 rubles for printing that and getting it into German hands. He suggested that I should approach Trotsky. This I did, bringing down upon my head the wrath of Trotsky, who threatened to arrest me as an agent of American capitalism who was trying to bribe him.

Immediately after this incident, however, there was opened up the bureau of international revolutionary propaganda, with an appropriation of 2,000,000 rubles spent upon newspapers, flyers, and pamphlets in the languages of the German and Austro-Hungarian empires.

The whole theory of Soviet propaganda has been "a relentless war of propaganda against those who wage a relentless war against us." That is the reason that such a ferocious propaganda offensive was waged against Germany. That is why in a milder form it was carried on against England and France. But because America did not lead the assault against the Soviet Government it, in turn, has left America out of the attack.

As a matter of fact, 99.9 per cent of all money was concentrated in an assault upon Germany.

I held no official position in this bureau but cooperated in the production of the illustrated paper which explained to the Germans how to make a revolution. Ultimately all this had its effect. Douglas Young, the British consul at Archangel, says: "Bolshevik propaganda had as much to do with the sudden collapse of Germany as our military operations."

For the time being, however, it did not avail to prevent the drive of the German army upon Petrograd. When this occurred in February, 1918, I joined the army that was being hurriedly recruited to stop this advance. I was then requested to organize a foreign-speaking detachment. A call for all foreigners to join an

* This refers to the preliminary pact signed on November 22, 1917, to discontinue military activities on the entire Russo-German front.

international legion was sent throughout Russia. The resulting contingent was not strong in numbers; it was strong in moral effect, in making Russians feel that there were some outsiders who were willing to fight with them. Thereafter, most of these people who had been so stridently crying out to the Russians, "Kill the Huns," valiantly fled when these Huns came within killing distance. For my many months' service I received 300 rubles—the pay of a regular soldier.

The whole motive of my course of action in Russia was to keep the German Imperialists from destroying the Soviet Republic and strangling the Russian people. I consistently used my energies in fighting them by propaganda, by military means, and by an espionage work against them which I organized in connection with a prominent American official, who can be called before this committee.

Some gentleman has stated here that I had been appointed a representative of the Soviet government. That he had it on the highest authority, from a Russian whose name he would not disclose lest he should be killed for it.

This is shrouded with terrible mystery—something which has been everywhere proclaimed openly as a fact. In May, 1918, there sprang up the idea of a Russian Bureau of Public Information in America, on the pattern of the American Bureau of Public Information operating in Russia. I was given credentials for the formation of such a bureau. I presented this matter to Mr. Arthur Bullard, head of the American Bureau in Russia, who said that it would be for the mutual interests of the two countries and he would use his influence for it. These credentials were likewise presented to Mr. Robins. They were shown all along the Trans-Siberian Line from Moscow to Vladivostok. This fact was printed in hundreds of Russian papers. The credentials were presented to the consul at Vladivostok and have passed through the hands of the Naval Intelligence Bureau, the Department of State, and the Department of Justice. The fact of this commission has been printed in scores of papers in America, particularly in *The Nation* and heralded from a hundred platforms. And yet, now, it is whispered in these chambers as a "dark secret."

When these credentials were given to me by the Soviet Government, I was definitely instructed in concurrence with the United States Government, to make it stand clear of any propaganda taint, and that particularly it should not present the claims of any one political party in Russia but should show the Soviets at their work.

In Washington I was informed that there could be no Russian Soviet Information bureau, because that government was not recognized.

Thereupon, I regarded that incident as closed and held my status to be that of an American citizen telling the truth as I saw it. In Russia as I spent my energies in fighting in every way against the German Imperialists, in their efforts to throttle the Russian people and their revolution, so here I have fought every imperialistic design amongst the allies that would throttle the Russian peasants and workers and would turn their natural love for America into hate. To that end I have presented reports to certain members of the State Department, to Justice Brandeis, to Colonel House, and through him to the President. I have presented my view of the facts through journals, organizations, and meetings of the middle business and educated class, neglecting the labor and socialist groups, the natural field for the "agitator."

"To the last syllable of recorded time," said Mr. Russell of the Root Mission, "mankind will have cause to regret that the people of America did not understand the people of Russia during their revolution. It does not promote that understanding to repeat those stories of loot and anarchy and murder, as though that were the chief occupation of the peasants' and workers' government."

My one idea has been to present the positive achievements of that government with the aim of promoting a closer cooperation between America and Russia and an understanding of what has happened in Russia in order that we may avoid the violences and cruelties of a brutal class war here. The American people want to hear this truth and are willing to pay for it. We, who have been fighting for fair play for the Soviets, have been absolutely without any funds except those supplied by the good will and graces of the American people. The other side seems to have had unlimited funds.

As to the motives and the facts involved in this statement I ask you to call the following witnesses who know of my activities in Russia and America: Col. Raymond Robins; Gregory Yarros, of the Associated Press; Jerome Davis, head of the YMCA in Russia for two years; Miss Bessie Beatty, editor of McCall's Magazine; Dr. Charles F. Kuntz, Iselin, N.J.; Mr. W. G. Humphries; Maj. Thomas D. Thacher.

All these people have been in Russia and take the same view of the Soviet government.

Williams was not of course unaware that in addressing the Subcommittee he was addressing a nation-wide audience. So he tried to cram in as much information about Russia and the Revolution and the Soviets as he possibly could. The result was an excellent lecture, meaty, eloquent, and far-ranging. Even the Senators succumbed, interrupting him only when they wanted further information or clarification. They were human, after all; they were curious; they wanted to learn. And this man seemed to know what he was talking about.

The question arose as to how objective was the information the witness was dispensing. Williams startled the Senators by avowing, in contrast to most of the preceding witnesses, frankly and proudly his pro-Soviet bias:

I do not pretend to have anything but a viewpoint—a partisan viewpoint, if you please—of the masses of the people with whom I spent my time, just as I believe that the viewpoint that has been generally expressed in this Committee is a partisan viewpoint of the people who have lived with those who have lost out in the Revolution, because the Revolution is a very unfortunate affair for some people, as it is fortunate for others. There are winners and losers—just as in everything else—and the losers suffer a great deal. I am not so devoid of all imagination as not to think of the suffering of the people who have lived in the roof-garden of life and have suddenly had to step out and go to work; and of the suffering also of the people who have been forcibly dispossessed of their property. I know something of their suffering and dismay. This has been reflected in America by almost every person that has been allowed to speak, because these people have lived with that class—the losers—who are full of anger and resentment, embitterment and rancor.

But, on the other hand, you must know that as there are people who lose out in a Revolution there are others who win; and the vast masses of the people are winners in this Revolution, and they are just as happy as the others are sad, and they hail the Revolution just as gloriously and joyfully as the others condemn it.

I am presenting the partisan viewpoint of the masses of the people toward the Revolution and the Soviet and the present leaders.

At the second session, Senator Wolcott brought up the question of bias once again, expressing surprise at Williams' attitude. "All the other witnesses that have come here," he observed, "have impressed me as being impartial, while you certainly admitted, as I recall, that you were confessedly in a sense, a partisan of the Revolution?"

This time, Williams was stung to more impassioned and vehement eloquence. Straightening up, his eyes flashing, he shot back:

Precisely. . . . I do not know of any witness who does not look at the matter from a particular biased standpoint. I do not try to persuade myself that I am unbiased, because I am biased by what I have seen. I have just read in the newspapers of three young fellows that were working with me, for whom I had the

greatest respect and honor, and these men who have got as much
of the divine spirit of love—and I say this reverently—almost as
much as Jesus Himself—three fellows between 19 and 26 years
of age. They have just been shot in Siberia. It is hard for me to
be cold and unmoved by it, because it is the same as if my brothers
had been shot. Therefore I am biased by that feeling that comes
all the time, when I speak about Russia. I know that the anti-
Soviet witnesses could not help but reflect the class they lived
with. We all persuade ourselves that we look at a question from
a very unprejudiced standpoint, but we are all biased. I am all
the time being biased by the fact that these men that I have been
living with and have had so much respect for, are being killed.
Sometimes it makes me mad, and sometimes I wonder that I keep
as restrained as I do.

If there was one thing the Senators seemed particularly upset about, it was the reports of what the
Bolsheviks did to the concept of the sacredness of
private property—confiscations, expropriations, re-
quisitions, nationalizations. The very thought that
such actions might be emulated by the poor and the
disinherited of other lands threw them into par-
oxysms of fear.

But Williams, smiling, reminded them of what
President Lincoln did to the concept of private property when he freed the Negro slaves. Ah, but his
purpose was to preserve the Union, not to challenge
the sanctity of private property, argued the Senators. True, answered Williams, but for the sake of
the nation's survival Lincoln did abolish the private
property rights of hundreds of thousands of Southern
slave holders; well, it was something of the same
logic that the Bolsheviks used in nationalizing the

lands, the factories, etc. They wished to preserve the Revolution!

The record does not show whether the Senators were convinced. At any rate, the matter was not pursued any further.

Almost as upsetting to the Senators were the stories of violence and Red Terror of which the previous witnesses had given them the goriest and most horrifying details.

Again Williams demurred. He didn't, of course, deny that there had been violence; he knew of no revolutions in history that were accomplished without some degree of violence, including the American revolution. But, by and large, the Bolshevik seizure of power in Petrograd was virtually bloodless. It was the counter-revolution and the foreign intervention that unleashed the killings, while the Bolsheviks naturally reacted. Even so, according to his calculations, only one in a thousand of the Russian population died in the struggle—and that, considering the depth and sweep of the Revolution, its all-embracing character, was perhaps not too terrible a price to pay.

The discussion continued back and forth. Finally wearied by the subject, Williams mildly exploded:

I will go on. I will leave this violence alone. May I make just this statement. I know that we are living in a very passionate time, and that it would be difficult for any committee to sit at

the time of the French Revolution and pass upon the facts before
it when it gets such discrepant facts from different sources, and I
realize the difficulties under which you labor. But when you bring
before the bar of history the Bolsheviks, charged with Red Terror,
and on the other side the White Guards and Black Hundreds,
charged with the White Terror, I know that when they raise their
hands, the gnarled and toil-stained hands of the peasants and
workers will be very white compared with the hands of these
ladies and gentlemen of privilege.

The Senators seemed to have been greatly moved
by the tales of immense suffering caused by the
Revolution. Williams did not deny, but urged that
the Revolution be seen in its dynamics and in historic perspective. He quoted Buckle's comment on
Edmund Burke who had turned against the French
Revolution because "His sympathy with present
suffering was so intense that he lost all memory of
the tyranny by which the sufferings were provoked."
He begged the Senators not to make the mistake
Burke made.

After many questions about the political structure
of the Soviet state, about democracy and dictatorship, and about the organization of work in shops
and factories, one Senator asked whether the witness
evaluated the Soviet Government as a success. Williams pointed to the brief existence of the Soviets
and refused to be categorical. Time, he said, will
tell. In the meantime, he did believe that the Soviet
structure represented a great social experiment which
might prove of inestimable value to the whole of

mankind. They would make mistakes, but they would learn. They might even learn certain things from us, and it was not impossible that we might learn some things from them.

At this point the following rather amusing colloquy took place:

Senator Wolcott: Mr. Williams, what I am going to ask you is somewhat irrelevant to the inquiry. . . . If the Soviet Government worked out satisfactorily in Russia, so you were convinced it is the best form of government yet invented by man, and thereupon you advocated it for the United States, you would be favorable to the idea that we should adopt it here after the fashion —in the manner—that the Russians adopted it; that is to say, without pursuing our constitutional methods to get it—by confiscation, in other words?

Mr. Williams: Senator, that is such a hypothetical question. I know that by the time the Soviet Government demonstrates itself it will be a number of years, and by that time I shall have grown old and conservative and hardened in my attitude toward life, and probably then I will jump at the idea of a new idea and beat it on the head, just like most people do when they reach a certain stage of life, and I might be such a conservative that I would take that attitude toward this new phenomenon then coming on our country.

There was laughter in the hearing room. The idea of Williams ever turning conservative seemed as preposterous then as it would seem now!

The speed and grace with which Williams turned tables on his inquisitors were astonishing. At one point the Senators sought to find out the degree of his knowledge and contacts with subversive elements in the United States. Did he know the leaders of the

IWW and did he agree with their philosophy? No, he knew little about the IWW, but insofar as it opposed political action in the struggle for betterment of the workers he disagreed with it. Did he know of any anarchists in the United States? Williams paused, thought for a moment, then grinning from ear to ear, confessed that he did. The Senators looked eager; the audience was astir.

"Yes," he said, "I have spoken before city clubs and other organizations and heard people say that the only way to treat the radicals was to string them up or shoot them down. These were men who believe in ruthless illegal methods. I call them anarchists in high places."

The Senators gasped. The audience roared. The press, with the exception of one paper, failed to report the incident.

VIII

In 1919 Williams spent so much time on the public platform that he had little left for writing. The only thing that year to appear under his name, besides the already mentioned pamphlet and a reprint of a speech he delivered in Chicago, was a small, 200-page book, *Lenin: The Man and His Work*. The first 120 pages comprising an introduction, a biographical sketch of Lenin, and a memoir called

"Ten Months with Lenin" were written by Williams.
The remaining pages contained portions of prospective books by Colonel Raymond Robins and the English journalist Arthur Ransome, both intimate impressions of Lenin. The book came out shortly after the second anniversary of the Bolshevik Revolution, and, despite its slimness and the somewhat casual way in which it was put together, the response in the press was remarkably good.

For two years Americans had been fed with the wildest rumors, tales and inventions about Lenin, concoctions from "special correspondents" in Paris, London, Copenhagen, and Stockholm, or rewrites of fanciful legends appearing in the Allied and German papers. Lenin was a peasant, the son of a serf; he was a great aristocrat, who while abroad lived in luxury, had servants galore, carried jewelled canes, wore silk pajamas, and was married to a great heiress; he was a great scholar, wore horn-rimmed glasses and a long beard; he had been murdered, jailed, and exiled from the Kremlin a hundred times, and people reported having seen him simultaneously in a Moscow prison, in Siberia, and in Barcelona, Spain; he was demoniacally clever; he had a mystical power over the masses, and so on and on.

But two years of this kind of nonsense began to pall. The victories of the Red Army began to have their effect on many American minds. The counter-revolutionary Russian generals—the idols of our press, and the recipients of our aid—were being annihilated by Lenin's worker and peasant "hordes" one after another: Wrangel, Yudenich, Kolchak were either gone or on the way out. Harsh facts, these, which no amount of lying about Lenin could hide. Williams' study came at the psychological moment.

Arthur Brisbane, the famous Hearst editor and columnist, hailed the book in a long front-page piece and urged readers to buy it.

The most mysterious, important character in the world today is Vladimir Ilyich Lenin. . . . The intelligent man wants to know about him, as he would want to know about a Messiah, or about the Black Death, if it came creeping from Asia. . . . To get information about a man ask his friends. . . . To learn about Lenin, read a book by his friends. . . .

The *Springfield Republican*, in an amazingly objective review, said: "The evidence, at all events, is too important to be overlooked. Those who fear the permanence and spread of the Soviet form of government will do well to watch and study Lenin and his methods closely."

The same point was stressed by all reviewers, whether friendly or inimical. Even the reviewer of the *New York Times*, a paper most unfriendly to Williams, while finding it difficult to swallow all the favorable things Williams and the others had to say about Lenin, was forced to acknowledge that "the book is worth reading" because it gave a portrait of Lenin. To be sure, "Much of the portrait is clearly overdrawn, and sometimes it is ridiculous, but it gives at least some of the truth, and since for the time, Lenin is a figure of importance in the world situation, it is interesting to get as much truth about him as can be got hold of, whether from enemy or friend."

All the reviewers commented especially on the vividness of Williams' portrayal. "Whatever may be thought of Mr. Williams' political and economic views," noted the review in the *New York Tribune* (written by the literary editor, Heywood Broun), "no one can deny his ability to tell a good story. The incidents he describes in the book are always interesting and often humorous. . . . The best of Mr. Williams' book is to be found in his personal reminiscences. . . . Mr. Williams' biography is an excellent first-hand sketch of a powerful and fascinating personality."

The fact that this work received such favorable comment suggested to Williams that he might write the major book he had in him. The time was auspicious. The great urgency of trying to save the Revolution from a widening of American and Allied intervention was rapidly subsiding. The Red Army and the Soviet partisan fighters were taking care of that: In the three months after the publication of *Lenin*, Denikin's armies were smashed; Kolchak's armies were annihilated; Vladivostok rejoined the Soviet Union; General Yudenitch, his armies smashed, was under arrest; Kolchak and his Prime Minister were executed; Allied intervention was drawing to an ignominious end—the British had evacuated Archangel and Murmansk, and the last American troops were about to be withdrawn from Vladivostok.

Prodded by his friends who had shared with him at least in part the Russian experience and had already published their accounts of it (*Six Red Months in Russia,* by Louise Bryant; *The Red Heart of Russia,* by Bessie Beatty; and *Ten Days that Shook the World,* by John Reed—all published in 1919), Williams settled down to write his account early in 1920. By the time *Through the Russian Revolution* was completed and published it was the summer of 1921. Victorious in the Civil War, the Bolshevik regime was now firmly entrenched. Among its American friends anxiety and curiosity about the Russian Revolution and its fate had sharply subsided. Books and articles, including translations from works by Lenin, Trotsky, Zinoviev, Bukharin, and others had become available in the meantime. Reed's *Ten Days that Shook the World* had achieved well-nigh universal acceptance as the most authentic record of events in 1917. Save for the chapters on the Far East, and some marvelous reproductions of stirring Soviet placards, Williams' book contained little, by way of event and episode, not found in the books of Reed, Louise Bryant and Bessie Beatty. What distinguished it abundantly from all other books on the subject was the majestic sweep, the grand perspective, the magisterial style; above all, the epic rhythms of a people in movement, inexorable, triumphant. But these great qualities did not vouchsafe for the book commensurate critical acclaim or distribution in the United States. Only a few reviewers recognized its claim to greatness. Upton Sinclair went all out:

> This book is, and I believe will remain for all time, the first book in the English language to which every writer about the Russian Revolution will turn. . . . The book is impassioned, vivid, stirring as a great drama. It is a work of art, by all odds the best book on the Russian Revolution.

No less ardent was Floyd Dell's praise:

> Albert Rhys Williams has written a book which recovers for us, in all its tragic and immortal loveliness, the poetry of the revolution's yesterday. . . . As every one knows, he went through the Revolution not only as an onlooker but as an active participant. And he has, not hastily but as a devoted and deliberate labor of love, made a record of those events that will stand as an enduring memorial to them to other generations than ours. He has captured in his ringing prose, the dramatic soul of that revolutionary time— its hopes, its tragedies, its triumphs are here set down with love and faith and tenderness. It is bright with all the fire that burned in the revolutionary heart of Russia. It is, for all the sad and terrible things it tells of, a happy book, it is the book of the Russian Revolution—the book of its achievement and its promise.

Almost a half century has passed since Sinclair's and Dell's reviews were penned. Their prophecies have been fulfilled. Though *Through the Russian*

Revolution had only one edition in this country, translations soon began to appear in other lands, drawing praise everywhere, and achieving large sales in some, particularly in Japan. The Russians, who had been busy publishing their own reminiscences, stories, novels, plays, and poems about the Revolution days, took three years before getting around to Williams' book (Reed's book fared better, because of Lenin's praise), but when it was finally published it was forthwith hailed as a great historical document and a literary masterpiece.

Pravda wrote:

The range of Williams' observations is stupendous: Petrograd in the throes of Revolution, the ferment in the villages, the fiery march of the Revolution across Siberia, and the first steps of intervention in the Far East. But he not only describes, with superb artistry he recreates the life, the spirit, the dynamics, the international sweep of the revolution in word pictures which etch themselves forever into one's memory. . . . Williams is not a Bolshevik. The more valuable then the profound, sincere appraisal of the ideals, facts, and people of the revolution that shines through all the pages.

The leading literary monthly *Krasnaia Nov'* agreed:

Absorbing, captivating book! . . . standing out brilliantly against the dull background of the mountains of books about Soviet Russia . . . tremendous intensity and artistic power . . . presenting a grandiose picture of the victorious march of the masses . . . the dynamics of the Great Revolution that stirred Russia from end to end. . .

Even the stodgily academic *Pechat' i Revolutsia* broke out into dithyrambs:

In contrast to other Western journalists, Williams sees not a revolt or chaos, but, on the contrary, the beginning of a great historical process, the appearance on the arena of history of the masses; the awakening in them of the sense of human worth and dignity. . . . The whole book is so dramatic, so heart-stirring, so superbly artistic that it is difficult to select the most thrilling parts . . . you see at once not only the understanding mind of the author, but a heart beating in unison with the great collective heart of the people.

A year later (1925) a translation of Williams' *Lenin: The Man and His Work* was published in Moscow, and it too received high praise for both its documentary and literary value.

For a foreign observer to receive such acclaim in a country where memories of the events described by him were still fresh in the minds of millions and where hundreds of native scholars, writers, and memoirists had themselves dealt with the same events, was a rare tribute indeed.

IX

With the completion of *Through the Russian Revolution* the most dramatic, inspiring, and creative period in Williams' life came to an end. Four glorious years. He had seen and actively participated in one of the decisive events in history: the first—and there is only *one* first—Socialist Revolution, a revolution involving scores of peoples and nationalities spread over one-sixth of the globe. He had circled the world to come back home to impart the glad tidings to his fellow countrymen. He had done this at a time when his country, misinformed and misled, was, to his infinite sorrow, waging military, political, economic, and psychological warfare against the infant Socialist Republic. Undeterred by hounding, threats, and calumny, he stood up in defense of the truth, summoning every ounce of energy and talent he had, functioning furiously as orator and writer, and producing two works which, in the opinion of critics he most admired, were "works of art" and "by all odds" the best on the Russian Revolution. Fate is rarely so munificent as to afford any one individual such glorious moments more than once.

In Russia the stormy days of revolution and civil war were over. War communism was being supplanted by a New Economic Policy, a partial restoration of capitalistic economy. In America, the press hailed the latest Russian development as a sign of Bolshevism's impending collapse from within. Washington's fear of the Bolshevik plague subsided, and so did the public's interest in things Russian. The few who remained interested were, judging by the small sale of Williams' book, less concerned with the Revolution's "heroic yesterday" than with its prosaic today. Williams was confident that all the press prophecies of a Bolshevik collapse were wishful nonsense, but not having been in Russia for almost three years, he could not support his optimism with firsthand information.

What to do?

He had for four years lived with the subject of the Soviet Union; it had become an inseparable part of him. The new phase in the Soviet development called for sympathetic understanding and honest depiction. Who was more qualified than he? Having long since given up all interest in the ministry, Williams packed up and went back to Russia.

Nothing was heard from him for the next couple of years.

Stories began to circulate that Williams had settled in Russia for good, that he had married an American girl, a scenario writer he had met in New York, that he had become a Soviet citizen, joined the Communist Party, and that the couple was living in a god-forsaken little village on the Volga. These rumors seemed to be confirmed by occasional pieces which after several years began to appear in American magazines. They dealt with rural Russia, and revealed such an intimate knowledge of peasant life and peasant lore, and such deep empathy with the peasant characters that one was prone to believe that Williams had not only assumed Soviet citizenship but had also acquired a Russian soul. In 1928, a collection of these pieces appeared under the title *The Russian Land*. Beautifully written, reminiscent in spots of Turgenev's *Sportsman's Sketches*, the book won plaudits for its literary artistry, but relatively few readers.

The material in *The Russian Land* was peripheral

to the vital problems of the Soviet Union in the twenties. The village, in the twenties, was largely the old Russian village, whereas the heart and mind of the revolution were in the cities, in the factories, and the shops. It was there that the revolution was girding its loins for the next advance, it was there that the great debates over policy between Trotsky and Stalin raged, it was there that the intellectual youth was making itself felt in a great outburst of artistic and literary creativity. By burying himself in the backwoods, Williams missed much of what other foreign writers, journalists and scholars (of whom there was a growing army now) saw and wrote about. Williams had fallen in love with the Russian peasant, and he sought to share his love with the reader, but by the end of the twenties the reader, if he was interested in Russia at all, was interested in something else entirely. And so Williams' book— full of the exotic, the bizarre, and the doomed— was hardly a best seller.

Shortly after the publication of the book, Williams reappeared on the American scene. All the stories about him—save the one that he had lived in the villages and that he was married to the American, Lucita Squier—proved to be false. He was and never contemplated being anything else but an American. Now that he was married and the book on rural Russia completed, his roving days were all but over. He came back to settle, raise a family, and plan a detailed work on the Russian Revolution —a book radically different from anything the professional historians would be likely to write, a book in which the central hero would be the Russian people.

After a round of house parties, receptions, and soirees, Williams again disappeared from the scene. He settled in Carmel, California; became the devoted father of a boy who was given the Welsh name, Rhys; lived an intense social life among the Left-wing elite on the coast (Lincoln Steffens, Ella Winter, many of the Hollywood writers and actors); made a trip to the Soviet Union (1930-1931); wrote an occasional piece in the magazines (but not in the avowedly Communist publications such as the *Worker* and the *New Masses*) and kept on collecting data and making notes for an encyclopedic book on the USSR. He wrote down questions and answers on every aspect of Soviet life that might possibly interest an American reader—the Five Year Plans, Collectivization, the Red Army, the Soviet Constitution, education, the arts, etc. The book, *The Soviets,* came out in 1937, just after the series of Stalinist purge trials which aroused universal horror and condemnation in the United States—an unfortunate time for a book friendly to the Soviets. It was a good, honest book, full of authentic information, illuminating comment, and distinguished for the excellence of the writing. The reviewers were fair enough, noting the author's "partisanship," but granting that it was rather intelligent, undogmatic partisanship. Among the Soviet sympathizers the book was welcomed as an antidote to the violent anti-Soviet propaganda that was coming from all sides—Fascists, Nazis, Coughlinites on the Right, Social Democrats, Lovestoneites, and Trotskyites on the Left. A few bold scholars recommended it as collateral reading in their courses as a corrective to the overwhelmingly anti-Soviet books on their reading lists.

However, in a period of bitter partisanship in the United States, the Soviet Union, and the rest of the world, the book's sweet reasonableness could arouse but little enthusiasm. Events in the next couple of years—the Soviet-Nazi pact, the partition of Poland, the attack on Finland and the resulting wholesale defections on the Left—inevitably reduced the book's readership and influence. In the winter of 1937-1938 Williams visited the USSR again and from there went to Spain to observe the Civil War.

The Nazi invasion of the Soviet Union and the magnificent resistance of the Red Army in face of the surprise attack caused a sudden change in American attitudes. In effect the USSR had now become our ally, and Williams hastened to meet the rising clamor for information about the Soviet Union and for explanations of the heroic character of the Soviet people's struggle against the Nazis by putting out an abridged and updated version of *The Soviets* under the title *The Russians, The People and Why They Fight*. This time the book caught on. It went into several printings and Williams was once again in the limelight as one of the best friends and interpreters of the Soviet people in America. One could hear him on the radio and read accounts of his speeches in the papers. During the summers of 1943-1944 he was one of the lecturers in a course at Cornell University on contemporary Russian civilization.

With the conclusion of the war, and with the Red Armies stationed in the heart of Europe, another shift in American sentiment occurred. The explosion of the atomic bombs over Hiroshima and Nagasaki, motivated not by military necessity but primarily as a warning to the Soviets to cease and desist, was the first stunning augury of the change. Soon all agencies of agitation and propaganda in the United States unleashed a concerted campaign of suspicion, calumny, and hatred against the Soviets. The Cold War was unleashed; McCarthyism was rampant. Holders of radical opinions, especially people known to have been friends of the Soviet Union, became political and social pariahs, their names anathema to editors and publishers and broadcasting stations. Williams was no exception. Once again he vanished from the scene, this time for good, for the country remained in the grip of the Cold War for the rest of Williams' life and beyond.

One might imagine that at least in the Soviet Union a grateful government and citizenry would remember and cherish the American who had for thirty tireless years devoted himself to fostering sympathy for them and understanding of their cause. Alas, that was not the case. Williams, like Reed, had committed one unforgivable sin: in his accounts of the Revolution in Russia, he failed to mention Stalin, while he mentioned Trotsky dozens of times. Accordingly, despite the accolades he and Reed received in the 1920's, their books and their names were consigned to oblivion upon Stalin's rise to power. Reed fared a little better than Williams. He had joined the Communist Party, had died before Stalin rose to supreme leadership, and had found his way into the Soviet pantheon when his remains were interred in the Kremlin wall. Williams never joined the party, and he lived to see his and Reed's books disappear from the Soviet shelves, not to be republished again during the Stalin years.

He accepted his lot philosophically, cheered by the thought that events had and would, he was sure, continue to vindicate his faith in the October Revolution, the Soviet Union, and socialism. The record so far was clear. One of his notes reads:

When, in October, 1917, the Soviets, led by the Bolsheviks, became the government, the so-called experts on Russia, journalists, publicists, historians, and socialists, declared "It will not last, at most a month or two!" but we knowing the Soviet people declared that the revolution would increasingly rally the masses to their government. As they had won the power they would keep in power; . . . they were here to stay. Life has proved us right.

When in 1921 the NEP was proclaimed, again the "experts" said that that was the end, but we who knew the Soviet people were not dismayed, sharing Lenin's confidence that the retreat was temporary, a breathing spell, and that the next advance toward Socialism was not too far away. Life has proved us right.

When the first Five Year Plan was launched in 1928, it was derided by capitalist experts as a "statistical dream," a "blueprint with astronomical figures." But we who knew the Soviet people unhesitatingly asserted that however colossal the projects, the Soviet people would be equal to the great challenge and would translate the dream into reality. Life has proved us right.

When the 300 divisions of Nazis, flushed with victory in the West, at the peak of their power, crossed over the Soviet border on that fateful day in June 1941, those so-called experts were boldly proclaiming that the Nazis would go through the Red Army like a knife through butter—that in three or four weeks the swastika would be fluttering from the towers of the Kremlin. But those of us who knew the Soviet people knew better. On June 24, in a cable to the Soviet Union, I expressed my conviction that the might of the Soviet people would prevail, and in due time the Red Flag with the hammer and sickle would be flying over the Reichstag in Berlin. And again life proved us right!

As for his neglect in the Soviet Union, Williams was not in the least bitter. They had had too much trouble of their own to give much thought to him. He was grieved by the brutal sectarian struggle of which he was a minor victim, but deeply grounded as he was in the history of the Church, he was not too shocked—human movements, no matter how noble their initial impulse, do develop ailments, but this does not detract from the splendor of the impulse

or the good that springs therefrom. Stalin, whatever
his virtues and faults, was not immortal; when he
went, the Soviet people would still be there, and so
would the socialist foundations they had built, and
the socialist ideal of justice. He was satisfied to
wait.

In the meantime, no longer young—he was ap-
proaching seventy—Williams turned his mind nos-
talgically to the glorious days of 1917. He dreamed
of writing once again about the Revolution and the
decisive role of the people in it—a role, he felt, not
sufficiently explored or stressed in any history he had
read. To recapture the past, he sent out young
scholars to hunt libraries and archives for data, newspapers published in Russia at the time, speeches,
articles, memoirs, etc. All their findings were copied,
labeled, and filed away. But before Williams had a
chance to utilize the material, he was struck down
by leukemia. Eternally optimistic, he did not abandon the project. Leukemia in an older person, he
argued, is not necessarily fatal, not if one takes care.
The scholars continued to search, and the files continued to grow, and Williams continued to savor it all
in happy anticipation. A happy man, sustained by
a happy dream.

He followed news from the USSR with as much
avidity as in the past. But, so absorbed was he in
reliving 1917, that neither the news of the Soviet
explosion of the atom bomb, nor the news of Stalin's

death evoked any comment from him in the notes he was in the habit of jotting down daily. It was the report of the pioneering Soviet shot into the cosmos, it was the Sputnik, that aroused Williams' greatest enthusiasm. He immediately wrote an article hailing the feat as the triumph of socialist science and industry and, since he no more had contacts in the USSR, had Lucita hand it over to a Soviet trade union official who happened to be in New York. The article soon appeared in the very influential trade union paper *Trud*. And this opened a new and happy chapter in Williams' life.

Touching letters from people he had known in Russia in the old days came pouring in in an incessant stream—requests for articles and comments, recent books containing references to him, collective letters from school children, and so on. Williams took infinite pains to answer the letters, sometimes in Russian. No blood transfusion did so much to perk up his spirit as did those letters. And no task was taken as seriously as filling requests for articles. Prominent Soviet visitors to the United States now made it their business to look in on the great old man who knew Lenin. For now that the image of Stalin and his period had been consigned to limbo, the whole trend in the Soviet Union was toward a revival of the image and inspiration of Lenin and his period.

Soon John Reed's *Ten Days that Shook the World*

appeared in new, large editions; and Williams was informed that a new edition of his *Through the Russian Revolution* was being prepared. He was invited to the Soviet Union, where he and Lucita received a royal welcome. He was placed in the Kremlin hospital where only famous homegrown and foreign communists are treated. He was asked to write an introduction to the new edition, which besides *Through the Russian Revolution* would contain everything he had written about Lenin.

After several months in the USSR, Williams returned to the United States refreshed, jubilant, though not cured. Then came copies of the new edition (100,000 copies!) with the eulogistic, indeed, loving introduction by Boris Polevoy. His seventy-eighth birthday was about a month away. Stroking the book caressingly, his blue eyes twinkling, he mused: It would be nice to live to the day when a Socialist America will appreciate and take pride in the fact that it was two Americans who together left to posterity the best firsthand accounts of the first Socialist Revolution in history. This was said half-jokingly, of course, but it did reflect Williams' deep longing to be accepted and appreciated by his own people, his own countrymen.

The writer of these lines would like to conclude his brief account of Williams' beautiful life with two personal recollections. The first is of Williams in 1919, shortly after he returned from Russia: gay, ebullient, radiating warmth and friendliness, his conversation sparkling with humorous observations, quips, ready quotations from the prophets and the poets, and enveloped in the aura of revolutionary romance. One occasion revived by a crumbling newspaper clipping rises in my memory with particular sharpness.

It was in midtown Manhattan and Williams was addressing a very decorous gathering of white-collar radicals and pacifists, fervently defending the workers and peasants of Russia and their Soviet government and denouncing our intervention in Russia's internal affairs, and our support of the counter-revolution. His passionate oratory held the audience spellbound.

Outside, hundreds of doughboys hooted, screamed, bellowed. Strains of "My country 'tis of thee, sweet land of liberty" drifted into the hall. Now and then a beer bottle came crashing through the rear windows. As the spirit of the audience began to sink, that of the speaker rose. "Let's invite them in and talk to them," he proposed with enthusiasm, "and make them see that they have no quarrel with their fellow workers and soldiers in Russia." The audience was taken aback, apprehensive. A distinguished radical (Max Eastman, I think) tiptoed to the outer doors, glanced across the reassuring police barrier at the rioting patriots, and with a skeptical smile tiptoed back. Red neckties and crimson carnations, timid badges of revolutionary sympathy, were surreptitiously stuffed into pockets. Those in the back seats moved away from the windows. But the speaker, cheerful and grinning, to the accompaniment of the cacophony of prejudice and bigotry, continued telling his heartwarming story of a "magnificent sunrise" and of a "sky shot through with riotous colors."

A happy warrior in the battle for American-Russian understanding—such was Williams in 1917-1918 and such he remained through the years. His faith in socialism and in the country that showed the world its practicality and realizability never flagged. It shines through every article and book he wrote after 1918, up to the very end.

The second recollection I would like to share with my readers is of a stroll Williams and I took in the woods of Mt. Desert Island, Maine, in late August, 1961, six months before his death. He and his family were staying on the estate of his devoted friend and admirer Mary Dreier. That morning, as we set out on our daily stroll, Williams was not feeling well. He had had a bad night, his bones ached, he had little energy; he needed, he thought, another blood transfusion, a very painful business. Also, he was harassed by the thought that *Izvestia*, the official organ of the Soviet Government, had several days earlier cabled a request for a piece to mark the forty-fourth anniversary of the October Revolution.

He had of late met so many such requests from Moscow that he felt completely drained. He just was not up to writing another word.

Tall, straight, his handsome head crowned with a silver mane, carrying a heavy cane, Williams looked like a legendary hero of some ancient myth. He loved the woods; he knew the names of every flower, tree, bird, or beast on the way. And he liked long strolls. But this time, he tired sooner than usual, so we sat down on a log to rest. He noticed the *Pravda* in my pocket. It had come that morning, and he had not yet glanced at it. I unfolded the paper that was wholly taken up with the recently adopted twenty-year plan for building Communism in the USSR. Williams perked up. He wanted the details. I read the essential parts aloud. And the more I read the more lively Williams became. His eyes sparkled. He demanded more and more detail. When I finished, he chuckled: "Wonderful. Even if a bit too sanguine. Well, if not twenty, let us say thirty years. But they'll get there."

He was now in a hurry to go back. His steps were springy, his voice resonant. "They'll get there, all right. No doubt of that."

That day, he sat down and dashed off the piece for *Izvestia*. It was his swan song, and a magnificent reaffirmation of his socialist faith. The concluding paragraphs, his last published words, may serve as this happy warrior's most appropriate epitaph:

To all the militant defenders of the Revolution, salutations! And deep regrets that they did not live to see the Soviet infant grow up into the giant and to find the high hopes and faith they had placed long ago in the Revolution now confirmed in this Manifesto. It is dynamic, stirring and vitalizing—like a blood transfusion—and infuses into one who had already overstayed his time on this planet the desire for a longer lease on life.

To live on in this exciting "springtime of humanity," and note what further headway the Revolution is making toward the realization of that age-old dream of mankind—the conquest by man of space and his further journeyings to the moon, the planets, and the stars!

To live on and note his progress in that not less daring and difficult enterprise—the conquest by man of himself—his advance on the road toward the good society in which everyone will receive according to his needs and from the Kingdom of Necessity pass into the Kingdom of Freedom.

Albert Rhys Williams died on February 27, 1962.

INTRODUCTION

IN Moscow I saw two peasant soldiers gazing
at a poster being stuck up on a *kiosk*.

"We can't read a word of it," they cried, indignant
tears in their eyes. "The Czar only wanted us to
plough and fight and pay taxes. He didn't want us
to read. He put out our eyes."

"To put out the eyes" of the masses, to put out
their minds and consciences, was the deliberate
policy of the Russian autocracy. For centuries the
people were steeped in ignorance, narcotized by the
church, terrorized by the Black Hundreds, dragooned
by the Cossacks. The protesters were thrown into
dungeons, exiled to hard labor in Siberian mines,
and hung up on gibbets.

In 1917 the social and economic fabric of the
land was shot to pieces. Ten million peasants
dragged from their ploughs were dying in the
trenches. Millions more were perishing of cold and
hunger in the cities while the corrupt ministers
intrigued with the Germans and the court held
bacchanalian revels with the notorious monk,
Rasputin. Even the Cadet, Milyukov, was forced
to say: "History does not know of another government so stupid, so dishonest, so cowardly, so
treacherous."

All governments rest upon the patience of the
poor. It seems everlasting, but there comes an end
to it. It came in Russia in March, 1917.

The masses felt that more vicious even than the

1

Kaiser in Berlin was their own Czar in Petrograd. Their cup of bitterness was full. They marched forth against the palaces to end it all. First, out of the Viborg district, came the working women crying for bread. Then long lines of workingmen. The police turned the bridges to prevent them entering the city, but they crossed on the ice. Looking at the red-flagged throngs from his window, Milyukov exclaimed: "There goes the Russian Revolution— and it will be crushed in fifteen minutes!"

But the workingmen came on in spite of Cossack patrols on the Nevsky. They came on in face of wilting fire from machine gun nests. They came on until the streets were littered with their bodies. Still they came on, singing and pleading until soldiers and Cossacks came over to the people's side, and on March 12 the Romanov dynasty, which had misruled Russia for 300 years, went crashing to its doom. Russia went mad with joy while the whole world rose up to applaud the downfall of the Czar.

It was mainly the workers and soldiers who made the Revolution. They had shed their blood for it. Now it was assumed that they would retire in the orthodox manner leaving affairs in the hands of their superiors. The people had taken the power away from the Czarists. Now appeared on the scene the bankers and lawyers, the professors and politicians, to take the power away from the people. They said:

"People, you have won a glorious victory. The next duty is the formation of a new state. It is a most difficult task, but fortunately, we, the educated, understand this business of governing. We shall set up a Provisional Government. Our responsibility is heavy, but as true patriots we will shoulder it,

Noble soldiers, go back to the trenches. Brave workingmen, go back to the machines. And peasants, you go back to the land."

Now the Russian masses were tractable and reasonable. So they let these bourgeois gentlemen form their "Provisional Government." But the Russian masses were intelligent, even if they were not literate. Most of them could not read or write. But they could think. So, before they went back to the trenches, the shops and the land, they set up little organizations of their own. In each munition factory the workers selected one of their number whom they trusted. In the shoe and cotton factories the men did likewise. So in the brickyards, the glass-works and other industries. These representatives elected directly from their jobs were called a *Soviet* (*Council*) *of Workmen Deputies.*

In like manner the armies formed *Soviets of Soldiers' Deputies,* the villages *Soviets of Peasant Deputies.*

These deputies were elected by trades and occupations, not by districts. The Soviets consequently were filled, not with glibly talking politicians, but with men who knew their business; miners who understood mining, machinists who understood machinery, peasants who understood land, soldiers who understood war, teachers who understood children.

The Soviets sprang up in every city, town, hamlet and regiment throughout Russia. Within a few weeks after the old state-apparatus of Czardom went to pieces, one-sixth the surface of the earth was dotted over with these new social organizations —no more striking phenomenon in all history.

The commander of the Russian battlesnip

Peresvet told me his story: "My ship was off the coast of Italy when the news arrived. As I announced the Czar's fall some sailors shouted, 'Long live the Soviet.' That very day on board ship a Soviet was formed, in all aspects like the one in Petrograd. I regard the Soviet as the natural organization of the Russian people, finding its root in the *mir* (commune) of the village and the *artel* (co-operative syndicate) of the city."

Others find the Soviet idea in the old New England town-meetings or the city assemblies of ancient Greece. But the Russian workingman's contact with the Soviet was much more direct than that. He had tried out the Soviet in the abortive Revolution of 1905. He had found it a good instrument then. He was using it now.

After the Czar's overthrow there was a short season of good will amongst all classes known as the "honeymoon of the Revolution." Then the big fight began—a battle royal between the bourgeoisie and the proletariat for the mastery of state power in Russia. On the one side the capitalists, landlords and finally the *intelligentsia* lining up behind the Provisional Government. On the other side the workmen, soldiers and peasants rallying to the Soviets.

I was set down in the midst of this colossal conflict. For fourteen months I lived in the villages with the peasants, in the trenches with the soldiers, and in the factories with the workers. I saw the Revolution thru their eyes and took part in most of the dramatic episodes.

I have used the names *Communist* and *Bolshevik* interchangeably, tho the party did not officially change its name to *Communist* until 1918.

In the French Revolution the great word was "Citizen." In the Russian Revolution the great word is "Comrade!"—*tovarishtch*. I have written it more simply *tovarish*.

For the right to use here some of my articles I am indebted to the editors of *Asia*, the *Yale Review*, the *Dial*, the *Nation*, the *New Republic*, and the *New York Evening Post*.

The visitor to Soviet Russia is struck by the multitudes of posters—in factories and barracks, on walls and railway-cars, on telephone-poles—everywhere. Whatever the Soviet does, it strives to make the people understand the reason for it. If there is a new call to arms, if rations must be cut down, if new schools or courses of instruction are opened, a poster promptly appears telling *why*, and how the people can co-operate. Some of these posters are crude and hurried, others are works of art. Six of them are reproduced in this book in almost the exact colors of the originals. The cost has been borne by friends of Russia, and the reader is particularly indebted to Mrs. Jessie Y. Kimball and Mr. Aaron Berkman.

On the next page is reproduced the first issue of the first revolutionary newspaper—the official *Soviet News (Izvestia)*. It was published on the day of the Czar's fall and every day since then.

ИЗВѢСТІЯ
ПЕТРОГРАДСКАГО СОВѢТА
Рабочихъ депутатовъ.

№ 1—28 февраля 1917 года.   № 1.

Къ населенію Петрограда и Россіи.
Отъ Совѣта Рабочихъ Депутатовъ.

Старая власть довела страну до полнаго развала, а народъ до голоданія. Терпѣть дальше стало невозможно. Населеніе Петрограда вышло на улицу, чтобы заявить о своемъ недовольствѣ. Его встрѣтили залпами. Вмѣсто хлѣба царское правительство дало народу свинецъ.

Но солдаты не захотѣли итти противъ народа и возстали противъ правительства. Вмѣстѣ съ народомъ они захватили оружіе, военные склады и рядъ важныхъ правительственныхъ учрежденій.

Борьба еще продолжается; она должна быть доведена до конца. Старая власть должна быть окончательно низвергнута и уступить мѣсто народному правленію. Въ этомъ спасеніе Россіи.

Для успѣшнаго завершенія борьбы въ интересахъ демократіи народъ долженъ создать свою собственную властную организацію.

Вчера 27 февраля въ столицѣ образовался Совѣтъ Рабочихъ Депутатовъ— изъ выборныхъ представителей заводовъ и фабрикъ, возставшихъ воинскихъ частей, а также демократическихъ и соціалистическихъ партій и группъ.

Совѣтъ Рабочихъ Депутатовъ засѣдающій въ Государственной Думѣ ставитъ своей основной задачей организацію народныхъ силъ и борьбу за окончательное упроченіе политической свободы и народнаго правленія въ Россіи.

Совѣтъ назначилъ районныхъ коммиссаровъ для установленія народной власти въ районахъ Петрограда.

Приглашаемъ все населеніе столицы немедленно сплотиться вокругъ Совѣта, образовать мѣстные комитеты въ районахъ и взять въ свои руки управленіе всѣми мѣстными дѣлами.

Всѣ вмѣстѣ, общими силами будемъ бороться за полное устраненіе стараго правительства и созывъ учредительнаго собранія, избраннаго на основѣ всеобщаго равнаго, прямого и тайнаго избирательнаго права.

Совѣтъ Рабочихъ Депутатовъ.

(For reproduction in English, see page 7.)

BOLSHEVIK POSTER IN RUSSIAN AND ARABIC CHARACTERS FOR THE PEOPLES
OF THE EAST: "PROLETARIANS OF ALL COUNTRIES, UNITE!"

НЕГРАМОТНЫЙ тот-же СЛЕПОЙ

ВСЮДУ ЕГО ЖДУТ НЕУДАЧИ И НЕСЧАСТЬЯ.

"THE ILLITERATE IS A BLIND MAN: EVERYWHERE PITFALLS AND MISFORTUNES AWAIT HIM."—SOVIET POSTER TO ENCOURAGE EDUCATION.

THE RED PEASANT, SOLDIER AND WORKINGMAN (*on the left*) TO THE COSSACK (*centre*) : COSSACK, WITH WHOM ARE YOU? WITH US OR WITH THEM?—(THE LANDLORDS, GENERALS AND CAPITALISTS).

The life of an illiterate is terribl
He lives in a dark forest. Everythin
frightens him. An owl hoots at night,
the illiterate thinks it is the were-wolf how
ing; he believes in devils and witches.
lightning strikes his hut, he says God is pun
ishing him for his sins; he does not know ho
to catch the lightning with a rod! The cro
is poor—he will pray to God: but if he knew how better t
cultivate Mother Earth, his harvest would be rich. He is cruel to animals—

SOVIET EDUCATIONAL POSTER.—CHILDREN OF DARKNESS AND SUPERST

iends of man. He does not know how
d them or utilize them. But when the
ate goes thru school—he, a blind man,
diately has his eyes opened. He begins to
stand everything; all things become clear to him.
ees what he did not see before. It is as if he had
red a hundred eyes; life for him begins to be a joy. All
rs begin to take a good turn. And if he is in trouble, he will take
e from his friend, the book—who will not deceive him—and he will
how to get out of his trouble.

INTO A SCHOOL: THEN EMERGING INTO LIGHT AND KNOWLEDGE.

Some father has driven
His daughter, disheveled,
Into the street,
Without cause or mercy.

The snow cuts her face,
The wind's breath is icy,
But the heart of the father
Is colder than these.

Is the father to blame
For mistreating his daughter?
He was taught by the priest
That woman is sin.

Now the Soviet teaches
A new vision of women,
As comrades of men,
Old woes are forgotten.

The social position of Russian peasant women under the old régime was
distinctly inferior to men and they were often treated
as drudges and menials.

Two old women lament
Old days of sorrow,
When prayers went unheard
And the grave was relief.

But no more does the stick
Fall upon women's shoulders.
Free and equal they march,
Comrades of men!

"Dry your tears, Women!
A new day is here,
When old superstitions
Bring no ignorant fear.

Shake off slavish bonds,
Discover your wings,
Fly from ancient darkness
To the light of new days."

When the Soviet later came into power it sought to make women conscious of their new rights and privileges. To this end the Soviet Government issued posters like this one: FORWARD TO THE LIGHT.

Poster Reproduction of the Famous Kremlin. The Russians Say: "Above Moscow is the Kremlin, and above the Kremlin are only the Stars." Inscribed on the Walls is the Slogan, "Long Live The Third International."

NEWS OF THE

PETROGRAD SOVIET

of Workmen Deputies.

№ 1 — March 13, 1917   **№ 1**

To the population of Petrograd and Russia
From the Soviet of Workmen's Deputies.

The old authorities brought the country to ruin and the people to starvation. It became impossible to endure it longer. The population of Petrograd came out in the streets to express its discontent. It was met with guns. Instead of bread, the government of the Czar gave the people bullets.

But the soldiers have refused to go against the people and have revolted against the government. Together with the civilians they have seized the armories the military stores and many important government institutions.

The struggle is still going on; it must be brought to an end. **The old power must be deposed and replaced by a people's government. This is the salvation of Russia.**

To secure a victorious end of this struggle in the interests of democracy, the people must create an organization of its own power.

Yesterday, March the 12th, a Soviet of Workmen Deputies was formed in the Capital. It consists of representatives elected from the shops and factories, the revolting military detachments and also from democratic and socialistic parties and groups.

The Soviet of Workmen Deputies now in session at the Imperial Duma faces as its basic problem, the organization of the people's forces in the battle for permanent political freedom and self-government in Russia.

The Soviet has appointed district commissars to execute the people's authority in the districts of Petrograd.

We call upon the inhabitants of the capital to rally around the Soviet, to form district committees and to take the administration of local affairs in their own hands.

All together, we unite our forces to fight for the complete destruction of the old government, and **for the calling of a Constituent Assembly, elected on the basis of a universal, equal, direct and secret ballot.**

The Soviet of Workers' Deputies.

(This is a reproduction in English of the Russian text on page 6.)

PART I

THE MAKERS OF THE REVOLUTION

WITH THE PEASANTS, WORKERS AND FIGHTERS

CHAPTER I

THE BOLSHEVIKS AND THE CITY

ON a white night of early June, 1917, I first entered Petrograd, the city that lies almost within the Arctic Circle. Tho it was midnight, the wide squares and *prospekts* bathed in the soft spectral light of this northern night were all alluring.

Past blue-domed barbaric churches and the silver rippling Catherine Canal we drove along the Neva, while across the river the slender spire of Peter and Paul rose like a golden needle. Then by the Winter Palace, the burnished dome of Saint Isaac's and countless shafts and statues to the memory of Czars who had gone.

But all these were monuments to rulers of the past. They had no hold on me for I was interested in the rulers of the present. I wanted to hear the great Kerensky then at the zenith of his spell-binding powers. I wanted to meet the ministers of the Provisional Government. I met many of them, heard them and talked with them. They were able, amiable and eloquent. But I felt they were not real representatives of the masses, that they were "Caliphs of the passing hour."

Instinctively I sought out the rulers of the future, the men in the Soviets elected directly out of the trenches, factories and farms. These Soviets had sprung up in almost every army city and village of Russia, over one-sixth of the surface of the earth. These local Soviets were now sending their delegates to the First All-Russian Congress of Soviets in Petrograd.

The First All-Russian Congress of Soviets. I found the Soviet in session in the Military Academy. A tablet recording the fact that "His Imperial Majesty, Nicholas II, made this place happy by his presence January 28, 1916," still hung on its walls, the one relic of the glittering past.

The gold-braided officers, the smiling courtiers, and lackeys had been swept from the halls. His Imperial Majesty, the Czar, was gone. His Republican Majesty, the Revolution, ruled here now, acclaimed by hundreds of black-bloused, khaki-clad delegates.

Here were men coming up from the ends of the earth. From the frozen Arctic and burning Turkestan they hailed, slant-eyed Tartars and fair-haired Cossacks, Russians, Big and Little, Poles, Letts and Lithuanians—all tribes and tongues and costumes. Here were toil-scarred delegates from the mines, the forge and the farm, battle-scarred soldiers from the trenches and sea-bronzed sailors from the five fleets of Russia. Here were the "March" revolutionists, colorless and quiet before the March storm blew the Czar from his throne, but now daubed with red revolutionary paint and calling themselves Socialists. Here were veterans of the Revolution, loyal to the cause thru long years of hunger, exile and Siberia, tried and tested by suffering.

Cheidze, the President of the Soviet Congress, asked me why I came to Russia. "Ostensibly as a journalist," I told him. "But the real reason is the Revolution. It was irresistible. It drew me here like a magnet. I am here because I could not stay away."

He asked me to address the Congress. The "Soviet News" (*Izvestia*) of July 8, reports my words thus:

Comrades: I bring you greetings from the Socialists of America. We do not venture to tell you here how to run a Revolution. Rather we come here to learn its lesson and to express our appreciation for your great achievements.

A dark cloud of despair and violence was hanging over mankind threatening to extinguish the torch of civilization in streams of blood. But you arose, comrades, and the torch flamed up anew. You have resurrected in all hearts everywhere a new faith in freedom.

Equality, Brotherhood, Democracy, are great and beautiful words. But to the unemployed millions they are merely words. To the 160,000 hungry children of New York they are hollow words. To the exploited classes of France and England they are mocking words. Your duty is to change these words into reality.

You have made the Political Revolution. Freed from the threat of German militarism your next task is the Social Revolution. Then the workers of the world will no longer look to

the West, but to the East—toward great Russia, to the Field
of Mars here, in Petrograd, where lie the first martyrs of your
Revolution.

"Long live free Russia!" "Long live the Revolution!" "Long
live Peace to the World!"

In his reply Cheidze made a plea for the workers
of all nations to bring pressure to bear on their governments to stop "the horrible butchery which is
disgracing humanity and beclouding the great days
of the birth of Russian freedom."

A storm of cheers, and the Congress took up the
order of the day—the Ukraine, Education, War-
Widows and Orphans, Provisioning the Front, Repairing the Railways, etc. This should have been
the business of the Provisional Government. But
that Government was flimsy and incompetent. Its
ministers were orating, wrangling, scheming against
one another and entertaining diplomats. But some-
body must do the hard work. By default it was
already passing into the hands of these Soviets of
the people.

This First Congress of Soviets was domi-
Enter the nated by the *intelligentsia*—doctors, en-
Bolsheviks. gineers, journalists. They belonged to
political parties known as Menshevik and
Socialist-Revolutionary. At the extreme left sat
107 delegates of a decided proletarian cast—plain
soldiers and workingmen. They were aggressive,
united and spoke with great earnestness. They were
often laughed and hooted down—always voted down.

One of the 10,000 city and village Soviets in which, as a peasant said, "we are teaching ourselves how to rule ourselves." This is the Petrograd Soviet to which 20,000 workers have been elected in four years.

The masses hearing Lenin express their demands. "*Under the pitiless pelting of facts I have been driven to the conclusion that if Lenin and 18 other Bolshevik (leaders) had perished, events in Russia would have taken much the same course. The robbed and oppressed masses—a hundred millions of men and women—moved toward the goal of their long unfulfilled desires like a flow of molten lava that no human force can dam or turn aside.*"—PROFESSOR E. A. ROSS.

"Those are the Bolsheviks," my bourgeois guide informed me, venomously. "Mostly fools, fanatics and German agents." That was all. And no more than that could one learn in hotel lobbies, salons, or diplomatic circles.

Happily, I went elsewhere for information. I went into the factory districts. In Nijni I met Sartov, a mechanic who invited me to his home. A long rifle stood in the corner of the main room.

"Every workingman has a gun now," Sartov explained. "Once we used it to fight for the Czar—now we fight for ourselves."

In another corner hung an *ikon* of Saint Nicholas, a tiny flame burning before it.

"My wife is still religious," Sartov apologized. "She believes in the Saint—thinks he will fetch me safely thru the Revolution. As tho a saint would help a Bolshevik!" he laughed. *"Yeh! Bogu!* There's no harm in it. Saints are queer devils. No telling what one of them may do."

The family slept on the floor, insisting that I take the bed, because I was an American. In this room I found another American. In the soft gleam of the ikon-light his face looked down at me from the wall, the great, homely, rugged face of Abraham Lincoln. From that pioneer's hut in the woods of Illinois he had made his way to this workingman's hut here upon the Volga. Across half a century, and half a world, the fire in Lincoln's heart had leaped to touch the heart of a Russian workman groping for the light.

As his wife paid her devotion to Saint Nicholas, the great Wonder-Worker, so he paid his devotion to Lincoln, the great Emancipator. He had given Lincoln's picture the place of honor in his home. And then he had done a startling thing. On the lapel of Lincoln's coat he had fixed a button, a large red button bearing on it the word, B-o-l-s-h-e-v-i-k.

Of Lincoln's life Sartov knew little. He knew only that he strove against injustice, freed the slaves, that he was reviled and persecuted. To Sartov, that was the earnest of his kinship with the Bolsheviks. As an act of highest tribute he had decorated Lincoln with this emblem of red.

I found that factories and boulevards were different worlds. A world of difference, too, in the way they said the word "Bolshevik." Spoken on the boulevards with a sneer and a curse, on the lips of the workers it was becoming a term of praise and honor.

The Bolsheviks did not mind the bourgeoisie. They were busy expounding their program to the workers. This program I got first hand from delegates coming up to the Soviet Congress from the Russian Army in France.

"Our demand is, not to continue the war, but to continue the Revolution," these Bolsheviks blurted out.

"Why are you talking about Revolution?" I asked,

taking the rôle of Devil's Advocate. "You have had your Revolution, haven't you? The Czar and his crowd are gone. That was what you were aiming at for the last hundred years, wasn't it?"

"Yes," they replied. "The Czar is gone, but the Revolution is just begun. The overthrow of the Czar is only an incident. The workers didn't take the government out of the hands of one ruling class, the monarchists, in order to put it into the hands of another ruling class, the bourgeoisie. No matter what name you give it, slavery is the same."

I said the world at large held that Russia's task now was to create a republic, like France or America; to establish in Russia the institutions of the West.

"But that is precisely what we don't want to do," they responded. "We don't cherish much admiration for your institutions or governments. We know that you have poverty, unemployment and oppression. Slums on one hand, palaces on the other. On the one side, capitalists fighting workmen with lock-outs, blacklists, lying press, and thugs. Workmen on the other side, fighting back with strikes, boycotts, bombs. We want to put an end to this war of the classes. We want to put an end to poverty. Only the workers can do this, only a communistic system. That is what we are going to have in Russia."

"In other words," I said, "you want to escape the laws of evolution. By some magic you expect suddenly to transfer Russia from a backward agricultural state into a highly organized co-operative commonwealth. You are going to jump out of the eighteenth century into the twenty-second."

"We are going to have a new social order," they replied, "but we don't depend on jumping or magic. We depend upon the massed power of the workmen and peasants."

"But where are the brains to do this?" I interrupted. "Think of the colossal ignorance of the masses."

"Brains!" they exclaimed hotly. "Do you think we bow down before the brains of our 'betters'? What could be more brainless and stupid and criminal than this war? And who are guilty of it? Not the working classes, but the governing classes in every country. Surely the ignorance and inexperience of workmen and peasants could not make a worse mess than generals and statesmen with all their brains and culture. We believe in the masses. We believe in their creative force. And we must make the Social Revolution anyhow."

"And why?" I asked.

"Because it is the next step in the evolution of the race. Once we had slavery. It gave way to feudalism. That in turn gave way to capitalism. Now capitalism must leave the stage. It has served its purpose. It has made possible large scale production, world-wide industrialism. But now it must make its exit. It is the breeder of imperialism and war, the strangler of labor, the destroyer of civilization. It must in its turn give place to the next phase —the system of Communism. It is the historic mission of the working-class to usher in this new social order. Tho Russia is a primitive backward land it is for us to begin the Social Revolution. It is for the working-class of other countries to carry it on."

A daring program—to build the world anew.

No wonder the ideas of James Duncan of the Root Mission seemed trivial as he came with tedious talk of craft unions, the union label, and the eight-hour day. His hearers were amused or bored. Next day a newspaper reported the two-hour speech thus: "Last night the Vice-President of the American Federation of Labor addressed the Soviets. Coming over the Pacific he evidently prepared two speeches, one for the Russian people and the other for the ignorant Eskimos—obviously last night he thought he was addressing the Eskimos."

For the Bolsheviks to put forward a big revolutionary program was one thing; to get it accepted by a nation of 160,000,000 was quite another—especially as the Bolshevik Party counted then not more than 150,000.

Bolsheviks Trained in America. Many factors, however, were conspiring to give Bolshevik ideas prestige with the people. In the first place the Bolsheviks understood the people. They were strong among the more literate strata, like the sailors, and comprised largely the artisans and laborers of the cities. Sprung directly from the people's loins they spoke the people's language, shared their sorrows and thought their thoughts.

It is not quite correct to say that the Bolsheviks understood the people. They *were* the people. So they were trusted. The Russian workingman, betrayed so long by the classes above him, puts faith only in his own.

This was brought home to a friend of mine in a grotesque manner. Krasnoschekov is his name, now President of the Far East Republic. Coming from the Workers' Institute in Chicago, he entered the lists as a champion of the workers. An able, eloquent man, he was elected President of the City Council of Nikolaievsk. The bourgeois paper promptly appeared with an assault upon him as an "immigrant roustabout."

"Citizens of great Russia," it asked, "do you not feel the shame of being ruled by a porter, a window cleaner from Chicago?"

Krasnoschekov wrote out a hot reply, pointing out his distinction in America as lawyer and educator. On the way to the newspaper with his article he turned in at the Soviet, wondering how much this assault had hurt him in the eyes of the workers.

"Tovarish Krasnoschekov!" someone shouted as he opened the door. With a cheer the men rose to their feet. *"Nash! Nash!"* (Ours! Ours!) they cried, grasping his hand. "We just read the paper, comrade. It made us all glad. We always liked you, tho we thought you were a bourgeois. Now we find out you are one of us, a real workingman, and we love you. We'll do anything for you."

Ninety-six per cent of the Bolshevik Party were workingmen. Of course the Party had its intelligentsia, not sprung directly from the soil. But Lenin and Trotzky lived close enough to the hunger line to know the thoughts of the poor.

The Bolsheviks were mostly young men not afraid of responsibility, not afraid to die,* and, in sharp contrast to the upper-classes, not afraid to work. Many of them became my friends, particularly the exiles returning on the immigrant tide now flowing back from America.

There was Yanishev, who was literally a workman of the world. Ten years earlier he had been driven out of Russia for inciting his fellow-peasants against the Czar. He had lived like a water-rat on the docks of Hamburg: he had dug coal in the pits of Austria and had poured steel in the foundries of France. In America he had been tanned in leather-vats, bleached in textile mills and clubbed in strike-lines. His travels had given him a knowledge of four languages and an ardent faith in Bolshevism. The peasant had become now an industrial proletarian.

Some satirist has defined a proletarian as a "talking workingman." Yanishev was not a talker by nature. But now he had to talk. The cry of millions

* Appendix I. The Death of a Red Regiment.

of his fellow-workers for the light drew the words to his lips and in mills and mines he spoke as no intellectual could speak. Night and day he toiled until midsummer came and he took me on a memorable trip to the villages.

Another comrade was Woskov, formerly agent of New York Carpenters' Union No. 1008, now in the Workers' Committee that ran the rifle factory at Sestroretsk. Another was Volodarsky, virtually a galley-slave of the Soviet and deliriously happy in it. Once he exclaimed to me: "I have had more real joy in these few weeks than any fifty men ought to have in all their lives!" There was Neibut, with his pack of books and with eyes glowing over the English in Brailsford's *The War of Steel and Gold!* To Bolshevik propaganda these immigrants brought Western speed and method. In Russian there is no word "efficient." These young zealots were prodigies of efficiency and energy.

The center of Bolshevik action was Petrograd. In this there is the fine irony of history. This city was the pride and glory of the great Czar Peter. He found a swamp here and left a brilliant capital. To make a foundation he sunk into these marshes forests of trees and quarries of stone. It is a colossal monument to Peter's iron will. At the same time it is a monument of colossal cruelty, for it is built not only on millions of wooden piles, but on millions of human bones.

Like cattle the workmen were herded in these

swamps to perish of cold and hunger and scurvy. As fast as they were swallowed up more serfs were driven in. They dug the soil with bare hands and sticks, carrying it off in caps and aprons. With thudding hammers, cracking whips, and groans of the dying, Petrograd rose like the Pyramids, in the tears and anguish of slaves.

Now the descendants of these slaves were in revolt. Petrograd had become the Head of the Revolution. Every day it started out missionaries on long crusading tours. Every day it poured out bales and carloads of Bolshevik gospel in print. In June, Petrograd was publishing *Pravda* (*Truth*),* *The Soldier, The Village Poor,* in millions of copies. "All done on German money," said the Allied observers, as ostrich-like, they sat with heads buried in the boulevard cafés, believing what they preferred to believe. Had they turned the corner they would have seen a long line of men filing past a desk, each laying on it a contribution, ten copecks, ten rubles, maybe a hundred. These were workers, soldiers, even peasants, doing their bit for the Bolshevik press.

The greater the success of the Bolsheviks, the louder the hue and cry against them. While the bourgeois press praised the sense and moderation of the other parties, it called for an iron fist for the Bolsheviks. While "Babushka" and Kerensky were

* Reproduction of this newspaper on pages 306-7.

given regal quarters in the Winter Palace, the Bolsheviks were thrown into jail.

In the past all parties suffered for their principles. Now it was chiefly the Bolsheviks who suffered. They were the martyrs of today. This gave them prestige. Persecution lifted them into prominence. The masses, now giving heed to Bolshevik doctrine, found it strangely akin to their own desires.

But it was not the sacrifice and enthusiasm of the Bolsheviks that was finally to bring the masses under their banner. More powerful allies were working with them. Hunger was their chief ally—a threefold hunger: a mass hunger for bread, and peace, and land.

In the rural Soviets rose again the ancient cry of the peasants, "The land belongs to God and the people." The city-workers left out God and cried, "The factories belong to the workers." At the front the soldiers proclaimed, "The war belongs to the devil. We want nothing to do with it. We want peace."

A great ferment was working in the masses. It set them organizing Land Committees, Factory Committees, Committees of the Front. It set them talking, so that Russia became a nation of a hundred million orators. It sent them into the streets in tremendous mass demonstrations.

One of the great Cathedrals of the Communist Faith—the Putilov Factory in Petrograd. Banners and speakers proclaim the International unity of all races and peoples.

Petrograd Demonstrates —The river of red flowing by the Admiralty. To the left is the *Street of Grand Noblemen* now called the *Street of Village Poverty* to remind men forever whence came the splendrous buildings.

CHAPTER II

THE spring and summer of 1917 was a series of demonstrations. In this Russia always excelled. Now the processions were longer, led not by priests but by the people, with red banners instead of *ikons,* and instead of church hymns, songs of revolution.

Who can forget Petrograd of July first! Soldiers in drab and olive, horsemen in blue and gold, white-bloused sailors from the fleet, black-bloused workmen from the mills, girls in vari-colored waists, surging thru the main arteries of the city. On each marcher a streamer, a flower, a riband of red; scarlet kerchiefs around the women's heads, red *rubashkas* on the men. Above, like crimson foam, sparkled and tossed a thousand banners of red.

As this human river flowed it sang.

Three years before I had seen the German war machine rolling down the valley of the Meuse on its drive towards Paris. The cliffs resounded then to ten thousand lusty German voices singing *"Deutschland über Alles,"* while ten thousand boots struck the pavement in unison. It was powerful but mechanical, and, like every act of those grey columns, ordered from above.

But the singing of these red columns was the spontaneous outpouring of a people's soul. Some one would strike up a revolutionary hymn; the deep resonant voices of the soldiers would lift the refrain, joined by the plaintive voices of the working-women; the hymn would rise, and fall, and die away; then, down the line, it would burst forth again—the whole street singing in harmony.

Past the golden dome of Saint Isaac's, past the minarets of the Mohammedan Mosque, marched forty creeds and races, welded into one by the fire of the Revolution. The mines, the mills, the slums and trenches were blotted from their minds. This was the day the people had made. They would rejoice and be glad in it.

But in their joy they did not forget those who, to bring this day, had marched bound and bleeding to exile and death on the plains of Siberia. Close at hand, too, were the martyrs of the March Revolution; a thousand of them lying in their red coffins on the Field of Mars. Here the militant strains of the *Marseillaise* gave way to the solemn measures of Chopin's *Funeral March*. With muffled drums and lowered banners, with bowed heads, they passed the long grave, weeping or in silence.

One incident, trivial in itself, but significant, marred the peace of the day. It was on Sadovaya where I was standing with Alex Gumberg, the little Russian-American, friend and pilot to so many Americans in the days of the Revolution. The wrath of the sailors and workingmen was roused by a red banner with the inscription *"Long live the Provisional Government."* They started to tear it down and in the mêlée some one shouted "The Cossacks are coming."

The very name of these ancient enemies of the people struck terror into the crowds. White-faced, they stampeded like a herd, trampling the fallen and yelling like madmen. Happily it was a false alarm. The ranks re-formed and with songs and cheers took up the march again.

But this procession was more than an outburst of emotion. It was sternly prophetic, its banners proclaiming: *"Factories to the Workers! Land to the Peasants! Peace to All the World! Down with the War! Down with the Secret Treaties! Down with the Capitalist Ministers!"*

This was the Bolshevik program crystallized into slogans for the masses. There were thousands of banners, so many that even the Bolsheviks were surprised. Those banners were signals indicating a big storm brewing. Everybody could see that, and everybody did see it, except those sent to Russia specifically commissioned to see it—the Root Mission for example. While these gentlemen were in revolutionary Russia they were absolutely isolated from the Revolution. As the Russian proverb goes: "they went to the circus, but they did not see the elephant."

On this July 1st the Americans were invited

to a special service in the Cathedral of Kazan.   In
the church they knelt to receive the kisses and bless-
ings of the priests, while the streets outside rang
with songs and cheers from the vast procession of
exalted people.   Blind men!   They did not see that
faith that day was not in the mass within those
musty walls, but in the masses without.

Yet they were no blinder than the rest of the
diplomats cheering the first glowing reports of
Kerensky's drive on the Eastern Front.   The drive,
like its leader, a dazzling success at first, turned into
a tragic fiasco.   It slaughtered 30,000 Russians,
shattered the morale of the army, enraged the people,
forced a cabinet crisis, and brought the disastrous
repercussion in Petrograd, the armed upheaval of
July sixteenth.

*The Armed
Demonstration.*
July 1st gave warning of the coming
storm.   July 16th saw it break in fury.
First long files of older peasant soldiers
with placards: *"Let the 40-year-old
men go home and harvest the crops."*   Then barrack,
slum and factory belching out torrents of men in
arms who converged on the Tauride Palace, and,
for two nights and a day, roared through its gates.
Armored cars, with sirens screaming and red flags
flying from the turrets, raced up and down the
streets.   Motor trucks, crammed with soldiers, bayonets jutting out on every side, dashed by like
giant porcupines on a rampage.   Stretched full

length on the car fenders lay sharpshooters, rifles projecting beyond the lamps, eyes on the watch for provocators.

This outpouring was much bigger than the river that ran thru these streets on July first, and more sinister, for it glittered with steel and hissed with curses—a long grey line of wrath. It was the spontaneous outburst of men against their rulers—ugly, reckless, furious.

Under a black banner marched a band of Anarchists, with Yarchuk the tailor at the head. On him was the stamp of the sweat-shop. Long bending over the needle had left him undersized. Now, in place of a needle, he was wielding a gun—the symbol of his deliverance from slavery to the needle.

Gumberg asked him, "What are your political demands?"

"Our political demands?" hesitated Yarchuk.

"To hell with the capitalists!" interjected a big sailor. "And our other political demands," he added, "are—to hell with the war and to hell with the whole damn Cabinet."

Backed up in an alley was a taxi-cab, the nozzles of two machine-guns poking thru the windows. In answer to our query, the driver pointed to a banner reading, *Down with the Capitalist Ministers.*

"We are tired of begging them not to starve and kill the people," he explained. "When we talk they won't listen; but wait till these two pups (*sobachki*) speak!" He patted the guns affectionately. "They will listen then all right."

A mob with nerves at trigger-tension, with such weapons in its hands, and such temper in its soul, did not need much provocation. And provocators were everywhere. Agents of the Black Hundred plied their trade of dissension among the crowds, inciting to riot and pogroms. They turned loose two hundred criminals from Kresty to pillage and loot. In the ensuing ruin they hoped to see the Revolution killed and the Czar restored. In some places they did bring on frightful slaughter.

At a tense moment, in the tight-packed concourse of the Tauride, a provocatory shot was fired. From that shot sprang a hundred. From every quarter rifles blazed, comrades firing point blank into comrades. The crowd screamed, crashed up against the pillars, surged back again, and then fell flat upon the ground. When the firing ceased, sixteen could not rise. During this massacre a military band two blocks away was playing the *Marseillaise*.

Fighting in the streets is panicky business. At night, with bullets spitting from hidden loopholes, from roofs above and cellar-ways below, with the enemy invisible and friends pouring volleys into friends, the crowds stampeded, back and forth, fleeing from a hail of bullets in one street only to plunge into leaden gusts sweeping thru the next.

Three times that night our feet slipped in blood on the pavement. Down the Nevsky was blazed a

The storm petrels of the Revolution—the sailors—first to raise the red flag in the fleet, always first to hurry to the rescue of the Soviets.

Escaping the bullets in the July Uprising by lying flat on the pavement. This picture is a hardy perennial. Any disturbance in Russia is liable to bring it forth again as the authentic photograph of the event.

trail of shattered windows and looted shops. The fighting ranged from little skirmishes, with nests of provocators, to the battle on Liteiny, which left twelve horses of the Cossacks stretched upon the cobbles. [Over these horses stood a big *izvoschik* (cabman), tears in his eyes. In time of Revolution the killing of 56 and wounding of 650 men might be endured, but the loss of 12 good horses was too much for an *izvoschik's* heart to bear.]

The Bolsheviks Control the Rising. Only Petrograd's long experience in barricade and street fighting, and the native good sense of the people, prevented the shambles from being more bloody than they were. Upon the chaotic insurgent masses was brought to bear a stabilizing force in tens of thousands of workingmen, backed by the directing mind of the Bolshevik Party. The Bolsheviks saw clearly that this uprising was a spontaneous elemental thing. They saw these masses striking out powerfully but rather blindly. They determined that they should strike to some purpose. They determined to let the full force of this demonstration reach the Soviet Central Executive Committee. This was a committee of 200 selected by the First All-Russian Congress of Soviets before it adjourned. It was in permanent session in the Tauride Palace, and upon it the masses were converging.

The Bolsheviks alone had influence over these

masses. All parties implored them to use it. Placing their speakers upon the central portico, they met each regiment and delegation with a short address.

From our vantage point we could view the whole concourse crammed with people, with here and there a man lifted upon his artillery horse, while many banners marked out a red current thru the solid mass.

Below us was a sea of upturned faces, the fears, and hopes, and angers written on them but half legible in the twilight of the Russian night. From down the street could be heard the roar of marching hosts, cheering the armored cars. The automobile searchlights focusing on the speaker, silhouetted him against the walls of the Palace, a gigantic figure in black. Every gesture, ten times magnified, cut a sweeping shadow across the white façade.

"Comrades," said this giant Bolshevik, "you want revolutionary action. The only way to get it is thru a revolutionary government. The Kerensky Government is revolutionary in name only. They promise land, but the landlords still have it. They promise bread, but the speculators still hold it. They promise to get from the Allies a declaration of the objects of the war, but the Allies simply tell us to go on fighting.

"In the cabinet a fundamental conflict rages between the Socialist and the bourgeois ministers. The result is a deadlock and nothing at all is done.

"You men of Petrograd come here to the Soviet

Executive Committee saying, 'Take the Government. Here are the bayonets to back you!' You want the Soviets to be the government. So do we Bolsheviks. But we remember that Petrograd is not all of Russia. So we are demanding that the Central Executive Committee call delegates from all over Russia. It is for this new congress to declare the Soviets the government of Russia."

Each crowd met this declaration with cheers and loud cries, *"Down with Kerensky"; "Down with the Bourgeois Government"; "All Power to the Soviets."*

"Avoid all violence and bloodshed," was the parting admonition to each contingent. "Do not listen to provocators. Do not delight your enemies by killing each other. You have amply shown your power. Now go home quietly. When the occasion for force arises we will call you."

In the swirling flood were cross currents made by the Anarchists, the Black Hundreds, German agents, hoodlums, and those volatile elements which always join the side with the most machine-guns. One thing was now clear to the Bolsheviks: the revolutionary workmen and soldiers around Petrograd were overwhelmingly *against* the Provisional Government and *for* the Soviet. They wanted the Soviet to be the government. But the Bolsheviks were afraid this would be a premature step. As they said, "Petrograd is not Russia. The other cities and the army at the front may not be ripe for such drastic action. Only delegates from the Soviets of all Russia can decide that."

Inside the Tauride the Bolsheviks were using every argument to persuade the members of the Soviet Executive Committee to call another All-Russian Congress. Outside the Tauride, they were using every exhortation to quiet and appease the clamoring masses. This was a task that taxed all their wits and resources.

The Sailors Demand
"All Power to the Soviets."

Some contingents came to the Tauride very belligerent. The Cronstadt sailors arrived in a particularly ugly temper. In barges they came up the river, eight thousand strong. Two of their number had been killed along the way. It had been no holiday excursion, and they had no intention of gazing at the walls of the Palace, filling the courtyard with futile clamor, then turning around and going home. They sent in a demand that the Soviet produce a Socialist Minister, and produce him at once.

Chernov, Minister of Agriculture, came out. He took for his rostrum the top of a cab.

"I come to tell you that three bourgeois Ministers have resigned. We now look to the future with great hope. Here are the laws which give the land to the peasant."

"Good," cried the hearers. "Will these laws be put into operation at once?"

"As soon as possible," Chernov answered.

"Soon as possible!" they mocked him. "No, no! We want it *now, now*. All the land for the peasant *now!* What have you been doing all these weeks anyhow?"

"I am not answerable to you for my deeds," Chernov replied, white with rage. "It is not you that put me in my office. It was the Peasants' Soviet. To them alone I make my reckoning."

At this rebuff a howl of derision went up from the sailors. With it went the cry: "Arrest Chernov! Arrest him!" A dozen hands stretched out to clutch the Minister and drag him off. Others sought to drag him back. In a vortex of fighting friends and foes, his clothes torn, the Minister was being borne away. But Trotzky, coming up, secured his release.

Meanwhile, Saakian scrambled up on the cab. He struck an attitude of stern command.

"Listen!" he cried. "Do you know who is now addressing you?"

"No," a voice called out. "And we don't give a damn."

"The man who is now addressing you," resumed Saakian, "is the Vice-President of the Central Executive Committee of the First All-Russian Congress of Soviets of Soldiers' and Workmen's Deputies."

This prodigious title instead of serving to impress and quiet the crowd, was greeted by laughter and cries of *"Down with him!"* (*doloi, doloi*). But he had come out to tame this mob, and with great vim he fired into it a fusillade of short abrupt sentences.

"My name—Saakian!" (The mob: "Down with him!")

"My party—Socialist Revolutionary!" ("Down with him!")

"My official religion—according to the passport— Armenian-Gregorian!" ("Down with him!")

"My real religion—Socialism!" ("Down with him!")

"My relation to the war—two brothers killed." A voice: "There should have been a third."

"My advice to you—trust us, your leaders and best friends. Stop this foolish demonstration. You are disgracing yourself, disgracing the Revolution, bringing disaster to Russia."

These sailors were already enraged. To slap them in the face thus was an idiotic act. Pandemonium broke loose. Again Trotzky to the rescue.

He steps upon the platform, the hero and idol of the Cronstadt sailors. He knows the temper of his hearers. He knows, today, they have no ears for censure.

"Revolutionary sailors, pride and flower of the revolutionary forces of Russia!" he began. "In this battle for the Social Revolution we fight together. Together, comrades, our fists beat upon the doors of this Palace until the ideals for which our blood has flowed shall at last be incarnated in the constitution of this country. Hard and long has been the

heroic struggle! But out of it will come a free life
for free men in a great free land. Am I not right?"
"Right you are, Trotzky," yells the crowd.
Trotzky moves away.
"But you haven't told us anything," they cry.
"What are you going to do about the Cabinet?"
They may be a mob, with an appetite for flattery,
but they are not so unthinking as to be pacified by
phrases, even from Trotzky.
"I am too hoarse to talk more," he pleads.
"Riazanov will tell you."
"No, you tell us!" Trotzky again mounts the cab.
"Only the All-Russian Congress can assume full
power of government. The Labor Section has
agreed to call this congress. The Military Section
will without doubt follow. In two weeks the dele-
gates can be here."
"Two weeks!" they cry in astonishment. "Two
weeks is too long. We want it *now!*"
But Trotzky prevails. The sailors acquiesce,
cheering the Soviets and the coming Revolution.
They move peacefully away, convinced that the
Second All-Russian Congress will be called.

Downing the Demonstra-
tion, then the Bolsheviks.
This is precisely what the
leaders in the Soviet Executive Committee do not want.
They are dead set against
the Soviet becoming the government. They have
many reasons to give. But the real reason is fear

of these very masses by whom they have been lifted to their exalted stations. The intelligentsia distrust the masses below them. At the same time they exaggerate the abilities and good intentions of the grand bourgeoisie above them.

They do not want the Soviets to take the power. They have no intention of calling a Second All-Russian Congress in two weeks, two months, or at all. But they are frightened by these turbulent crowds crashing into the courtyard, hammering at the doors. Their tactics are to placate the mob, and they seek help from the Bolsheviks. At the same time these intelligentsia play another game. They join the Provisional Government in calling regiments from the front "to quell the mutiny and restore order in the city."

On the third day the troops arrive. Bicycle battalions, the reserve regiments, and then long grim lines of horsemen, the sun glancing on the tips of their lances. They are the Cossacks, ancient foes of the revolutionists, bringing dread to the workers and joy to the bourgeoisie. The avenues are filled now with well-dressed throngs cheering the Cossacks, crying *"Shoot the rabble." "String up the Bolsheviks."*

A wave of reaction runs thru the city. Insurgent regiments are disarmed. The death penalty is restored. The Bolshevik papers are suppressed. Forged documents attesting the Bolsheviks as German agents are handed to the press. Alexandrov,

the Czar's prosecutor, hales them before the bar,
indicted for high treason under section 108 of the
Penal Code. Leaders like Trotzky and Kollontai
are thrown into prison. Lenin and Zinoviev are
driven into hiding. In all quarters sudden seizures,
assaults and murder of workingmen.

In the early morning of July 18th I am suddenly
wakened by piercing cries from the Nevsky. With
the clattering of horses' hoofs are mingled shouts,
desperate pleas for mercy, curses—one terrible
blood-curdling scream. Then, the thud of a falling
body, the groans of a man dying, and silence. An
officer coming in explains that some workingmen
had been caught pasting up Bolshevik posters along
the Nevsky. A squad of Cossacks had ridden them
down, lashing out with whips and sabres, cleaving
one man open, and leaving him dead on the pavement.

At this new turn of events the bourgeoisie are
elated. Ill-based elation! They do not know that
the screams of this murdered workman will penetrate the furthermost corners of Russia, rousing his
comrades to wrath and arms. This July day they
cheer the Volynsk regiment, as with band playing it
enters the city to suppress this uprising, whose purpose is to offer all power to the Soviets. Ill-starred
cheers! They do not know that on a coming November night they will see this regiment in the forefront
of the rising that triumphantly delivers all power to
the Soviets.

The troops are called in to conquer Petrograd; but in the end Petrograd conquers them. The infection of this Bolshevik stronghold is irresistible. It is a huge blast furnace of the Revolution, burning away all dross and indifference. No matter how cold and sluggish they may enter the city, out of it they go fired by the spirit of the Revolution.

The city rose in tears and blood, in hunger and cold, in the forced labor of myriads of the starved and beaten. Their bones lie buried deep in the mud below. But their outraged spirits seem to live again in the Petrograd workingmen of today— spirits powerful and avenging. The serfs of Peter built the city; presently their descendants will be coming into their own.

It does not appear thus in midsummer 1917. The black shadow of reaction hovers over them. But the Bolsheviks bide their time. History, they feel, is on their side. Their ideas are working out in the villages, in the fleet and at the front.

To these places I now make my way.

CHAPTER III

A PEASANT INTERLUDE

G O out among the forests and the people,"
said Bakunin.

"In the capitals the orators thunder and rage
But in the village is the silence of centuries."

We craved a taste of this silence. Three months
we had heard the roar of Revolution. I was
saturated with it: Yanishev was exhausted by it. His
voice had failed thru incessant speaking and he had
been ordered by the Bolshevik Party to take a ten
days' respite. So we started out for the Volga basin
bound for the little village of Spasskoye (Salvation),
from which Yanishev had been driven out in 1907.

It was high noon one August day when we left
the Moscow train and set out on the road leading
across the fields. Sun-drenched in these last weeks
of summer, the fields had turned into wide rolling
seas of yellow grain, dotted here and there with
islands of green. These were the tree-shaded peasant
villages of the province of Vladimir. From a rise
in the road we could count sixteen of them, each
with its great white church capped with glistening
domes. It was a holiday and the distant belfries were

flooding the fields with music as the sun had flooded them with color.

After the cities this was to me a land of peace and quiet. But to Yanishev it was a land of poignant memories. After ten years of wandering the exile was returning home.

"In that village over there," he said, pointing to the west, "my father was a teacher. The people liked his teaching, but one day the gendarmes came, closed the school, and led him off. In that next village Vera lived. She was very pretty and very kind and she was my sweetheart. I was too bashful to tell her then, and now it is too late. She is in Siberia. In the woods yonder a few of us used to meet to talk about the revolution. One night the Cossacks came riding down on us. That bridge is where they killed Yegor, the bravest of our comrades."

It was not a happy home-coming for the exile. Every turn in the road started up some recollection. Handkerchief in hand Yanishev walked along, pretending that it was only perspiration he was wiping from his face.

As we came across the village green of Spasskoye we saw an old peasant in a bright blue smock sitting on a bench before his hut. He shaded his eyes, puzzled by the appearance of these two dust-stained foreigners. Then in joyful recognition he cried "Mikhail Petrovich!" and throwing his arms around Yanishev, kissed him on both cheeks. Then

he turned to me.   I told him that my name was
Albert.

"And your father's name?" he inquired gravely.

"David," I replied.

"Albert Davidovich (Albert, son of David), welcome to the home of Ivan Ivanov.   We are poor,
but may God give you his richest blessing."

Ivan Ivanov stood straight as an arrow, long-
bearded, clear-eyed, hard-muscled.   But it was
not his strength of body, nor his warmth of feeling,
nor his quaint formality of speech that struck me.   It
was his quiet dignity.   It was the dignity of a natural
object, a tree whose roots run deep into the soil.
And it was indeed out of the soil of this *mir* that
Ivan Ivanov for sixty years had drawn his suste-
nance, as had his fathers for generations.   His
little *izba* was made of logs, its deep thatched roof
now green with weeds, its garden gay with flowers.

Ivan's wife, Tatyana, and daughter, Avdotia,
having saluted us, brought a table from the house.
On it they set a samovar, and lifting its top, placed
eggs along the steaming sides.   Ivan and his household made the sign of the cross and we sat down
at the table.

"Of what we are rich in, we gladly give you," said
Ivan, (*Chem bogaty, ty ee rady*).

The women brought in a big bowl of cabbage-
soup (*shtchee*), and for each person a wooden spoon.
Every one was supposed to dip his soup from the
common bowl.   Seeing this, I stood not upon the

order of the dipping, but dipped at once. When the first bowl was empty, they brought a second, full of porridge (*kasha*). It was followed by a bowl of boiled raisins. Ivan presided at the samovar, dispensing tea, black bread and cucumbers. It was a special feast, for this was a special holiday in Spasskoye.

Even the crows seemed to be aware of it. Great flocks wheeling overhead threw swift cloud-shadows across the ground, or alighted on the church roof and covered it completely. The domes, all green or glistening gold, would in a minute be blackest jet.

I told Ivan that in America farmers killed crows because they ate the grain.

"Yes," said Ivan, "our crows eat the grain. But they eat the field-mice, too. And even if they are crows, they are like us and want to live."

Tatyana held a like attitude toward the flies that swarmed around the table. Descending on a piece of sugar they would turn it as black as the crow-covered church.

"Never mind the flies," said Tatyana. "Poor things, in a month or two they'll be dead, anyhow."

The Village Takes a Holiday. It was the Feast of Transfiguration, and from all the countryside around came the poor, the crippled and the aged. Again and again we heard the tapping of a cane and a plaintive voice asking alms *radi Christa,* for the Christ's sake.

Yanishev and I dropped a few copecks into the bags they thrust before them. The women followed with large pieces cut from the big black loaves, while Ivan solemnly deposited in each sack a great green cucumber. Cucumbers were scarce this year, so it was truly a gift of love. But whether we gave cucumbers or bread or copecks, back to each of us came the plaintive sing-song blessing of the beggar.

Even the roughest, poorest Russian peasant is moved to profound pity by the spectacle of human misery. His own life teaches him the meaning of pain and privation. But this does not dull his sympathy; it makes him the more sensitive to the sufferings of others.

To Ivan the city workingmen cooped up in their hot dusty streets were "poor fellows" (*bedniakee*); the criminals locked up in jails were "unfortunates" (*neschastnenkie*); while a group of war-prisoners in Austrian uniforms cut him deepest of all. They seemed jolly enough as they came rollicking by, and I said so.

"But they are so far away from home," said Ivan. "How can they be happy?"

"Well," I said, "here am I, farther from home than they are, and I am happy."

"Yes," assented the others, "that is right."

"No," said Ivan Ivanov, "that is wrong. Albert Davidovich is here because he wanted to come. The prisoners are here because we made them come."

Naturally two foreigners sitting at the table of

Ivan Ivanov made a sensation among the natives of Spasskoye. But the elders did not let their curiosity overcome their sense of the proprieties. Only a few children came down, and fixed their gaze upon us. I smiled at the children and they looked thunderstruck. Again I smiled, and three of them almost fell backwards. This seemed a peculiar reaction to my friendly overtures. At the third smile they cried, *"Zolotiyeh zooby!"* and clasping hands they ran away. Before I could grasp the meaning of this behavior they came rushing back with a score of recruits. In semi-circle they stood around the table with all their wistful eyes converged on me. There was nothing for me to do but smile again. "Yes, yes!" they cried. *"Zolotiyeh zooby!* He is the man with golden teeth!" This was why my smile had startled them. And what could be more marvelous than the arrival of a foreigner whose mouth grew golden teeth? Had I arrived in Spasskoye with a golden crown upon my head I could not have more deeply stirred the community than by wearing a golden crown upon my tooth. But this I learned on the morrow.

Now from the farther end of the village came the strains of music. There was a chorus of young voices accompanied by the thrumming of the *balalaika*, the clanging of cymbals and the throbbing of a kind of tambourine (*bouben*). Clearer and nearer came the music, until suddenly around the corner of the church emerged the procession of players and singers. The girls were in the gay rich costumes of the peasants; the boys wore smocks of green and orange and brightest hue, belted by cords with tasseled ends. The boys played the instruments, while the girls sang in response to the precentor, a clean-looking, tousle-haired lad of seventeen, one of the last to be drafted to the front. In clear lusty voice, with abandon of emotion he sang an old folk-song, adding new verses of his own as he strode along. Later he wrote them down for me.

> At the window a birch tree stands
>   The golden days are gone
> Pity us, fair maidens all,
>   We are now recruits!
>
> Why have they taken me as a soldier?
>   I, my father's only son?
> The reason probably is this,
>   I've courted the maidens all too long.
>
> From the trenches a lad steps out
>   Crying, "Oh, my fathers!
> All my comrades have been killed!
>   Soon my turn will come."
>
> Why, my darling, don't you meet me
>   In the midst of fields?
> Don't you feel some pain or sorrow
>   That a soldier boy am I?
>
> Father, mother, dig a grave,
>   Bury me deep below.
> For my courting, for my freedom,
>   Bury my naughty head.

Three times they circled the village green. Then gathering on the grass before the church, they sang

and danced till morning. The rush and joyous fling
of the dancers, the colors of their costumes lit by the
pine-torches, the laughter and snatches of song rising
out of the dark, the young lovers with their caresses
frank and unashamed, the church bell at intervals
crashing like a great temple gong and the startled
birds wheeling overhead, all combined to create an
impression of primitive energy and beauty. It carried me back across the centuries to the days when
the race was young, and men drew life and inspiration directly from the soil.

Yanishev Tells
of America.

It was a dream world, an idyllic commune, bound together in a fellowship
of toil and play and feasting. With
its spell upon me I made my way to
the *izba*, opened the door, and came suddenly face
to face with the twentieth century again. It was in
the person and words of Yanishev, Yanishev the artisan, the Socialist and the Internationalist. To the
peasants ringed around him he was describing the
America of today. It was not the usual story of the
bitter experiences of the Russian in America, the
story of slums and strikes and poverty that thousands
of returning exiles have spread over Russia. Yanishev, with husky voice but face aglow, was telling the
wonders of America. To peasants with houses one
story high he pictured the houses of New York,
forty, fifty and sixty stories high. To men who had
never seen a shop larger than the blacksmith's, he

told of great plants where a hundred trip hammers pounded night and day. From their serene Muscovite plain he took them to great cities with subway trains tearing up the night, Great White Ways flooded with pleasure-seekers, and clanging factories where millions surged in and out.

The villagers listened attentively. They were not overawed or wonderstruck. Yet we could not complain of any lack of appreciation.

"The Americans do wonderful things," said one old mujik, shaking our hands.

"Yes," agreed his companion, "they do things more wonderful than even the *leshey* (the wood spirit)."

But in their kindly comments we felt a certain reserve, as if they were trying to be polite to strangers. Next morning a conversation overheard by chance gave us their real opinion.

Ivan was speaking. "No wonder Albert and Mikhail are white-faced and tired. Think of being brought up in a country like that." And Tatyana said, "It's a hard life we live, but God knows it looks harder over there."

I glimpsed for the first time a truth that grew clearer as the months went by. The peasant has a mind of his own, which he uses to make judgments of his own. This is startling to the foreigner, to whom the Russian peasant is a shambling creature of the earth, immersed in the night of mediaevalism, chained by superstition, steeped in poverty. It is startling to discover that this peasant, unable to read or write, is able to think.

His thought is primal, elemental, with the stamp of the soil on it. It reflects the centuries of living on the far-stretching plains and steppes under the wide Russian sky and through the long winter. He brings a fresh untutored mind to bear upon all questions in a manner penetrating and often disconcerting. He challenges our long-held convictions. He revises our estimate of western civilization. It is not at all obvious to him that it is worth the price we pay for it. He is not mesmerized by machinery, efficiency, production. He asks, "What is it for? Does it make men happier? Does it make them more friendly?"

His conclusions are not always profound. Sometimes they are only naïve and curious. When the *mir* assembled on Monday morning the village Elder (*starosta*) politely extended to me the greetings of the village. He said apologetically that the children had brought home a report about my golden teeth, but that it did not seem reasonable, and they didn't know whether to believe it or not. There was nothing to do but demonstrate. I opened my mouth while the Elder peered long and intently into it and then gravely confirmed the report. Thereupon the seventy bearded patriarchs formed in line while I stood with mouth agape. Each gazed his fill and then moved along to give place to the next man

The paradoxes of Russia—the peasants, shrewd and superstitious, cruel and kind, communistic and individualistic, baffling to Tolstoy; irritating to Gorky. What will they make of the new Russia?

Author with the wood-choppers starting for the forests.

Across the fields with the children gleaning the oats and rye.

until all the members of the *mir* had filed past my open mouth.

I had to explain that it is the custom of Americans to put cement and gold and silver in their crumbling teeth. One old man of eighty, whose fine clean teeth showed not the slightest need of dentistry, gave his opinion that Americans must eat food very strange and strong to work such havoc. Several said it might be all right for Americans to have golden teeth, but that it would never do for Russians, who were always drinking so much tea and such very hot tea that it would surely melt the gold. At this point Ivan Ivanov, who had been enjoying the prestige of harboring the unusual visitors, spoke up. He insisted that his tea was as hot as any in the village, and testified that he had drawn at least ten glasses for me, yet there had been no melting.

Abroad the term "American" is almost synonymous with "man of wealth." Gold on my eye-glasses and on my fountain pen convinced them that I must be a man of super-wealth. Yet I came to marvel at their lavish display of gold quite as much as they at mine. For this peasant village had gold in abundance, only it was not on the persons of the villagers. It was in their church. As one stepped thru the church doors there loomed up a beautiful reredos twenty or thirty feet high, covered with a glistening sheen of gold. At one time the villagers had raised ten thousand rubles to decorate this temple.

While this little village was far removed from the

currents of Europe and America, still there were
marks of culture and civilization advancing from the
West. There were cigarettes and Singer sewing-
machines, men whose limbs had been shot off by
machine-guns, and two boys from the factory-
towns with store-clothes and celluloid collars—ugly
contrasts to the smocks and kaftans of the village.

One night standing before a neighbor's hut we
were startled to hear thru the curtains a soft and
modulated voice asking *"Parlez-vous Français?"* It
was a pretty peasant girl raised in the village but
with all the airs and graces which belong to a girl
raised in a court. She had served in a French household in Petrograd and had come home to give birth
to her child.

Thus in varied ways the outside world was filter-
ing into the village stirring it from the slumber of
centuries. Stories of big cities and of lands across
the seas came by way of prisoners and soldiers, trad-
ers and *zemstvo* men. It resulted in a strange mis-
cellany of ideas about foreign lands—a curious com-
pound of facts and fancies. One time a grotesque
half-fact about America was brought home to me
pointedly and in an embarrassing manner.

We were at the supper table and I was explaining that in my note-book I was writing down all the
customs and habits of the Russians that struck me
as strange and peculiar.

"For example," I said, "instead of having individual dishes you eat out of one great common bowl.

That is a curious custom." "Yes," said Ivan. "I suppose we are a curious people."

"And that big stove! It takes up a third of the room. You bake bread in it. You sleep on top of it. You get inside and take a steam bath in it. You do everything with it and in a most peculiar manner." "Yes," nodded Ivan again, "I suppose we are a peculiar people."

I felt something step on my foot. I thought it was a dog but it proved to be a pig. "There!" I exclaimed. "That is the most peculiar custom of all. You let pigs and chickens walk right into your dining-room."

At this moment the baby in Avdotia's arms began kicking its feet up and down upon the table in baby fashion. Addressing the child, she said, "Here, baby! Take your feet off the table. Remember you are not in America." And turning to me she added courteously, "What peculiar customs you have there in America."

We Harvest the Crops. It was the day after the holiday, and the visitors from neighboring towns still tarried. There were games and dancing on the village green; and a band of children, having come into possession of an accordion, paraded solemnly about, singing the songs of yesterday, quaint little understudies of their elder brothers and sisters. An after-the-holiday lethargy lingered over most of the village. But not over the household of Ivan Ivanov. Everybody was busy there. Avdotia was twisting straw into bands to bind the sheaves. Tatyana was plaiting strips of bark and shaping them into sandals. Olga, Avdotia's elder child, was forcibly teaching the cat to drink tea. Ivan sharpened the scythes, and we all set out for the fields.

At this move the young people came out of the *izbas*. "Please don't go to the fields. Stay at home," they teased. As we proceeded they became quite serious. I asked why we should not go.

"If one family starts for the fields all the others follow," they said. "Then our holiday fun will be over. Please don't go!"

But the ripened harvest was calling. The sun was shining, and there was no telling how soon the rains would fall. So Ivan marched along, and when, fifteen minutes later, we reached a rise of ground, we looked back to see the paths dotted with black figures making for the fields. Like a beehive the village was sending out its workers to garner its food-stores for the oncoming winter. As we reached the rye-field Yanishev quoted from Nekrassov's national epic, *Who Can Be Happy and Free in Russia?*

> "You full yellow cornfields!
> To look at you now
> One would never imagine
> How sorely God's people
> Had toiled to array you.
> 'Tis not by warm dewdrops

That you have been moistened;
   The sweat of the peasant
Has fallen on you.

"The peasants are gladdened
   At sight of the oats,
And the rye and the barley,
   But not by the wheat,
For it feeds but the chosen.
   'We love you not, Wheat!
But the rye and the barley
   We love—they are kind,
They feed all men alike.'"

As each one turned to his task I joined in the
work, fetching water, tying sheaves, swinging a
scythe, watching the light-brown stalks come tumbling down. The scythe demands skill and practice.
So the figure I cut and the swathe I cut were not
heroic, nor did I add to the prestige of American
reapers. Ivan was too polite to criticize my tech-
nique but I could see that it was inciting him to suppressed merriment. In his comment to Avdotia I
picked up the Russian word for camel. I was
indeed hunched over like a camel while Ivan Ivanov
stood erect, handling his scythe like a master-
craftsman. I turned upon Ivan and accused him of
likening me to a camel. He was embarrassed. But
when he saw that I was amused, and admitted my
likeness to that humped creature, he laughed and
laughed.

"Tatyana! Mikhail!" he roared. "Albert Davidovich says that when he cuts the grain he looks like
a camel. Ho! ho! ho!" Two or three times after

that he broke into sudden laughter. The camel must have helped him thru many weary wastes in the long winter.

Writers dwell upon the laziness of the Russian peasant. Watching the mujik lounging around market places and vodka-shops gives one that impression. But trying to keep up with the mujik in the fields very quickly takes it away. With the sun beating down on their heads and the dust rising from under their feet they mowed and raked and bound and stacked until the last straw had been gleaned from the field. Then they tramped back into the village.

The Peasants Wary of Bolshevism. Since our arrival the villagers had been asking Yanishev to make a speech. In the early evening there arrived a delegation beseeching him.

"Think of it," said Yanishev. "Ten years ago if these peasants had suspected that I was a Socialist they would have come to kill me. Now, knowing that I am a Bolshevik, they come begging me to talk. Things have gone a long, long way since then."

Yanishev was not a gifted man unless it be a gift to be deeply sensitive to the sorrows of the world. Tormented by the sufferings of others, he had chosen privation for himself. As an artisan in America he earned six dollars a day. Out of this he took enough for a cheap room and meals. With the rest he bought "literature" and carried it from door to door

In the poor quarters of Boston, Detroit, Moscow and Marseilles, they still speak of Yanishev as the comrade who gave everything to the cause.

In Tokio a fellow-exile once found an excited coolie trying to drag Yanishev, protesting, into a rickshaw. "I just got in his rickshaw," Yanishev explained, "and he began pulling and sweating like a horse. I may be a fool, but I can't let a man work like a beast for me. So I paid him and got out. I'll never get into a rickshaw again."

Since his return to Russia he had travelled night and day addressing enormous crowds until his voice failed him and he could only whisper and gesture He had come to his home village to recuperate. But even here the Revolution would not let him rest.

"Will Mikhail Petrovich give us a little speech?" the peasants pleaded. "Only a little speech."

Yanishev could not deny them. The committee drew a wagon out upon the village green and when the throng was thick around it, Yanishev mounted this rostrum and began telling the Bolshevik story of the Revolution, the War, and the Land.

They stood listening while evening darkened into night. Then they brought torches, and Yanishev talked on. His voice grew husky. They brought him water, tea and *kvass*. His voice failed, and they waited patiently till it came back again. These peasants who had labored all day in the fields stood there late into the night, more eager to gather stores for their mind than they had been to gather food for their bodies. It was a symbolic sight, this torch of knowledge flaming in the darkness of the village— one of tens of thousands scattered over the Ukrainian steppes, the plains of Muscovy and the far stretches of Siberia. In hundreds of them that night torches were flaming and other Yanishevs were telling the story of the Revolution.

So much reverence and age-old longings in those eager faces pressing around the speaker. So much hunger in these questions rising out of the dark. Yanishev toiled on until he was utterly exhausted. Only when he could go no further did they reluctantly disperse. I listened to their comments. Were these "ignorant illiterate mujiks" ready to swallow this new doctrine, to be swayed by the passion of a propagandist?

"Mikhail Petrovich is a good man," they were saying. "We know that he has gone far and seen many things. What he believes may be good for some people, but we do not know whether it is good for us." Yanishev had poured out his soul, explaining, expounding the creed of Bolshevism—and not a single convert. Yanishev himself said so, as he dragged himself up into the hayloft where we had gone to escape from the stuffy cabin. One young peasant, Fedossiev, seemed to divine the loneliness and spiritual emptiness of a preacher who gives his best and seemingly is rejected.

"It is all so new, Mikhail Petrovich," he said. "We are a slow people. We must have time to think it over and talk it over. Only today we reaped the grain in the fields; it was months and months ago that we sowed it in the ground."

I tried to add a reassuring word. "Never mind," whispered Yanishev, with the zealot's confidence in the ultimate triumph of his faith. "Of course, they will believe." He lay in collapse on the hay, his body trembling and coughing, but with serenity in his face.

I doubted. But Yanishev was right. Eight months later he made another speech on the village green. It was on invitation of the Communist Party of the village of Spasskoye. Fedossiev was chairman of the meeting.

Yanishev Talks of the Land.   Morning brought many peasants to the door with questions. Above all was the problem of the land. The Bolshevik solution at that time was, "Leave it to the local land committees. Let them take over the great estates and put them into the hands of the people." The peasants pointed out that this did not solve the land problem of Spasskoye, for here there were no crown or church or private domains.

"All the land around here already belongs to us," said the Elder. "It is too little, for God gives us many children. The Bolsheviks may be as good as Mikhail Petrovich says they are, but if they take the government, can they make more land? No. Only God can do that. We want a government with money enough to send us to Siberia or to any place where there is land in plenty. Will the Bolsheviks do that?"

Yanishev explained the colonizing scheme, and then turned to the agricultural commune which the Bolsheviks were projecting for Russia. It was ultimately to change the *mir* into a cooperative large-scale farming enterprise. He pointed out the wastage of the present system in Spasskoye. Here, as usual, the land was divided into four sections. One was held for common pasturage. To make sure of a fair division of the good, the bad and the medium ground, each peasant was allotted a field in each of these respective sections. Yanishev pointed out the time lost in going from field to field. He showed the gain that would come if the fields, instead of being cut into checkerboards, were worked as a unit on a grand scale. He pictured the gang-plow and the harvester at work. Two of the peasants had seen their magic performances in another province and testified that for working they were regular "devils" (*tcherti*).

"And will America send them to us?" the peasants asked.

"For a while," Yanishev replied. "Then we shall build great shops and make them right here in Russia."

Again he took his hearers out of their quiet rural haunts into the roar and clamor of a great modern plant. And again there was that same uneasy reaction to his tale. They were more afraid than enamoured of modern industrialism. They wanted our wonderful machinery. But they thought it would be a dubious blessing if they must pay the price of seeing chimneys belching black smoke-clouds over their land of green and white. The peasants dread the idea of "being cooked in a factory boiler." Necessity goaded some of them into mines and mills, but since the Revolution they have gone flocking back to the land.

Besides their social questions, there were many personal problems that confronted Yanishev. Should he recommend his political creed by compromising his personal convictions? For example, should he who had left the Greek Church, make the sign of the cross before and after meals. Yanishev decided against it and prepared himself for questions from Ivan Ivanov. But though the old peasant looked perplexed and his wife grieved when Yanishev omitted the ceremony, they never asked for explanations.

In Russia the customary salutation to the toiler in the fields is "God's help to you." (*Bog v pomoshch*). Yanishev decided to use that greeting instead of the formal "Good morning." He also stood thru the long service for Fedossiev's baby. In Russian villages bells toll often for the death of a child.

"Many children God gives us," said the Elder. "And to keep bread in the mouths of those that live we must not neglect the fields." So the others went to their work while the priest and the parents, Yanishev and I, went to the church. Beside the mother stood her nine children. Each year she had borne a child and, ranged according to age, they formed a flight of steps with here and there a gap. That year the child had died. And now this year's child was dead. It was a tiny thing, no larger than the lily beside it, so small and fragile in its little blue coffin, with the massive walls and pillars of the church rising around it.

This village of Spasskoye was fortunate in its priest. He was a kind and sympathetic man, liked and trusted by the people. Tho called so often to say the children's mass, he was trying not to make it a thing of routine. Gently he lit the candles on the coffin, laid the cross on the baby's breast, and began the mass, filling the church with his resonant voice. Priest and deacon chanted the service, while father, mother and children crossed themselves and knelt and touched their foreheads to the floor. Opposite the priest Yanishev stood stolidly with half-bowed head.

They faced each other with the mystery of life and death between them; the one a priest of the Holy Orthodox church, the other a prophet of the Social Revolution; the one consecrating himself to making children happy and secure in the paradise beyond, the other devoting his life to making the earth secure and happy for living children.

. . . . .

I went with Yanishev upon many of his mission-
ary journeys thru the Russian towns and cities.
From the skilled artisans in the textile-center of
Ivanovo, we ranged thru all ranks of the proletarians
down to the slum of the thieves in Moscow, im-
mortalized in Maxim Gorky's *The Night Asylum*.
But always the thoughts of Yanishev were going
back to the villages.

Six months later I said good-bye to him at the
Fourth Soviet Congress in Moscow. Clinging to his
arm was a woman of seventy, very withered and
bent. Yanishev introduced her reverently as his
"teacher." Beyond the confines of Russia or outside the working-classes her name was quite unknown. But to the young rebels among the workers
and peasants her name was everything. With them
she had shared hardship, pain and prison. The long
years of toil and hunger had left her white and
feeble, an object inspiring pity until one saw her
eyes. In them were still the fires which had kindled
the spirits of scores of young men like Yanishev
and sent them out as flaming apostles of the Social
Revolution. For the Revolution she had given her
life, but had hardly dared dream that she would
see it.

Now it had come and she was sitting among her
own, with hands clasped in the hand of her young
disciple. True, industry was in ruin, the Germans
were at the gates, and hunger and cold walked
thru the city, yet as she sat in the ancient Hall of

Nobles, listening to Lenin, she was seeing the new day coming, bringing peace to all people and to her a chance to live on the land.

"We both came from the land and we both love it," she whispered to me. "And when the Revolution is complete Mikhail and I are going back to live in the villages." *

* Appendix III. The Burial of Yanishev.

CHAPTER IV

THE MAN ON HORSEBACK

IN the summer of 1917 I travelled far and wide thru Russia. From all sides rose the lamentation of a stricken people. I heard it in the textile mills of Ivanovo, the Fair grounds of Nijni and the market-squares of Kiev. It came to me from the holds of steamers on the Volga and at night from rafts and barges drifting down the Dnieper. The burden of the people's sorrow was the war, "The cursed war!"

Everywhere I saw the blight and wreckage of war. In the Ukraine I drove out over those rolling lands which made Gogol exclaim: "You steppes! O God! How lovely you are!" We stopped at a little village folded in the hills and about three hundred women, forty old men and boys and a score of crippled soldiers gathered round our *zemstvo* wagon. When I stood up to address them I asked: "How many ever heard of Washington?" One lad raised his hand. "How many have heard of Lincoln?" Three hands. "Kerensky?" About ninety. "Lenin?" Ninety again. "Tolstoi?" One hundred and fifty hands.

They enjoyed this, laughing together at the for-

65

eigner and his funny accent. Then a foolish blunder.
I asked, "Who of you have lost someone in the war?"
Nearly every hand went up, and a wail swept thru
that laughing throng, like a winter wind moaning in
the trees. Two old peasants fell against the wagon-
wheels sobbing, and shaking my platform. A lad
ran out of the crowd, crying: "My brother—they
killed my brother!" And the women, drawing their
platoks to their eyes, or clasped in each other's
arms, wept and wept, until I wondered where all the
tears could come from. Who would have dreamed
that behind those placid faces lay so much grief?

This was but one of the thousands of Russian villages which the war had stripped of every able-
bodied man. It was one of countless villages to
which the wounded came crawling back, crippled,
eyeless, or armless. Millions never returned at all.
They lay in that great grave, 1500 miles long
stretching from the Black Sea to the Baltic—the
Russian front against the Germans. There peasants
with only clubs in their hands, driven up against the
machine guns of the Germans, were mowed down
en masse.

There were plenty of guns in Archangel. They
had even been loaded on cars, and started for the
front. But merchants who wanted those cars for
their wares, slipped a few thousand rubles to the officials; so, ten miles out of Archangel, the munitions
were dumped and the cars shunted back to be re-

loaded with champagnes, automobiles, and Parisian dresses.

Life was gay and dazzling in Petrograd and the big cities—big profits in this war business—but it was cold and bloody business for 12,000,000 soldiers driven into the trenches by order of the Czar.

And now under Kerensky there were still 12,000,-000 under arms. They were conscripts, dragged from ploughs and workshops to have guns thrust in their hands. The ruling-class used every device to keep those weapons in the soldiers' hands. It waved the flag and screamed "Victory and glory." It organized Women's Battalions of Death crying "Shame on you men to let girls do your fighting." It placed machine-guns in the rear of rebelling regiments declaring certain death to those who retreated. But all to no avail.

The Soldiers in Revolt. In thousands the soldiers were throwing down their guns and streaming from the front. Like plagues of locusts they came, clogging railways, highways and waterways. They swarmed down on trains, packing roofs and platforms, clinging to car-steps like clusters of grapes, sometimes evicting passengers from their berths. A Y. M. C. A. man swears he saw this sign: "*Tovarish Soldiers:* Please do not throw passengers out of the window after the train is in motion." Perhaps an exaggeration. But they did throw our suitcases out of the window.

It happened on a trip I made to Moscow with Alex Gumberg. Our compartment was crowded, and the Russians, having almost hermetically sealed door and window against the night air, went blissfully to sleep. The place, soon steaming like a Turkish bath, became unbearable. To let in a breath of air, I slid the door open, then joined the sleepers. In the morning I woke to a harsh surprise. Our suitcases were gone.

"Some *tovarish* robbers in uniform threw them out of the window and then jumped off the train," explained the old conductor. His consolation for our grief was that they had likewise stolen the baggage of an officer in the next compartment. We grieved not so much for the loss of our clothes as for the invaluable passports, notebooks and letters of introduction our bags contained.

Two weeks later we got another surprise—a summons from the station-master in Moscow. There was one of our suitcases forwarded to us by the robbers. It contained none of our clothes but all our documents and the officers' papers—not a single one was missing.

After all, considering the plight of the hordes of deserting soldiers that swept across the land, one wonders not at the number of thefts and excesses they committed but at the fewness of them. And if the tales of awful conditions in the trenches were true, the wonder is not that so many soldiers deserted but that so many still remained at the front.

I wanted to see conditions for myself. Many times I tried to get a pass to the front. At last in September I succeeded. With John Reed and Boris Reinstein, I started for the Riga Sector.

With us was a Russian priest, a big bearded fellow, gentle and amiable, but with a terrible thirst for tea and conversation. On the door of our compartment the guard slapped up a sign that said: *"American Mission."* Under this aegis we slept and ate as the train crept thru the autumn drizzle and the priest talked endlessly on about his soldiers.

"In the old text of the church prayers," he said, "God is called *Czar of Heaven* and the Virgin, *Czarina*. We've had to leave that out. The people won't have God insulted, they say. The priest prays for peace to all nations. Whereupon the soldiers cry out, 'Add "without annexations and indemnities" '. Then we pray for travellers, for the sick and the suffering. And the soldiers cry 'Pray also for the deserters'. The Revolution has made havoc with the Faith, yet the masses of soldiers are religious. Much can still be done in the name of the cross.

"But the Imperialists tried to do too much with it. 'On with the war!' they cried. 'On with the war, until we plant the cross glittering over the dome of Saint Sophia's in Constantinople.' And the soldiers replied: 'Yes! But before we plant the cross on Saint Sophia's, thousands of crosses will be planted on our graves. We don't want Constantinople. We want to go home. We don't want other people to take our land away from us. Neither will we fight to take other people's land away from them.' "

But even if they had the will to fight, what could they fight with? At Wenden, the old city of the Teutonic Knights, we were set down in the midst of an army in ruins. Out of a gray sky the rain poured down, turning roads into rivers, and the soldiers' hearts into lead. Out of the trenches gaunt skeletons rose up to stare at us. We saw famine-stricken men falling on fields of turnips to devour them raw. We saw men walking barefoot in the stubbled fields, summer uniforms arriving at the beginning of winter, horses dropping dead in mud up to their bellies. Above the lines brazenly hovered the armored planes of the enemy watching every move. There were no air-craft guns, no food, no clothes. And to crown all, no faith in their superiors.

Because their officers and government would or could do nothing for them the soldiers were doing things for themselves. On all sides, even in trenches and gun-positions, new Soviets were springing up. Here in Wenden there were three—(*Is-ko-sol, Is-ko-lat, Is-ko-strel*).

We were guests of the last, the Soviet of Lettish Sharp-Shooters, the most literate, the most valiant, the most revolutionary of all. For protection against the German planes, they convened in a tree-screened valley, ten thousand brown uniforms blending with the autumn tinted leaves. Even with the threat above them, every mention of Kerensky's name drew gales of laughter, every mention of peace thunders of applause.

"We are not cowards or traitors," declared the spokesmen. "But we refuse to fight until we know what we are fighting for. We are told this is a war for democracy. We do not believe it. We believe the Allies are land-grabbers like the Germans. Let them show that they are not. Let them declare their peace terms. Let them publish the secret-treaties. Let the Provisional Government show it is not hand in glove with the Imperialists. Then we will lay down our lives in battle to the last man."

This was the root of the debacle of the great Russian armies. Not primarily that they had nothing to fight *with* but that they felt they had nothing to fight *for*.

Backed by the workingmen the soldiers were determined that the war should stop.

Fate of the Man on Horseback. The bourgeoisie backed by the Allies and the General Staff were equally determined that the war should go on. Continuing the war would give three things to the bourgeoisie: (1) It would continue to give them enormous profits out of army contracts. (2) In case of victory it would give them, as their share in the loot, the Straits and Constantinople. (3) It would give them a chance of staving off the ever more insistent demands of the masses for land and factories.

They were following the wisdom of Catherine the Great who said: "The way to save our empire from the encroachment of the people is to engage in war and thus substitute national passions for social aspirations." Now the social aspirations of the Russian masses were endangering the bourgeois empires of land and capital. But if the war could go on, the day of reckoning with the masses would be postponed. The energies absorbed in carrying on the war could not be used in carrying on the Revolution. "On with the war to a victorious end!" became the rallying cry of the bourgeoisie.

But the Kerensky government no longer could control the soldiers. They no longer responded to the eloquence of this romantic man of words. The bourgeoisie set out to find a Man of the Sword. . . . "Russia must have a strong man who will tolerate no revolutionary nonsense, but who will rule with an iron hand," they said. "Let us have a Dictator."

For their Man on Horseback they picked the Cossack General, Kornilov. At the conference in Moscow he had won the hearts of the bourgeoisie by calling for a policy of blood and iron. On his own initiative he had introduced capital punishment in the army. With machine guns he had destroyed battalions of refractory soldiers and placed their stiffened corpses in rows along the fences. He declared that only drastic medicine of this kind could cure the ills of Russia.

On September 9, Kornilov issued a proclamation declaring: "Our great country is dying. Under pressure of the Bolshevik majority in the Soviet, the Kerensky government is acting in complete accord with the plans of the German General Staff. Let all who believe in God and the temples pray to the Lord to manifest the miracle of saving our native land."

He drew 70,000 picked troops from the front. Many of them were Mohammedans—his Turkoman bodyguard, his Tartar horsemen and Circassian mountaineers. On the hilts of their swords the officers swore that when Petrograd was taken, the atheist Socialists would be forced to finish building the great mosque or be shot. With aeroplanes, British armored cars and the blood-thirsty Savage Division, he advanced on Petrograd in the name of God and Allah.

But he did not take it.

In the name of the Soviets and the Revolution the masses rose as one man to the defense of the capital. Kornilov was declared a traitor and an outlaw. Arsenals were opened and guns put in the hands of the workingmen. Red Guards patrolled the streets, trenches were dug, barricades hastily erected. Moslem Socialists rode into the Savage Division and in the name of Marx and Mohammed exhorted the mountaineers not to advance against the Revolution.

Their pleas and arguments prevailed. The forces of Kornilov melted away and the "Dictator" was captured without firing a single shot. The bourgeoisie were depressed as the White Hope of the Counter-Revolution went down so easily before the blows of the Revolution.

The proletarians were correspondingly elated. They saw the strength and unity of their forces.

They felt anew the solidarity binding together all sections of the toiling masses. Trench and factory acclaimed one another. Soldiers and workingmen paid special tribute to the sailors for the big part they played in this affair.

CHAPTER V

W HEN the news of Kornilov's advance on Petrograd was flashed to Kronstadt and the Baltic fleet, it aroused the sailors like a thunderbolt. From their ships and island citadel they came pouring out in tens of thousands and bivouacked on the Field of Mars. They stood guard at all the nerve centres of the city, the railways and the Winter Palace. With the big sailor Dybenko leading, they drove headlong into the midst of Kornilov's soldiers exhorting them not to advance. They put the fear of the Revolution into the hearts of the Whites and the fire and zest of the Revolution into the blood of their fellow Reds.

In July Trotzky had hailed them as "Pride and Flower of the Revolutionary Forces!" When they had been damned on all sides for some brash deeds at Kronstadt he had said: "Yes, but when a counter-revolutionary general tries to throw a noose around the neck of the Revolution, the Cadets will grease the rope with soap, while the sailors will come to fight and die with us together!"

So it proved in this adventure of Kornilov. And it was always so. All over Russia I had met these blue-bloused men with the roll of the sea in their

75

carriage and the tang of the salt winds in their blood. Everywhere they went expounding the doctrines of Socialism. I had heard them in forum and market-places stirring the sluggish to action. I had seen them in remote villages starting the flow of food to the cities. Later when the Yunkers rose against the Soviets I was to see these sailors heading the storming party that rushed the telephone-station and dug the Yunkers from their nests. Always they were first to sense danger to the Revolution, always first to hurry to its rescue.

The Revolution was precious to the Russian sailor because it meant deliverance from the past. That past was a nightmare. The old Russian naval officers came exclusively from the privileged caste. The count against them was that they imposed, not a rigid discipline, but one that was arbitrary and personal. The weal of a sailor was at the mercy of the whims, jealousies and insane rage of petty officers whom he despised. He was treated like a dog and humiliated by signs that read: "For Dogs and Sailors."

Like the soldier's, the sailor's replies to his superior were limited to the three phrases: "Quite so" (*tak tochno*) "No indeed" (*nekak niet*) "Glad to try my best" (*rad staratsa*), with the salutation, "Your nobility." Any added remark might bring him a blow in the face. The most trivial offense met with the most severe penalty. In four years 2527 men were executed, sent to the penitentiary or

Obliterating the Past. Colossal statue of Czar Alexander III being dismantled after the Soviet came into power. Note the workman at extreme top fixing rope on the crown. (*See next page.*)

"How are the mighty fallen!"   Children gazing into the bronze head from the dismantled statue of Czar Alexander III.

to hard labor. All done in the name of the Czar.

Now the Czars were gone; their very names were being blotted out. The ships were being re-christened with names fitting the new republican order.

By this ceremony the *Emperor Paul the First* became *The Republic*. The *Emperor Alexander II* emerged from its baptism of paint as the *Dawn of Liberty*. Here was revolution enough to make these ancient autocrats turn in their graves. But it was even harder on the living Czar and his son. The *Czarevitch* was renamed the *Citizen*, while *Nicholas II* came forth as the good ship *Comrade*. Comrade! This ex-Czar, now living in exile in Tobolsk, knew that the meanest coal-heaver was now a "Comrade."

The new names appeared in gold on the jaunty ribboned caps of the sailors. And the sailors appeared everywhere as missionaries of Liberty, Comradeship and the Republic.

To make these changes in the names of the ships was very easy. Yet they were not mere surface changes, but symbolized a change in reality. They were the outward and visible signs of an inward and spiritual fact—the democratization of a great fleet.

The Sailors Rule the Navy. In September I had my first contact with the sailor at home. It was at Helsingfors where the Baltic fleet stood as a barricade on the water-road to Petrograd. Tied up to the dock was the *Polar Star*, the yacht of the former Czar. Our guide, an old ex-officer, pointed out a strip of yellow wood that ran around the ship.

"That moulding is of best mahogany," he whispered to us. "It cost twenty-five thousand rubles, but these damned Bolsheviks are too lazy now to keep it polished, so they painted it yellow. In my day a sailor was a sailor; he knew that his job was to scrub and polish, and he tended to his job. If he didn't we knocked him down. But the devil is loose among them now. Think of it! On this very yacht belonging to the Czar himself, ordinary seamen sit about making laws for managing the ships, the fleet and the country. And they don't stop there. They talk about managing the world. Internationalism and democracy they call it, but I call it downright treason and insanity."

There in brief was the issue between the old régime and the new. In the old order, discipline and control were superimposed from above; in the new, they proceeded from the men themselves. The old was a fleet of officers, the new a fleet of sailors. In the change a new set of values had been created. Now the polishing of the sailor's wits upon democracy and internationalism had higher rating than polishing the brass and mahogany.

The second index of the temper of the new fleet came to us as we climbed the gangway of the *Polar Star*, where Rasputin and his associates once had their fling. Here Bessie Beatty, the American correspondent, was gravely informed that the presence

of her sex upon the ships was taboo—it was one of
the new rules of the Soviet of Sailors. The captain
was polite, much adorned with gold braid, but very
helpless.

"I can do nothing at all," he explained dolefully. "Everything is in the hands of the 'Committee'."

"But she has come ten thousand versts to see the
fleet."

"Well, we can see what the Committee says," he
answered.

The messenger came back with a special dis-
pensation from the Committee and we were on our
way again. Everywhere members of the crew would
challenge the presence of a woman in our party,
politely capitulating, however, as the captain explained, "By special permit of the Committee."

This Central Committee of the Baltic Sea, or, as
it was familiarly known, the *Centrobalt,* sat in the
great cabin *de luxe.* It was simply a Soviet of the
ships. Each contingent of 1,000 sailors had a representative in the committee, which consisted of 65
members, 45 of whom were Bolsheviks. There were
four general departments: Administrative, Political,
War and Marine, transacting all the affairs of the
fleet. The captain had one of the former princes'
suites, but from the great cabin he was debarred.
Happily my credentials were an open sesame to the
committee and the cabin.

The irony of history! Here in these chairs a

few months ago lolled a mediaeval autocrat with his ladies and his lackeys. Now big bronzed seamen sat in them, hammering out problems of the most advanced Socialism. The cabin had been cleared for action. The piano and many decorations had been placed in a museum. The tables and lounges were covered with brown canvas burlap. The grand salon was now a workshop. Here hard at work were ordinary seamen suddenly turned legislators, directors and clerks. They were a bit awkward in their new role, but they clung to it with desperate earnestness, sixteen hours a day. For they were dreamers gripped by an idea, the drive and scope of which appear in the following address:

To the Representative of the American Social Democracy, Albert Williams, in Reply to his Greetings.

The Russian democracy in the person of the representatives of the Baltic Fleet sends warm greetings to the proletariat of all countries and hearty thanks for the greetings from our brothers in America.

Comrade Williams is the first swallow come flying across to us on the cold waves of the Baltic Sea, which now for over three years has been dyed by the blood of the sons of one family, the International.

The Russian proletariat will strive, up to its last breath, to unite everybody under the red banner of the International. When starting the Revolution, we did not have in view a Political Revolution alone. The task of all true fighters for freedom is the making of a Social Revolution. For this the advance guard of the Revolution, in the person of the sailors of the Russian Fleet, and the workmen, will fight to the end.

The flame of the Russian Revolution, we are sure, will spread over the world and light a fire in the hearts of the workers of all lands, and we shall obtain support in our struggle for a speedy general peace.

The free Baltic Fleet impatiently awaits the moment when it can go to America and relate there all that Russia suffered under the yoke of Czarism, and what it is feeling now when the banner of the struggle for the freedom of peoples is unfurled.

LONG LIFE TO THE AMERICAN SOCIAL-DEMOCRACY.
LONG LIVE THE PROLETARIAT OF ALL LANDS.
LONG LIVE THE INTERNATIONAL.
LONG LIVE GENERAL PEACE.
The Central Committee of the Baltic Fleet, Fourth Convention.

On this table where in good will and amity they had written this address to me, these sailors dipped their pens in vitriol and wrote another. It was addressed to their Commander-in-Chief, Kerensky. He was unable to explain his part in the Kornilov mix-up and had just made an offensive reference to the sailors. They returned the compliment in this wise:

We demand the immediate removal from the Government of the "Socialist" political adventurer, Kerensky, who is ruining the great Revolution by his shameless political blackmail in behalf of the bourgeoisie.

To you, Kerensky, traitor to the Revolution, we send our curses. When our comrades are drowning in the Gulf of Riga, and when all of us, as one man, stand ready to lay down our lives for freedom, ready to die in open fight on the sea or on the barricades, you strive to destroy the forces of the fleet. To you we send our maledictions. . . .

This day, however, the men were in festive mood. They were happy over a big fund just raised for their soldier comrades on the Riga front, and now were playing host to their first foreign comrade. The Secretary of the Committee escorted me on the pilot-boat to his battleship, the *Republic*. The entire crew was on deck cheering our approach across the waters. After an official welcome there were loud demands for a speech. My knowledge of Russian was very meagre then, and my interpreter knew but little English. I had to fall back on the current revolutionary phrases. But the mere reiteration of the new battle cries had power to charm these new disciples of Socialism. The sounding of these slogans in my foreign accent drew an outburst of applause that echoed like a salvo from all the ship's batteries.

It was in these waters that the historic meeting between the Kaiser and the Czar had been staged. The applause could not have been more thunderous (certainly not so spontaneous) than when, as an American Internationalist, I shook hands with Averishkin, the Russian Internationalist, on the bridge of this battleship off the coast of Finland.

A Ship's Menu,
a Club and a College.

After our love-feast on deck we retired to the quarters of the ship's committee. I was plied with innumerable questions about the American navy, ranging from "Do American navy officers reflect solely the viewpoint of the upper classes?" to "Are American battleships kept as clean as this one of ours?" As we talked, eggs and steak were brought to me, while each member of the committee was served with a large plate of potatoes. I commented on the difference in the dishes.

"Yours is officer's fare, ours is sailor's," they explained.

"Then why did you make a revolution?" I asked banteringly.

They laughed and said, "The Revolution has given us what we wanted most—freedom. We are masters of our ships. We are masters of our own lives. We have our own courts. We can have shore-leave when not on duty. Off duty we have the right to wear civilian clothes. We do not demand everything of the Revolution."

The world-wide rise of the workers, however, is based on their desire, not solely for the first necessities of life, but for a larger part in its amenities. Driving through Helsingfors one night we missed the usual bands of sailors rolling down the streets. Suddenly we were brought sharply up before a building with façade and dimensions of a great modern hotel. We entered and were guided by the music to the dining-hall. There, in a room set with palms and glistening with mirrors and silver, sat the diners, listening to Chopin and Tchaikovsky, interspersed with occasional ragtime from the American conductor. It was a hotel of the first class, but instead of the usual clientele of a big hotel—bankers, speculators, politicians, adventurers and ornate ladies—it was crowded with bronzed seamen of the war fleet of the Russian Republic, who had commandeered the entire building. Thru its curtained halls now streamed a procession of laughing, jesting, arguing sailors in their suits of blue.

Outside in big letters was the sign *"Sailors' Club"* with its motto, "A welcome to all the sailors of the world." It opened with ten thousand dues-paying members, ninety per cent of whom were literate. The club boasted a much-used magazine room, the nucleus of a library, and an excellent illustrated weekly, *The Seaman (Moryak)*.

They had founded, too, a "University," with courses ranging from the most elementary to the most advanced. In the committee on curriculum I blunderingly asked the chairman from what university he came.

"No university, no school," he replied regretfully. "I come from the dark people, but I am a revolutionist. We did away with the Czar, but a worse enemy is ignorance. We shall do away with that. That is the only way to get a democratic fleet. Now we have a democratic machine, but most of our officers have not the democratic spirit. We must train our officers out of the ranks." In his courses he had enlisted professors from the university, men from the scientific societies and some officers.

How did all this new discipline and comfort affect the fleet? Opinions differed. Many officers said that in destroying the old discipline the technical efficiency was lowered. Others said that consider-

ing its ordeal by war and revolution the fleet was in
good trim. As the test of its moral efficiency, they
pointed to the battle of the Monsund Isles. Out-
numbered by the Germans, and out-distanced in
speed and gun-range, these revolutionary sailors had
fought a brilliant engagement with the enemy. All
admitted that their fighting morale was superb.

There was no doubt of the enthusiasm of the
sailors for their fleet. They had a feeling of communal ownership in it. When the pilot-boat carried
me away from the *Republic,* Averishkin with a gesture that took in all the gray ships riding in the bay,
exclaimed, "Our fleet! Our fleet! We shall make
it the best fleet in the world. May it always fight
for justice!" Then, as if looking thru the gray
mists which hung above the water and beyond the
red mists of the world war, he added, "Until we make
the Social Revolution and the end of all wars."

In Russia this Social Revolution was coming on
apace and these men of the fleet were shortly to be
in the vortex of it.

PART II

THE REVOLUTION AND THE DAYS
AFTER

AMONG THE WHITES AND THE REDS

CHAPTER VI

"ALL POWER TO THE SOVIET"

A NOTHER winter is bearing down upon hungry, heartsick Russia. The last October leaves are falling from the trees, and the last bit of confidence in the government is falling with them.

Everywhere recklessness and orgies of speculation. Food trains are looted. Floods of paper money pour from the presses. In the newspapers endless columns of hold-ups, murders and suicides. Night life and gambling-halls run full blast with enormous stakes won and lost.

Reaction is open and arrogant. Kornilov, instead of being tried for high treason, is lauded as the Great Patriot by the bourgeoisie. But with them patriotism is tawdry talk and a sham. They pray for the Germans to come and cut off Petrograd, the Head of the Revolution.

Rodzianko, ex-President of the Duma, brazenly writes: "Let the Germans take the city. Tho they destroy the fleet they will throttle the Soviets." The big insurance companies announce one-third off in rates after the German occupation. "Winter

89

always was Russia's best friend," say the bourgeoisie. "It may rid us of this cursed Revolution."

Despair Foments Rebellion. Winter, sweeping down out of the North, hailed by the privileged, brings terror to the suffering masses. As the mercury drops toward zero, the prices of food and fuel go soaring up. The bread ration grows shorter. The queues of shivering women standing all night in the icy streets grow longer. Lockouts and strikes add to the millions of workless. The rancor in the hearts of the masses flares out in bitter speeches like this from a Viborg workingman:

"Patience, patience, they are always counselling us. But what have they done to make us patient? Has Kerensky given us more to eat than the Czar? More words and promises—yes! But not more food. All night long we wait in the lines for shoes and bread and meat, while, like fools, we write '*Liberty*' on our banners. The only liberty we have is the same old liberty to slave and starve."

It is a sorry showing after eight months of pleading and parading thru the streets. All they have got are lame feet, aching arms, and the privilege of starving and freezing in the presence of mocking red banners: *"Land to the Peasants!" "Factories to the Workers!" "Peace to all the World!"*

But no longer do they carry their red banners thru the streets. They are done with appealing and beseeching. In a mood born of despair and disillusion they are acting now—reckless, violent, iconoclastic, but—acting.

In the cities revolting employees are driving mill-owners out of their offices. Managers try to stop it, and are thrown into wheel-barrows and ridden out of the plant. Machinery is put out of gear, materials spoiled, industry brought to a standstill.

In the army soldiers are throwing down their guns and deserting the front in hundreds of thousands. Emissaries try to stop them with frantic appeals. They may as well appeal to a landslide. "If no decisive steps for peace are taken by November first," the soldiers say, "all the trenches will be emptied. The entire army will rush to the rear." In the fleet is open insubordination.

In the country, peasants are overrunning the estates. I ask Baron Nolde, "What is it that the peasants want on your estate?"

"My estate," he answers.

"How are they going to get it?"

"They've got it."

In some places these seizures are accompanied by wanton spoliation. The skies around Tambov are reddened with flames from the burning hay-ricks and manor-houses. Landlords flee for their lives. The infuriated peasants laugh at the orators trying to quiet them. Troops sent down to suppress the outbursts go over to the side of the peasants.

Russia is plunging headlong towards the abyss.

Over this spectacle of misery and ruin presides a handful of talkers called the Provisional Government. It is almost a corpse, treated to hypodermic injections of threats and promises from the Allies. Before tasks calling for the strength of a giant it is weak as a baby. To all demands of the people it has just one reply, "Wait." First, it was "Wait till the end of the war." Now, "Wait till the Constituent Assembly."

But the people will wait no longer. Their last shred of faith in the government is gone. They have faith in themselves; faith that they alone can save Russia from going over the precipice to ruin and night; faith alone in the institutions of their own making. They look now to the new authority created out of their own midst. They look to the Soviets.

"Let the Soviets Be the Government." Summer and fall have seen the steady growth of the Soviets. They have drawn to themselves the vital forces in each community. They have been schools for the training of the people, giving them confidence. The net-work of local Soviets has been wrought into a wide firmly built organization, a new structure which has risen within the shell of the old. As the old apparatus was going to pieces, the new one was taking over its functions. The Soviets in many ways were already acting as a government. It was necessary only to

proclaim them the government.   Then the Soviets
would be in name what they were already in reality.

From the depths now lifted up a mighty cry:
"All power to the Soviets."   The demand of the
capital in July became the demand of the country.
Like wildfire it swept thru the land.   Sailors on the
Baltic Fleet flung it out to their comrades on the
Black and White and Yellow seas, and from them
it came echoing back.   Farm and factory, barracks
and battlefront joined in the cry, swelling louder,
more insistent every hour.

Petrograd came thundering into the chorus on
Sunday, November 4th, in sixty enormous mass
meetings.   Trotzky having read the Reply of the
Baltic Fleet to my Greetings asked me to speak
at the People's House.

Here great waves of human beings dashed against
the doors, swirled inside and sluiced along the corridors.   They poured into the halls, filling them
full, splashing hundreds up on the girders where
they hung like garlands of foam.   Out of the eddying throngs, a mighty voice rose and fell and broke
like surf, thundering on the shore—hundreds of
thousands of throats roaring *"Down with the Provisional Government."   "All Power to the Soviets."*
Hundreds of thousands of hands were raised in a
pledge to fight and die for the Soviets.

The patience of the poor at an end; the pawns and
cannon-fodder in revolt!   The dark masses, long
inert, but roused at last, refusing longer to be brow-

beaten or hypnotized by the word-juggling of statesmen, scorning their threats, laughing at their promises, take the initiative into their own hands, demanding of their "leaders" to move forward into
revolution or resign. For the first time the slaves
and the exploited, consciously choosing the time of
their deliverance, vote for insurrection, investing
themselves with the government of one-sixth of the
world. A big venture for men unschooled in state
affairs. Are they equal to these tasks? Can they
control the currents now being loosed in the city?
At any rate these masses show complete control of
themselves. From these blood-stirring revolutionary
meetings they pour forth in orderly fashion.

The poor frightened bourgeoisie are reassured.
They see no houses looted, no shops wrecked, no
white-collared gentry shot down in the streets. To
their minds, therefore, all is well; there will be no
insurrection. The true import of this restraint quite
escapes them. The people indulge in no sporadic
outbursts because they have better use for their
energies. They have a Revolution to make, not a
riot. And a Revolution requires order, plan, labor—
much hard intensive labor.

The Masses Conducting
their Revolution.

These insurgent masses go
home to organize committees,
draw up lists, form Red Cross
units, collect rifles. Hands
lifted in a vote for Revolution now are holding guns.

They get ready for the forces of the Counter-Revolution now mobilizing against them. In Smolny sits the Military Revolutionary Committee from which these masses take orders. There is another committee, the Committee of a Hundred Thousand; that is, the masses themselves. There are no by-streets, no barracks, no buildings where this committee does not penetrate. It reaches into the councils of the Black Hundred, the Kerensky Government, the intelligentsia. With porters, waiters, cabmen, conductors, soldiers and sailors, it covers the city like a net. They see everything, hear everything, report everything to headquarters. Thus, forewarned, they can checkmate every move of the enemy. Every attempt to strangle or sidetrack the Revolution they paralyze at once.

Attempt is made to break the faith of the masses in their leaders by furious assault upon them. Kerensky cries from the tribunal "Lenin, the state criminal, inciting to pillage . . . and the most terrible massacres which will cover with eternal shame the name of free Russia." Immediately the masses reply by bringing Lenin out of hiding with a tremendous ovation and turning Smolny into an arsenal to guard him.

Attempt is made to drown the Revolution in blood and disorder. The Dark Forces keep calling the people to rise up and slaughter Jews and Socialist leaders. Forthwith the workmen placard the city with posters saying "Citizens! We call upon you to maintain complete quiet and self-possession. The cause of order is in strong hands. At the first instance of robbery and shooting, the criminals will be wiped off the face of the earth."

Attempts are made to isolate the different sections of the revolutionists. Telephones are cut off between Soviets and barracks; immediately communications are established by setting up telephonograph apparatus. The Yunkers turn the bridges, cutting off the working-class districts; the Kronstadt sailors close them again. The offices of the Communist papers are locked and sealed, cutting off the flow of news; the Red Guards break the seals and set the presses running again.

Attempt is made to suppress the Revolution by force of arms. Kerensky begins calling "dependable" troops into the city; that is, troops that may be depended upon to shoot down the rising workers. Among these are the Zenith Battery and the Cyclists' Battalion. Along the highroads on which these units are advancing into the city the Revolution posts its forces. They attack the enemy, not with guns but with ideas. They subject these troops to a withering fire of arguments and pleas. Result: these troops that are being rushed to the city to crush the Revolution enter instead to aid and abet it.

To these zealots of the Communist faith, all soldiers succumb, even the Cossacks. "Brother Cossacks!" reads the appeal to them, "you are being incited against us by grafters, parasites, landlords and by our own Cossack generals who wish to crush our Revolution. Comrade Cossacks! Do not fall in with this plan of Cain." And the Cossacks likewise line up under the banner of the Revolution.

CHAPTER VII

WHILE Petrograd is in a tumult of clashing patrols and contending voices, men from all over Russia come pouring into the city. They are delegates to the Second All-Russian Congress of Soviets convening at Smolny. All eyes are turned towards Smolny.

Formerly a school for the daughters of the nobility, Smolny is now the center of the Soviets. It stands on the Neva, a huge stately structure, cold and grey by day. But by night, glowing with a hundred lamp-lit windows, it looms up like a great temple—a temple of Revolution. The two watch fires before its porticos, tended by long-coated soldiers, flame like altar-fires. Here are centered the hopes and prayers of untold millions of the poor and disinherited. Here they look for release from age-long suffering and tyranny. Here are wrought out for them issues of life and death.

That night I saw a laborer, gaunt, shabbily-clad, plodding down a dark street. Lifting his head suddenly he saw the massive façade of Smolny, glowing golden thru the falling snow. Pulling off his cap, he stood a moment with bared head and outstretched arms. Then crying out, *"The Commune! The People! The Revolution!"* he ran forward and merged with the throng streaming thru the gates.

Out of war, exile, dungeons, Siberia, come these delegates to Smolny. For years no news of old comrades. Suddenly, cries of recognition, a rush into one another's arms, a few words, a moment's embrace, then a hastening on to conferences, caucuses, endless meetings.

Smolny is now one big forum, roaring like a gigantic smithy with orators calling to arms, audiences whistling or stamping, the gavel pounding for order, the sentries grounding arms, machine-guns rumbling across the cement floors, crashing choruses of revolutionary hymns, thundering ovations for Lenin and Zinoviev as they emerge from underground.

Everything at high speed, tense and growing tenser every minute. The leading workers are dynamos of energy; sleepless, tireless, nerveless miracles of men, facing momentous questions of Revolution.

At ten-forty on this night of November 7th, opens the historic meeting so big with consequences for the future of Russia and the whole world. From their party caucuses the delegates file into the great assembly-hall. Dan, the anti-Bolshevik chairman, is on the platform ringing the bell for order and declares, "The first session of the Second Congress of Soviets is now open."

First comes the election of the governing body of the congress (the presidium). The Bolsheviks get

14 members. All other parties get 11. The old governing body steps down and the Bolshevik leaders, recently the outcasts and outlaws of Russia, take their places. The Right parties, composed largely of intelligentsia, open with an attack on credentials and orders of the day. Discussion is their forte. They delight in academic issues. They raise fine points of principle and procedure.

Then, suddenly out of the night, a rumbling shock brings the delegates to their feet, wondering. It is the boom of cannon, the cruiser *Aurora* firing over the Winter Palace. Dull and muffled out of the distance it comes with steady, regular rhythm, a requiem tolling the death of the old order, a salutation to the new. It is the voice of the masses thundering to the delegates the demand for *"All Power to the Soviets."* So the question is acutely put to the Congress: "Will you now declare the Soviets the government of Russia, and give legal basis to the new authority?"

The Intelligentsia Desert. Now comes one of the startling paradoxes of history, and one of its colossal tragedies—the refusal of the intelligentsia. Among the delegates were scores of these intellectuals. They had made the "dark people" the object of their devotion. "Going to the people" was a religion. For them they had suffered poverty, prison and exile. They had stirred the quiescent masses with revolutionary ideas, inciting them to revolt. The character and nobility of the masses had been ceaselessly extolled. In short, the intelligentsia had made a god of the people. Now the people were rising with the wrath and thunder of a god, imperious and arbitrary. They were acting like a god.

But the intelligentsia reject a god who will not listen to them and over whom they have lost control. Straightway the intelligentsia became atheists. They disavow all faith in their former god, the people. They deny their right to rebellion.

Like Frankenstein before this monster of their own creation, the intelligentsia quail, trembling with fear, trembling with rage. It is a bastard thing, a devil, a terrible calamity, plunging Russia into chaos, "a criminal rebellion against authority." They hurl themselves against it, storming, cursing, beseeching, raving. As delegates they refuse to recognize this Revolution. They refuse to allow this Congress to declare the Soviets the government of Russia.

So futile! So impotent! They may as well refuse to recognize a tidal wave, or an erupting volcano as to refuse to recognize this Revolution. This Revolution is elemental, inexorable. It is everywhere, in the barracks, in the trenches, in the factories, in the streets. It is here in this congress, officially, in hundreds of workmen, soldier and peasant delegates. It is here unofficially in the masses crowding every inch of space, climbing up on pillars and window-sills, making the assembly hall white with fog from their close-packed steaming bodies, electric with the intensity of their feelings.

The people are here to see that their revolutionary will is done; that the congress declares the Soviets the government of Russia. On this point they are inflexible. Every attempt to becloud the issue, every effort to paralyze or evade their will evokes blasts of angry protest.

The parties of the Right have long resolutions to offer. The crowd is impatient. "No more resolutions! No more words! We want deeds! We want the Soviet!"

The intelligentsia, as usual, wish to compromise the issue by a coalition of all parties. "Only one coalition possible," is the retort. "The coalition of workers, soldiers and peasants."

Martov calls out for "a peaceful solution of the impending civil war." "Victory! Victory!—the only possible solution," is the answering cry.

The officer Kutchin tries to terrify them with the idea that the Soviets are isolated, and that the whole army is against them. "Liar! Staff!" yell the soldiers. "You speak for the staff—not the men in the trenches. We soldiers demand 'All Power to the Soviets!'"

Their will is steel. No entreaties or threats avail to break or bend it. Nothing can deflect them from their goal.

Finally stung to fury, Abramovich cries out, "We cannot remain here and be responsible for these

crimes. We invite all delegates to leave this congress." With a dramatic gesture he steps from the
platform and stalks towards the door. About eighty
delegates rise from their seats and push their way
after him.

"Let them go," cries Trotzky, "let them go!
They are just so much refuse that will be swept into
the garbage-heap of history."

In a storm of hoots, jeers and taunts of "Rene-
gades! Traitors!" from the proletarians, the intelligentsia pass out of the hall and out of the
Revolution. A supreme tragedy! The intelligentsia
rejecting the Revolution they had helped to create,
deserting the masses in the crisis of their struggle.
Supreme folly, too. They do not isolate the Soviets,
they only isolate themselves. Behind the Soviets
are rolling up solid battalions of support.

The Soviets Proclaimed the Government. Every minute brings news of
fresh conquests of the Revo-
lution—the arrest of ministers,
the seizure of the State Bank,
telegraph station, telephone station, the staff headquarters. One by one the centers of power are
passing into the hands of the people. The spectral
authority of the old government is crumbling before the hammer strokes of the insurgents.

A commissar, breathless and mud-spattered from
riding, climbs the platform to announce: "The
garrison of Tsarskoye Selo for the Soviets. It stands

guard at the gates of Petrograd." From another: "The Cyclists' Battalion for the Soviets. Not a single man found willing to shed the blood of his brothers." Then Krylenko, staggering up, telegram in hand: "Greetings to the Soviet from the Twelfth Army! The Soldiers' Committee is taking over the command of the Northern Front."

And finally at the end of this tumultuous night, out of this strife of tongues and clash of wills, the simple declaration: *"The Provisional Government is deposed. Based upon the will of the great majority of workers, soldiers and peasants, the Congress of Soviets assumes the power. The Soviet authority will at once propose an immediate democratic peace to all nations, an immediate truce on all fronts. It will assure the free transfer of lands . . . etc."*

Pandemonium! Men weeping in one another's arms. Couriers jumping up and racing away. Telegraph and telephone buzzing and humming. Autos starting off to the battle-front; aeroplanes speeding away across rivers and plains. Wireless flashing across the seas. All messengers of the great news!

The will of the revolutionary masses has triumphed. The Soviets are the government.

This historic session ends at six o'clock in the morning. The delegates, reeling from the toxin of fatigue, hollow-eyed from sleeplessness, but exultant, stumble down the stone stairs and thru the gates of Smolny. Outside it is still dark and chill, but a red dawn is breaking in the east.

One of the crack Bolshevik regiments marching to Smolny under banners emblazoned with *All Power to the Soviets, Long Live the Revolution.*

On the night of November 7 we saw the Winter Palace (*left*) stormed by the Red Guards. Here they are massed before the base of the Alexander column (*right*).

CHAPTER VIII

LOOTING THE WINTER PALACE

THE Russian poet, Tyutchev, writes:

"Blessed is he who visited this world
In moments of its fateful deeds:
The highest Gods invited him to come,
A guest, with them to sit at feast
And be a witness of their mighty spectacle."

Twice blessed were five Americans: Louise Bryant, John Reed, Bessie Beatty, Gumberg and myself. We were spectators of the great drama enacted in the halls of Smolny: we also saw the other big event of the night of November 7th—the taking of the Winter Palace.

We had been sitting in Smolny, gripped by the pleas of the speakers, when out of the night that other voice crashed into the lighted hall—the cannon of the cruiser *Aurora,* firing at the Winter Palace. Steady, insistent, came the ominous beat of the cannon, breaking the spell of the speakers upon us. We could not resist its call and hurried away.

Outside, a big motor-truck with engines throbbing was starting for the city. We climbed aboard and tore thru the night, a plunging comet, flying a tail of white posters in our wake. From alleys and doorways dim figures darted out to snatch them up and read:

Къ Гражданамъ Россіи.

Временное Правительство низложено. Государственная власть перешла въ руки органа Петроградскаго Совѣта Рабочихъ и Солдатскихъ Депутатовъ Военно-Революціоннаго Комитета, стоящаго во главѣ Петроградскаго пролетаріата и гарнизона.

Дѣло, за которое боролся народъ: немедленное предложеніе демократическаго мира, отмѣна помѣщичьей собственности на землю, рабочій контроль надъ производствомъ, созданіе Совѣтскаго Правительства — это дѣло обезпечено.

ДА ЗДРАВСТВУЕТЪ РЕВОЛЮЦІЯ РАБОЧИХЪ, СОЛДАТЪ И КРЕСТЬЯНЪ!

Военно-Революціонный Комитетъ
при Петроградскомъ Совѣтѣ
Рабочихъ и Солдатскихъ Депутатовъ.

25 октября 1917 г. 10 ч. утра.

To the Citizens of Russia:

The Provisional Government is deposed. The State power has passed into the hands of the organ of the Petrograd Soviet of Workers' and Soldiers' Deputies, the Military Revolutionary Committee, which stands at the head of the Petrograd proletariat and garrison.

The aims for which the people were fighting – immediate proposal of a democratic peace, abolition of landlord property-rights in the land, labor control over production, creation of a Soviet Government, – these aims have been achieved.

LONG LIVE THE REVOLUTION OF WORKMEN, SOLDIERS AND PEASANTS!

Military-Revolutionary Committee
of the Petrograd Soviet of
Workers and Soldier's' Deputies.

November 7, 1917

[*Reproduction in English of the Russian text on opposite page.*]

This announcement is a trifle previous. The ministers of the Provisional Government, minus Kerensky, still sit at council in the Winter Palace. That is why the guns of the *Aurora* are in action. They are thundering into the ears of the ministers the summons to surrender. True, only blank shells are firing now, but they set the air shivering, shaking the building and the nerves of the ministers within.

As we come into the Palace Square the booming of the guns dies away. The rifles no longer crackle thru the dark. The Red Guards are crawling out to carry off their dead and dying. Out of the night a voice cries, "The Yunkers surrender." But mindful of their losses, the besieging sailors and soldiers cling to cover.

The Mob Enters the Palace. New throngs gather on the Nevsky. Forming a column, they pour thru the Red Arch and creep forward, silent. Near the barricade they emerge into the light blazing from within the Palace. They scale the rampart of logs, and storm thru the iron gateway into the open doors of the east wing—the mob swarming in behind them.

From cold and darkness, these proletarians come suddenly into warmth and light. From huts and barracks they pass into glittering salons and gilded chambers. This is indeed Revolution—the builders entering into the Palace they built.

And such a building! Ornate with statues of gold

and bronze, and carpeted with Oriental rugs, its rooms hung with tapestries and paintings, and flooded with a million lights from the twinkling crystal chandeliers, its cellars crammed with rare wines and liquors of ancient vintage. Riches beyond their dreams are within their grasp. Why not grasp them?

A terrible lust lays hold of the mob—the lust that ravishing beauty incites in the long starved and long denied—the lust of loot. Even we, as spectators, are not immune to it. It burns up the last vestige of restraint and leaves one passion flaming in the veins—the passion to sack and pillage. Their eyes fall upon this treasure-trove, and their hands follow.

Along the walls of the vaulted chamber we enter there runs a row of huge packing-cases. With the butts of their rifles, the soldiers batter open the boxes, spilling out streams of curtains, linen, clocks, vases and plates.

Scorning such petty booty, the throngs swirl past to richer hunting-grounds. The vanguard presses forward thru gorgeous chambers opening into ever more gorgeous ones, lined with cabinets and wardrobes. They fall upon them with shouts of expectant joy. Then cries of anger and chagrin. They find mirrors shattered, panels kicked in, drawers rifled— everywhere the trail of vandals who have gone before. The Yunkers have taken the cream of the plunder.

So much is gone! So much intenser, then, the

struggle for what remains. Who shall gainsay them the right to this Palace and its contents? All of it came out of their sweat and the sweat of their fathers. It is theirs by right of creation. It is theirs, too, by right of conquest. By the smoking guns in their hands and the courage in their hearts they have taken it. But how long can they keep it? For a century it was the Czar's. Yesterday it was Kerensky's. Today it is theirs. Tomorrow it shall be —whose? No one can tell. This day the Revolution gives. Next day the Counter-Revolution may snatch away. Now while the prize is theirs shall they not make the most of it? Here where courtiers wantoned for a century shall they not revel for a night? Their outraged past, the feverish present, the uncertain future—everything urges them to grasp what they can now.

Pandemonium breaks loose in the Palace. It rolls and echoes with myriad sounds. Tearing of cloth and wood, clatter of glass from splintered windows, clumping of heavy boots upon the parquet floor, the crashing of a thousand voices against the ceiling. Voices jubilant, then jangling over division of the spoils. Voices hoarse, high-pitched, muttering, cursing.

Then another voice breaks into this babel—the clear, compelling voice of the Revolution. It speaks thru the tongues of its ardent votaries, the Petrograd workingmen. There is just a handful of them, weazened and undersized, but into the ranks of

these big peasant soldiers they plunge, crying out—
"Take nothing. The Revolution forbids it. No
looting. This is the property of the people."

Children piping against a cyclone, dwarfs attacking an army of giants. So seem these protesters, trying to stem with words the onslaught of soldiers
flushed with conquest, pillage-bent. The mob goes
on pillaging. Why should it heed the protest of a
handful of workmen?

The Restraining Hand
of Revolution.
But these workmen will be
heeded. Back of their words
they feel the will of the Revolution. It makes them fearless
and aggressive. They turn upon the big soldiers
with fury, hurl epithets into their faces, wrest the
booty out of their hands. In a short time they have
them on the defensive.

A big peasant making off with a heavy woolen
blanket is waylaid by a little workingman. He
grabs hold of the blanket, tugs away at one end of
it, scolding the big fellow like a child.

"Let go the blanket," growls the peasant, his
face convulsed with rage. "It's mine."

"No, no," the workingman cries, "it's not yours.
It belongs to all the people. Nothing goes out of
the Palace tonight."

"Well, this blanket goes out tonight. It's cold in
the barracks!"

"I'm sorry you're cold, *tovarish*. Better for you

to suffer cold than the Revolution to suffer disgrace by your looting."

"Devil take you," exclaims the peasant. "What did we make the Revolution for, anyhow? Wasn't it to give clothes and food to the people?"

"Yes, *tovarish*, the Revolution will give everything you need in due time, but not tonight. If anything goes out of here we will be called hooligans and robbers—not true Socialists. Our enemies will say that we came here not for revolution, but for loot. So we must take nothing. For this is the property of the people. Let us guard it for the honor of the Revolution."

"Socialism! The Revolution! Property of the People!" With this formula the peasant saw his blanket taken away from him. Always these abstract ideas adorned with capital letters taking things away from him. Once it was done with "Czardom, The Glory of God." Now it was being done with "Socialism, Revolution, Property of the People."

Still there was something in this last concept that the peasant could grasp. It was in line with his communal training. As it took hold of his brain his hold on the blanket relaxed, and with a last tragic look at his precious treasure he shambled away. Later I saw him expounding to another soldier. He was talking about the "Property of the People."

Relentlessly the workingmen press home their advantage, using every tactic, pleading, explaining,

threatening. In an alcove is a Bolshevik workingman, furiously shaking one hand at three soldiers,
the other hand on his revolver.

"I hold you responsible, if you touch that desk,"
he cries.

"Hold us responsible!" jeer the soldiers. "Who
are you? You broke into the Palace just as we
did. We are responsible to no one but ourselves."

"You are responsible to the Revolution," retorts
the workingman sternly. So deadly earnest is he
that these men feel in him the authority of the Revolution. They hear and obey.

The Revolution loosed the daring and ardor in
these masses. It used them to storm the Palace.
Now it leashes them in. Out of bedlam it brings
forth a controlling power—quieting, imposing order,
posting sentries.

"All out! Clear the Palace!" sounds thru the
corridors, and the throng begins to flow toward the
doors. At each exit stands a self-appointed Committee of Search and Inspection. They lay hold of
each man as he comes along, exploring his pockets,
shirt and even his boots, gathering in a varied line of
souvenirs; statuettes, candles, clothes-hangers, dam-
ask, vases. The owners plead like children for their
trophies, but the committee is adamant repeating
constantly, "Nothing goes out of the Palace tonight."

And nothing does go out that night on the persons
of the Red Guards, tho prowlers and vandals later
on make off with many valuables.

The commissars now turn to the Provisional Government and their defenders. They are rounded up and escorted to the exit. First, come the ministers, seized in session around the green baize table in the Hall of State. They file down in silence. From the crowd inside not a word or a jeer. But from the mob outside rises a blast of denunciation when a sailor calls for an automobile. "Make them walk, they have ridden long enough," the mob yells, making a lunge at the frightened ministers. The Red Sailors, with fixed bayonets, close around their captives and lead them out across the bridges of the Neva. Towering above all the convoy is Tereschenko, the Ukrainian capitalist, bound now from the Ministry of Foreign Affairs to the Prison of Peter-Paul, reversing the journey of the Bolshevik, Trotzky, from the Prison of Peter-Paul to the office of Foreign Affairs.

The Yunkers were led out to cries of "Provocators! Traitors! Murderers!"—a sorry crestfallen lot. That morning each Yunker had vowed to us that he would fight until just one bullet was left. This last one, he would put thru his own brain rather than surrender to the Bolsheviks. Now he was giving up his arms to these Bolsheviks, solemnly promising never to take weapons against them again. (Unhappy fellows! They were to break their promise.)

Last of the captives to leave the Palace were the members of the Women's Battalion. Most of them were of proletarian birth. "Shame! Shame!" cried the Red Guards, "Working-women fighting against workingmen." To drive home the indignation they felt, some grabbed the girls by the arms, shaking and scolding them.

This was about the sum total of the casualties among the soldier girls, tho later one of them committed suicide. Next day the hostile press spread tales of gruesome atrocities against the Women's Battalion, alongside of stories of sack and pillage of the Palace by the Red Guards.

Yet nothing is more alien to the essential nature of the working-class than destructiveness. Were it not so, history might have a different story to tell of the morning of November eighth. It might have to record that the magnificent edifice of the Czars was left a heap of crumbling stones and smoking embers by the vengeance of a long-suffering people.

For a century it had stood there upon the Neva, a cold and heartless thing. The people had looked to it for light, and it had brought forth darkness. They had cried to it for compassion, and it had answered with the lash, the knout, the burning of villages, exile in Siberia. One winter morning in 1905 thousands of them had come here, defenseless, petitioning the Little Father for redress of wrongs. The Palace had answered with rifle and cannon, reddening the snow with their blood. To the masses the building was a monument of cruelty and oppression. Had they razed it to the ground, it would have been but one more instance of the wrath of an outraged people, removing from their eyes forever the hated symbol of their suffering.

Instead they proceeded to remove the historic landmark from all likelihood of damage.

Kerensky had done the opposite. He had recklessly put the Winter Palace in the arena of conflict by making it the center of his cabinet and his own sleeping quarters. But the representatives of these storming masses who had captured the Palace, declared that it was not theirs nor the Soviets', but the heritage of all. By Soviet decree it was made the Museum of the People. The custody of it was formally placed in the hands of a committee of artists.

A New Attitude Towards Property. So events gave the lie to another dire prophecy. Kerensky, Dan and other of the intelligentsia had shrieked against the Revolution, predicting a hideous orgy of crime and plunder, the loosing of the basest passions of the mob. Once the hungry and embittered masses got in motion, they said, like a maddened herd they would go trampling down, wrecking, and destroying everything. "Even Gorky was prophesying the end of the world" (Trotzky).

And now the Revolution has come. There are, indeed, isolated acts of vandalism; rich-clad bourgeois still return home minus their great fur coats;

mobs work havoc before the Revolution can rein them in.

But there is one outstanding fact. The first fruits of the Revolution are law and order. Never was Petrograd safer than after passing into the hands of the masses. Unprecedented quiet reigns in the streets. Hold-ups and robberies drop almost to zero. Robbers and thugs quail before the iron hand of the proletariat.

It is not merely negative restraint—order rising out of fear. The Revolution begets a singular respect for the rights of property. In the shattered windows of the shops, within hands' reach of passing men in desperate need, are foodstuffs and clothing. They remain untouched. There is something pathetic in the sight of hungry men having food within their grasp and not grasping it, something awesome in the constraint engendered by the Revolution. It exerts its subtle influence everywhere. Into the far-off villages it reaches. No longer are the peasants burning the great estates.

Yet it is the upper classes who assert that in them lies true respect of the sanctity of property. A curious claim at the end of the World War for which the governing classes are responsible. By their fiat, cities were given to the torch, the face of the land covered with ashes, the bottom of the sea strewn with ships, the structure of civilization shot to pieces, and even now still more terrible instruments of destruction are being prepared.

What basis is there for true respect of property in the bourgeoisie? Actually they produce little or nothing. To the privileged, property is something that comes by cleverness, by chance inheritance, by stroke of fortune. With them it is largely a matter of titles, deeds and papers.

But to the working classes, property is a thing of tears and blood. It is an exhausting act of creation. They know its cost in aching muscles and breaking backs.

> "With shoulders back and breast astrain,
> And bathed in sweat that falls like rain,
> Thru midday heat with gasping song,
> He drags the heavy barge along."

goes the song of the Volga boatmen.

What men have brought forth in pain and labor they cannot wantonly annihilate, any more than a mother can destroy her child. They, out of whose thews and muscles the thing has issued, will best guard and cherish it. Knowing its cost, they feel its sacredness. Even before works of art the rude, untaught masses stand with reverence. Only vaguely do they glimpse their meaning. But they see in them the incarnation of effort. And all labor is holy.

The Social Revolution is in truth the apotheosis of the rights of property. It invests it with a new sanctity. By transferring property into the hands of the producers it gives the keeping of wealth into the hands of its natural and zealous guardians—the makers of it. The creators are the best conservators.

CHAPTER IX

RED GUARDS, WHITE GUARDS AND BLACKGUARDS

THE Soviets declared themselves the government on November 7. But it was one thing to take power; another thing to keep it. It was one thing to write out decrees; another to back them with bayonets.

The Soviets soon found a big fight on their hands. They found, too, a crippled military-apparatus to fight with. It was all out of gear, sabotaged by officers. The Revolutionary General Staff could not straighten out the tangle from above. It appealed directly to the workers.

They uncovered stores of benzine and motors, whipping the transport into shape. They assembled guns, gun-carriages, and horses, to form artillery-units. They requisitioned provisions, forage, and Red Cross supplies, rushing them to the front. They seized 10,000 rifles being shipped to Kaledin and distributed them among the factories.

The stamp of hammers in the factories gives way to the tramp of marching feet. The foreman's orders give way to the commands of sailors drilling awkward squads. Thru the streets hurry the motor cars spreading this call to arms:

РАЙОННЫМЪ
Совѣтамъ Рабочихъ Депутатовъ
Фабрично-Заводскимъ Комитетамъ

ПРИКАЗЪ.

Корниловскія банды Керенскаго угро-
жаютъ подступамъ къ столицѣ. Отданы
всѣ необходимыя распоряженія для того,
чтобы безпощадно раздавить контръ-ре-
волюціонное покушеніе противъ народа
и его завоеваній.

Армія и Красная Гвардія революціи нуждаются въ не-
медленной поддержкѣ рабочихъ.

Приказываемъ районнымъ Совѣтамъ и фабр.-зав. Комитетамъ:

1) выдвинуть наибольшее количество рабочихъ для рытья окоповъ,
воздвиганія баррикадъ и укрѣпленія проволочныхъ загражденій;

2) гдѣ для этого потребуется прекращеніе работъ на
фабрикахъ и заводахъ, немедленно исполнить;

3) собрать всю имѣющуюся въ запасѣ колючую и простую про-
волоку, а равно всѣ орудія, необходимыя для рытья окоповъ и возведенія баррикадъ;

4) все имѣющееся оружіе имѣть при себѣ;

5) соблюдать строжайшую дисциплину и быть готовыми поддержать
армію революціи всѣми средствами.

Предсѣдатель Петроградскаго Совѣта Раб. и Солд. Депутатовъ
Народный Комиссаръ ЛЕВЪ ТРОЦКІЙ.

Предсѣдатель Военно-Революціоннаго Комитета
Главнокомандующій ПОДВОЙСКІЙ.

TO THE DISTRICT
SOVIETS OF WORKER'S DEPUTIES AND SHOP-FACTORY COMMITTEES

ORDER

THE KORNILOV BANDS OF KERENSKY ARE THREATENING THE OUTSKIRTS OF OUR CAPITAL. ALL NECESSARY ORDERS HAVE BEEN GIVEN TO CRUSH MERCILESSLY EVERY COUNTER-REVOLUTIONARY ATTEMPT AGAINST THE PEOPLE AND ITS CONQUESTS.

THE ARMY AND THE RED GUARD OF THE REVOLUTION ARE IN NEED OF IMMEDIATE SUPPORT OF THE WORKERS.

THE DISTRICT SOVIETS AND SHOP-FACTORY COMMITTEES ARE ORDERED:

1) To bring forward the largest possible number of workers to dig trenches, erect barricades and set up wire defenses;

2) Wherever necessary for this purpose to **SUSPEND WORK** in shops and factories, it must be done **IMMEDIATELY.**

3) To collect all available plain and barbed wire, as well as all tools **FOR DIGGING TRENCHES AND ERECTING BARRICADES;**

4) **ALL AVAILABLE ARMS TO BE CARRIED ON PERSONS;**

5) Strictest discipline must be preserved and all must be ready to support the Army of the Revolution to the utmost.

President of the Petrograd Soviet of Workers & Soldiers Deputies
People's Commissar LEV TROTSKY.

President of the Military-Revolutionary Committee
Chief Commander PODVOISKY.

[Reproduction in English of the Russian text on opposite page.]

121

In answer, everywhere appear workmen with cart-ridge belts outside of overcoats, blankets strapped on their backs, spades, tea-kettles and revolvers tied on with strings. Long, irregular lines of slant-ing bayonets winding thru the dark.

Red Petrograd rises in arms to repel the Counter-Revolutionary forces marching up out of the south. Over the roofs, now hoarse, now shrill, comes the sound of factory-whistles blowing the tocsin to war.

On all roads leading out of the city pours a torrent of men, women and boys, carrying kit-bags, picks, rifles and bombs. A drab and motley throng. No banners, no drums to cheer them on. Plunging trucks splash them with mud, freezing slush oozes thru their shoes, winds from the Baltic chill to the bone. But they push on to the front, unresting, as the grey day turns to sullen night. Behind them the city flings its lights into the sky, and still they press forward into the dark. Fields and forests are swarming now with dim shapes, pitching tents, build-ing camp-fires, cutting trenches, stretching wire. One brief day, and tens of thousands have moved out twenty miles from Petrograd, and stand, a bulwark of living flesh against the forces of the Counter-Revolution.

To military experts it is a rag-tag army, a rabble. But in this "rabble" there is a drive and power not reckoned with in the books of strategy. These dark masses are exalted with visions of a new world. Their veins burn with a crusading fire. They fight with reckless abandon, often with skill. They plunge forward into the black copse against hidden foes. They stand up to the charging Cossacks and tear them from their horses. They lie flat before the machine gun fire. Bursting shells send them fleeing but they rally again. They carry back the stricken, binding their wounds. Into the ears of their dying comrades they whisper, *"The Revolution! The People!"* They die, gasping out *"Long live the Soviet! Peace is coming!"*

Disorder, confusion, panic, of course, in these raw levies of the shops and slums. But the ardor of these hungry, work-scarred men and women, fighting for their faith, is more effective than the organized battalions of their foes. It destroys these battalions. It shatters their morale. Hardened Cossacks come, see and are conquered by it. "Loyal" divisions, ordered to the front, flatly refuse to shoot down these workmen-soldiers. The whole opposition crumples up or melts away. Kerensky flees from the front in disguise. The commander of the grand armies that were to crush the Bolsheviks cannot find a corporal's guard to fly with him. The proletarians are victors all along the line.

The Whites take the Telephone Station. While the Soviet masses are battling on the plains outside Petrograd, the Counter-Revolution rises suddenly in the rear. It sets out to paralyze the Soviet power at its base in the city.

The Yunkers, who were paroled after their capture at the Winter Palace, break their parole to join this White Guard uprising. They are detailed to seize the telephone station.

The telephone station is one of the vital centers of the city; from it run a million wires, which like a million nerves, help make the city a unit. In Petrograd the telephone station is housed in a massive stone citadel on the Morskaya. Here some Soviet sentries are posted. Thru the tedium of the day they have one thing to look forward to—the change of sentries at night.

Night comes and with it twenty men marching down the street. The sentries think it is the relief-squad bringing them liberty. But it is not. It is a squad of officers and Yunkers disguised as Reds. Their guns are slung slant-wise in orthodox Red Guard fashion. They give the Red Guard pass-word to the sentries. In good faith the sentries stack guns and turn to go. In a flash twenty revolvers are pointed at their heads.

"*Tovarishe!*" (Comrades!) exclaim the astounded Reds.

"You damned swine!" shout the officers. "Get into that hall there, and keep your mouths shut or we will blow your heads open."

The doors slam behind the bewildered sentries, who find, not release and freedom, but imprisonment at the hands of the Whites. The telephone station is in the hands of the Counter-Revolution.

In the morning the new masters finished fortifying the place under the supervision of a French officer. Suddenly the officer turned on me with a stern, "What are you doing here?"

"Correspondent—American," I replied. "Dropped in to see what was up."

"Your passport," he demanded. I produced it. He was impressed and apologized. "Of course, this is none of my business. Like you, I just glanced in to see what was happening." But he went on directing the work.

On both sides of the archway the Yunkers ran out barricades of boxes, automobiles and piles of logs. They levied toll on passing autos, bringing in supplies and weapons, and corralled all passers-by who might possibly serve as soldiers of the Soviet.

A great prize came their way in the person of Antonov, the Soviet Commissar of War. Driving by in his auto, he was suddenly yanked from the seat; and before he could recover from the shock, he was behind barred doors. With the fate of the Revolution hanging in the balance, he found himself a prisoner of the Counter-Revolutionists. His anguish at being jailed was only exceeded by their joy at jailing him. They were jubilant. For among the unorganized masses of revolutionary Petrograd, leaders were as yet desperately few. They knew— according to all the laws of military science—that the masses, leaderless, could not move effectively against their citadel; and the master military brain of the Reds was now in their hands.

The Revolution Rallies its Forces. Some things these officers did **not** know. They did not know that the Revolution was not dependent upon any single brain, or set of brains, but upon the collective brains of the Russian masses. They did not know how deeply the Revolution had roused the brain, the initiative, and the resources of these masses, and wrought them into a living unit. They did not know that the Revolution was a living organism, self-sustaining, self-directing, rallying at the danger-call all its latent powers for self-preservation.

When an evil germ enters the blood of the human organism the whole body senses the danger, as if an alarm had been sent out. Along a hundred arteries the special corpuscles or phagocytes come hurrying to attack the poison-centre. Fastening on the intruder, they attempt to expel it. This is not the conscious act of the brain. It is the unconscious intelligence inherent in the human organism.

Now into the body of Red Petrograd, threatening its very life, enters the malignant poison of the Counter-Revolution. The reaction is immediate. Spontaneously along a hundred streets and arteries, the corpuscles (in this case red ones) come hurrying to the contagion centre—the telephone station.

Ping! Crash! A bullet splintering a log announces the arrival of the first Red corpuscle carrying a gun. Ping! Ping! Crash! Crash! A gust of lead, biting stone-chips from the wall, heralds the advent of more attacking units.

Peering thru the barricades, the Counter-Revolutionists already see swarms of Red Guards at the ends of the street. The sight of them arouses an old Czarist officer to savagery. "Turn on the guns!" he shouts. "Kill the rabble!" Up and down the streets they let loose a storm of rifle and machine-gun fire. Like a canyon the street is filled with noise and ricochetting bullets. But there are no Red corpses. The revolutionary masses have no appetite for martyrdom. Provokingly they refuse to be killed.

It is different from former days. Then the mobs obligingly put themselves in the way of the guns. In hundreds they were spattered over the Winter Palace Square, blown to pieces by the artillery, trampled under the hoofs of the Cossacks, massacred by machine guns. It was so easy! How easy now, too, to annihilate them, if they would but rush the barricades.

But the Revolution is careful of its material. It has made these masses cautious. It has taught them the first lesson in strategy: find out what your enemy wants you to do, and then don't do it. The barricades, the Reds see, are intended to destroy them; they intend to destroy the barricades.

They inspect them and decide the tactics of assault. They pick out every vantage-point. They hide behind stone pillars. They scale walls. They crawl along the copings. They lie flat upon the roofs. They ambuscade themselves in windows and chimney-pots. From every angle they train their guns upon the barricades. Then suddenly they open fire, raking the barricades with hails of lead. As precipitately as they began, they stop, and steal up into new positions. Another outburst and another silence. The officers begin to feel like trapped animals, around whom invisible hunters are drawing a circle of fire.

New units are constantly arriving, filling the gaps in the circle. The ring draws tighter and tighter and seals up the Counter-Revolution in the centre. Then, having isolated its plague-spot the Revolution prepares to eradicate it.

A gale of bullets forces the Whites to abandon the barricade and find refuge under the archway. Behind stone ramparts, now, they pause for counsel. The first plan is to make a sortie, break thru the Red cordon and escape. But this they see is suicide. A scout crawls out on the roof and is driven back, a ball thru his shoulder. They play for time, begging a peace parley, but the besiegers reply:

"Three days ago we captured you in the Winter Palace; we paroled you then. You broke your parole. You shot down our comrades. We do not trust you."

They sue for amnesty, offering to give up Antonov.

"Antonov! We'll take him ourselves," the Reds reply. "Harm him and we'll kill you—every one of you."

Red Guards Tricked by the Red Cross Car. Desperate situations induce desperate ventures.

"Oh, for a Red Cross car," sighed an officer. "The Reds might let that thru their lines."

"Well, if we haven't the car, we've got the crosses," said another officer, producing four big Red Cross labels. He pasted them on front, sides and back of an auto. At once it looked like a Red Cross car.

Two officers took the front seat. One at the wheel, the other with his hand on the auto pocket and a revolver in his hand. A haggard man, half crazed with fear, the father of one of the Yunkers climbed into the rear.

"Jump in and come along," said the officers to me. The Whites always took it for granted that anyone in bourgeois dress was on the bourgeois side. Even many who knew of the revolutionary activity of men like John Reed, for example, and myself, assumed it was only a ruse to get the confidence of the Bolsheviks.

I climbed into the car and the hood was pushed thru the archway. At sight of the Red Cross the firing of the Red Guard ceased. Slowly and anxiously we drove up to the Red lines. The soldiers, sailors and workmen received us, guns in hand.

"Well, what do you want?" they glowered.

"Many of our men are badly wounded. No bandages, no medicines," the officer at the wheel explained. "We want to go to Red Cross quarters and get supplies. Our men are suffering terribly."

"Let 'em suffer," growled one of the sailors with an oath. "Haven't they made our men suffer? And we had just paroled them—the damned liars."

To this, one of the other sailors cried, "No, *tovarish.*" To us in the car they said, "All right. Pass thru. Hurry."

We swept on up the street, while behind us the fusillade against the telephone station began again.

"Not bad fellows after all, those Red Guards," I interjected.

"Fools! (*Doorake*). What you call in English 'damn fools', eh?" They laughed hysterically again.

We ran down the French Quay at terrific speed, making a wide detour in order to throw possible pursuers off our track. A sharp turn brought us up before the Engineers' Castle. The big gates opened to let us in and a minute later we were in a salon filled with officers—Russian, French and British. The staff heard the report on the crisis at the telephone station and ordered the immediate dispatch of an armored car and reinforcements. There were a few other details, some words with a Czarist general, and we turned to go.

"Wait a minute," interrupted the general, "let me give you something useful to take back with you." He sat down at a table and laid out some papers, in size and shape like credentials of the Soviet. Picking up a stamp he brought it down sharply on the first credential. There were the magic words *"War Revolutionary Committee"* in form and letter just like the seal of the Soviet. If that was not a stolen Soviet stamp it was an exact replica. No one could detect the imitation. In Russia this sort of forgery is a fine art.

"Trotzky himself couldn't give you a better credential than that," the general remarked, handing it over. "In uncertain times like these, one always carries the proper kind of papers," he continued facetiously, imprinting the Soviet seal on two more credentials. "There you are! Ready for any emergency. Fill it out with bad writing and misspelled words and you have a first-class Bolshevik pass for any place you want to go. And by the way," he added, passing over some black iron globes about the size of baseballs, "a few of these will come in handy."

"Hand grenades?" I queried.

"No," the general answered. "They are pills. Capsules. Medicine for Reds. Give a Red Guard one of these in the right place and it's a sure cure for Bolshevism, Revolution, Socialism and everything else that ails him. What, eh?" he cried, tremendously pleased with his wit. "A Red Cross car full of pills!"

Again our car was headed back to the telephone

station. But in the last half hour the streets had changed. Red sentries were posted on nearly every corner. They were largely peasants whom fate had torn from the country quiet and thrown down into this city, all agog with Revolutionists and Counter-Revolutionists and no mark to tell the two apart.

They were puzzled as we bore down on them waving our papers, pointing to the Red Cross sign on our car and yelling out, "Aid to the wounded *tovarishe*." While they were trying to collect their wits we went sweeping past. One after another was rushed off his feet, until we came to a big peasant standing guard in the center of the Millionaya. With rifle raised he barred the way and brought us up with a sudden halt.

"Idiot!" shouted the officers. "Don't you see that this is a Red Cross car? Don't waste time while the *tovarishe* are dying."

"Are you *tovarishe* too?" asked the peasant, eyeing the officers' uniforms suspiciously.

"Of course we are. Too long have the bourgeoisie drunk the people's blood! Down with the traitor Counter-Revolutionists," said the officers, mouthing shibboleths of the Revolution.

"And do I live to see the day when officers come over to the help of the dark people?" said the old peasant half to himself. It was too much. He couldn't quite believe it and asked for our papers.

With his finger tracing the lines he painfully spelled out each word. As the peasant read the officer's paper the officer, hand on pistol, read the peasant's face. That peasant never knew how close he stood to death. If he had said "No. You cannot pass," the officer would have blown out his brains. His permit to let us go was his own permit to live. He didn't know the seal on our paper was forged. He only saw it was like his own, so he said, "Yes!" and we were off again.

Once more we came to the Red cordon around the telephone station. It was a nervous moment for the officers. Under pretence of bringing life and succor to wounded Whites they were bringing death and wounds to the Reds. These Reds did not know that. Tho they had had a taste of the treachery of the Counter-Revolution, they did not suspect that it would flout all moral laws and violate its own codes. So when these officers begged quick passage for their car in the name of humanity, the Red Guards answered, "All right, Red Cross. Hurry thru."

The lines opened and a minute later our car with its load of hand-grenades slipped under the archway of the station, hailed by shouts of joy from the imprisoned Whites. They were glad for the hand-grenades and for the latest military information. But they were gladdest of all to learn of the armored car coming to their relief.

CHAPTER X

MERCY OR DEATH TO THE WHITES?

IT was a black outlook for the White Guards hemmed inside the telephone station. But now comes this jubilant news that an armored car is hurrying to their rescue. They gaze intently down the street for the first glimpse of it.

As it comes swinging in from the Nevsky, they hail it with cheers. Like a great iron steed it lumbers along and stops before the barricades. Cheers again from the Whites. Ill-starred cheers! They do not know that they are cheering their end. They do not know that this is not their car; it has passed into the hands of the Reds. It is a Trojan horse, within whose armored belly are concealed the soldiers of the Revolution. It slews about until its muzzle is pointed thru the archway. Then suddenly it spouts a stream of lead as a garden hose spouts water. Screams now instead of cheers! Tumbling over boxes and one another, the officers, in one shrieking, tangled mass, go crashing thru the hallway and up the stairs.

Poetic justice! Here where a few hours earlier these Counter-Revolutionists pressed their revolvers

Bolsheviks with one of the armored cars that quelled the White uprising. The cars were christened *Proletariat, International, The Red Commune, Lenin*, etc.

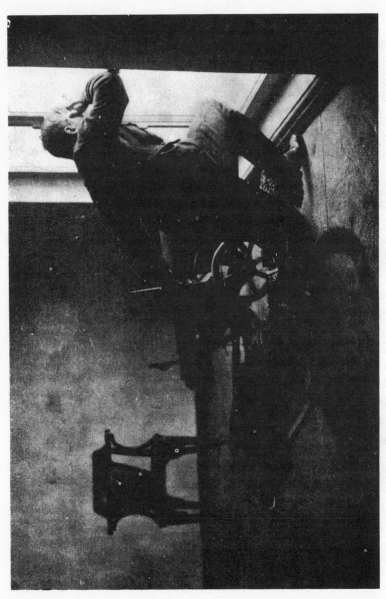

Fighting from doors and windows in the War of the Reds and Whites. Despite the *rat-tat-tat* of the machine-guns, the theatres and market-places were crowded.

against the temples of the Revolution, the Revolution presses its machine guns against their temples.

The White Guards in a Funk. At the top of the stairway the Whites disentangle themselves, not to make a stand, but to run better.

Ten resolute men could have held this stairway against a thousand. But there are not ten men to do it. There is not one. There is only a panic-stricken pack, in the clutch of a fear that drains the blood from their faces, the reason from their brains. All courage gone. All prudence gone. Gone even the herd-instinct of unity in the face of common peril.

"Sauve qui peut," (let him save himself who can) becomes the cry of the older officers.

They fling away caps, belts and swords; insignia of honor now become badges of shame and death. They rip off shoulder straps, gold-braid and buttons. They plead for a workman's costume, a cloak, an overcoat—anything to disguise their rank. An officer coming upon a greasy blouse hanging on a peg becomes a maniac with joy. A captain finding the apron of a cook puts it on, plunges his arms in flour and already white from terror becomes the whitest White Guard in all Russia.

But for most of them there is no cover save the darkness of closets, booths and attic corners. Into these they crawl like hunted animals in collapse. To treachery against their enemies these officers now add treason to their allies. They had led the Yunkers into this trap. Now the trap is closing, and the officers abandon them.

First to rally their wits, the Yunkers begin to cry out, "Our officers! Where are our officers?" No answer to their cries. "Damn the cowards!" they shout. "They have deserted us."

Rage at this betrayal fuses the Yunkers together. Their best tactics would be to hold the stairway, but they shrink away from it. Red vengeance crouching at the foot fills them with dread. It will not let them move forward. They fall back into a thick walled room with a narrow entrance. There, like rats clustering in a hole, they wait the onrush of the Red tide that may come rising up the stairway, flooding the corridors, drowning them out.

To some of these young fellows, sprung from the middle-class, this is a doubly tragic ending. Death at the hands of peasants and workers with whom they have no quarrel! But, caught in this camp of the Counter-Revolution, they must share its doom. They know how richly they deserve it. This sense of guilt unnerves them. Their guns fall from their hands. They slink down on chairs and tables, moaning, their eyes fixed on the entrance thru which the Red tide is to come crashing in. They listen for the swirl of the first wave flinging itself on the stairway; hammering on the door.

Save their own hammering pulses there is not a sound.

Reds, Whites and Girls Petrified by Fear. There is another chamber of torture in this building. It holds Antonov, the Red sentries, and all captives bagged by the Whites during the day. They sit helpless, locked in their prison, while outside rages the battle sealing the fate of their Revolution, and their own fate. No one comes to tell them how the battle goes. Only thru the thick walls comes the muffled crackle of rifles, the crash of falling glass.

Now all these noises abruptly cease. What does it mean? The triumph of the Counter-Revolution? The Whites victorious? What next? The opening of the door? The firing-squad lining them up before a wall? Bandages tied round their eyes? The report of rifles? Their own death? The death of the Revolution? So they muse, heads sunk in hands, while the clock above the door pitilessly tells off the seconds. Each stroke may be the last. Awaiting that last, they sit straining to hear the tread of the firing-squad, coming down the corridor. But save for the ticking clock, not a sound.

Still another torture chamber, this one filled with women. It is the top floor, with hundreds of telephone girls huddled around the switch-boards. The eight-hour bombardment, the stampede of the officers, their frenzied cries for help, have shattered the nerves of these girls and their minds run wild. They run to wild stories of Bolshevik atrocities, the rape of the Women's Battalion, crimes imputed to these Red hordes swarming into the court-yard below.

In their fevered imagination they are already victims of a like brutality, writhing in the arms of these monsters. They break into tears. They write frantic little last farewells. They cling together in white-faced groups, listening for the first yells of the ruffians, the thumping of their boots along the hall. But there are no thumping boots—only their own thumping hearts.

The building becomes quiet as a tomb. It is not the quiet of the dead, but tense and vibrant, the silence of hundreds of living beings paralyzed with terror. The silence is contagious. It passes thru the walls and lays hold of the Red throngs outside. They in turn become still, stricken by the same paralysis of fear. They shrink away from the stairway lest it belch out clouds of gas, a fusillade of bombs. Hundreds outside in terror of the Whites within! Hundreds inside in terror of the Reds without! Thousands of human beings torturing each other.

Inside the building this ordeal by silence becomes unendurable. I, at least, can endure it no longer. For relief I run forward, not knowing where; anywhere to get away from the silence. Opening a side-door by accident I catapult into the chamber filled with Yunkers. They jump as tho it is the crack of doom.

"American correspondent," they gasp. "O! Help us! Help us!"

"How can I?" I falter. "What shall I do?"

"Something—anything!" they implore. "Only save us."

Some one says, "Antonov." The others catch up the name, repeating it like an incantation. "Antonov. Yes, Antonov. Go to Antonov. Downstairs—Antonov. Quick, before it is too late—Antonov!" They point the way.

In a minute I make another headlong entrance before another astounded audience—the captive Reds and Antonov.

"You are all free. The officers have fled. The Yunkers surrender. They beg you to save them. Any terms. All they ask is their lives. Only hurry, hurry."

In a moment this prisoner Antonov awaiting death becomes the arbiter of death. The condemned is asked to be the judge. A startling change! But the face of this little, tired overworked Revolutionist did not change. If the thought of revenge flashed into his mind, it as quickly flashed out again. "So I am not to be a corpse but a commander," he said wanly. "Next thing is to see the Yunkers is it? Very well." He put on his hat and walked upstairs to the Yunkers.

"Antonov! *Gospadeen* Antonov! Commander

Antonov!" they wailed. "Spare our lives. We know we are guilty. But we throw ourselves on the mercy of the Revolution."

Sorry ending to a gay adventure! In the morning sallying out to kill Bolsheviks and in the evening begging Bolsheviks for their own lives. Saying *"Tovarish"* as one might say "swine," then breathing it reverently as a term of honor.

"Tovarish Antonov," they implored, "give us your word as a Bolshevik, a true Bolshevik. Give us your word for our safety."

"My word," said Antonov. "I give it."

"They may not take your word, *Tovarish* Antonov," muttered one poor wretch. "They may kill us anyhow."

"If they kill you," assured Antonov, "they must first kill me."

"But we don't want to be killed," whimpered the poor fellow.

The Mob Decrees Death to the White Guards. Antonov could not conceal his contempt. Turning into the hall, he started down the stairs. To the taut nerves every step sounded like the detonation of a gun.

The Red throng outside heard the steps and raised their rifles expecting a fusillade. And then this surprise! Antonov, their own leader!

"Nash! Nash!" (Ours! Ours!) acclaimed a hundred voices. "Antonov! Long live Antonov!" rose

from another hundred throats. The shout raised in the courtyard was caught up in the street and the crowd surged forward crying, "The officers, Antonov? Where are the officers and the *Yunkers?*"

"Done for," announced Antonov. "Their arms are down."

Like the bursting of a dam came the roar from a thousand throats. Yells of triumph and howls of rage proclaiming "Death to the officers! Death to the Yunkers!"

Good reason for the Whites to tremble! At the mercy of those to whom they had forfeited all claims for mercy. Not by fighting, but by fighting foully they had roused this volcano of wrath. In the eyes of these soldiers and workmen the Whites were murderers of the Red comrades, assassinators of the Revolution, miscreants to be exterminated like vermin. Fear only had kept the Reds from plunging up the stairway. Now all cause for caution was gone. The infuriated men stormed forward filling the night with their cries, "Wipe out the butchers! Kill the White Devils! Kill every one of them!"

A torch here and there in the blackness lit up the bearded faces of peasants, soldier-faces, the faces of city artisans grimed and thin, and in the front rank the open, alert countenances of the big sailors from the Baltic fleet. On all of them, in flashing eyes, and clenched jaws vengeance was written, the terrible vengeance of the long-suffering. Pressed from the rear, the mass lunged forward against the stairway where Antonov stood, calm and impassive, but looking so frail and helpless before this avalanche of men.

Raising his hand and voice, Antonov cried out, "*Tovarishe,* you cannot kill them. The Yunkers have surrendered. They are our prisoners."

The throng was stunned. Then in a hoarse cry of resentment it found its voice. "No! No! They are not our prisoners," it protested. "They are dead men."

"They have given up their arms," continued Antonov. "I have given them their lives."

"You may give them their lives. We don't. We give them the bayonet!" bawled a big peasant turning to the crowd for approval.

"The bayonet! Yes, we give them the bayonet!" they howled in a blast of approbation.

Antonov faced the tornado. Drawing a big revolver, he waved it aloft, crying out, "I have given the Yunkers my word for their safety. You understand! I will back my word with this."

The crowd gasped. This was incredible.

"What's this? What do you mean?" they demanded.

Clutching his revolver, finger on the trigger, Antonov repeated his warning: "I promised them their lives. I will back that promise with this."

"Traitor! Renegade!" a hundred voices thundered at him. "Defender of the White Guards!" a big sailor flung in his face. "You want to save the rascals. But you can't. We'll kill them."

"The first man who lays his hands on a prisoner—*I will kill him on the spot!*" Antonov spoke slowly, with emphasis on each word. *"You understand! I will shoot him dead!"*

"Shoot us?" queried the affronted sailors.

"Shoot us! Shoot us!" bellowed the whole indignant mob.

For it was just that—a mob, with all the vehement passions of the mob. A mob with every primitive instinct inflamed and ascendant: cruel, brutal, lusting for blood. In it flamed the savagery of the wolf, the ferocity of the tiger. A huge beast drawn out of the jungles of the city, stirred up by these White hunters, wounded, and bleeding from its wounds, all day exasperated and tormented, at last, in a paroxysm of joy and rage it was about to pounce upon its tormentors and tear them to pieces. At this moment this little man stepped between it and its prey! To me the most emotional thing in the whole revolution is this little man standing in that stairway, so unemotionally looking that mob in the eye; rather, in its thousand glaring eyes. There was pallor in his face, but no tremor in his limbs. And no quaver in his voice, as he said again slowly and solemnly, "The first man who tries to kill a Yunker, I will kill him."

The sheer audacity, the impudence of it took their breath away.

"What do you mean?" they yelled. "To save these officers, Counter-Revolutionists, you kill us workmen—Revolutionists?"

"Revolutionists!" retorted Antonov, derisively. "Revolutionists! Where do I see Revolutionists here? You dare call yourselves Revolutionists? *You,* who think of killing helpless men and prisoners!" His taunt went home. The crowd winced as tho struck by a whip.

"Listen!" he went on. "Do you know what you are doing? Do you realize where this madness leads? When you kill a captive White Guard you are not killing the Counter-Revolution, you are killing the Revolution. For this Revolution I gave twenty years of my life in exile and in prison. Do you think that I, a Revolutionist, will stand by and watch Revolutionists crucify the Revolution?"

"But if they had *us* there would be no quarter," bellowed a peasant, "they would kill us."

"True, they would kill us," answered Antonov. "What of that? They are not Revolutionists. They belong to the old order, to the Czar and the knout, to murder and death. But *we* belong to the Revolution. And the Revolution means something better. It means liberty and life for all. That's why you give it your life and blood. But you must give it more. You must give it your reason. Above the satisfaction of your passions you must put service to the Revolution. For the triumph of the Revolu-

tion you have been brave. Now, for the honor of
the Revolution be merciful. You love the Revolution. I only ask you not to kill the thing you love."

He was aflame, his face incandescent, his arms
and voice imploring. His whole being, focussing
itself in that last appeal, left him exhausted.

"Speak to them, comrade!" he entreated.

Four weeks earlier I had spoken to these sailors
from the turret of their battleship *The Republic*.
As I stepped to the front they recognized me.

"The American *tovarish*," they shouted.

Loudly and fervently I spoke about the Revolution, about the battle waged thruout Russia for
land and freedom, about their own betrayal by the
White Guards and the justice in their wrath. But
the eyes of the world turned to them as the fighting
vanguard of the Social Revolution. Would they take
the old bloody path of retaliation or blaze the way to
a nobler code? They had shown themselves daring
for the preservation of the Revolution. Would they
show themselves magnanimous for its glory?

It was an effective speech at the outset. But not
because of its content. The recitation of the Lord's
Prayer or Webster's Oration would have been almost
as effective. Not one in a hundred understood what
I was saying. For I spoke in English.

But these words—strange and foreign—crackling
out in the dark held them and made them pause—
precisely what Antonov was working for—that this

hurricane of passion might subside a little, to gain time for another impulse to get the upper hand.

The Mob Disciplined by the Revolution. For while this was a mob, it was a revolutionary mob. Deep-rooted in the hearts of at least half this workman-soldier crowd was one powerful abiding loyalty—the Revolution. The word was a fetich. Their dreams and hopes and longings were all woven around "The Revolution." They were its servants. It was their master.

True, at this moment another master held them, displacing every idea of the Revolution. Revenge was in the saddle, recklessly lashing the mob along. But this was temporary. The permanent allegiance of their lives was to the Revolution. Given the chance it would rise up, expel the usurper, assert its authority, and again control its followers. Antonov did not stand alone against a multitude. In that mob, there were a thousand Antonovs, sharing with him the same high zeal for the Revolution. Antonov was just one unit of that mob, flesh of its flesh, spirit of its spirit, sharing its antagonism to the Yunkers and officers, aflame with its same hot passions.

Antonov happened to be first of this mob to rein in his passions, the first in whose consciousness the Revolution replaced revenge. The change made in his heart by concept of the Revolution would like-wise be wrought in the hearts of the soldiers and workers. This Antonov knew. By repeating the magic word "Revolution" he sought to bring them to their revolutionary selves; he sought to evoke revolutionary order out of chaos. And he did.

Before our eyes we saw again the ancient miracle of the Word—the stilling of the tempest. The howling and the raging died away, save for here and there an angry voice still persisting. But as Woskov interpreted my words, and Antonov spoke again, these centres of dissent subsided. Chastened and in a receptive mood, these soldiers and sailors were substituting for their own will to revenge the will of the Revolution. Only let them understand that will.

"What is it, Antonov?" they cried. "What do you want us to do?"

"To treat the Yunkers as prisoners of war," said Antonov. "To carry out the terms of surrender. I have pledged these Yunkers their lives. I ask you to back my pledge with yours."

The mob became a Soviet. A sailor spoke; then two soldiers and a workingman. The vote was taken by show of hands. A hundred battle-stained hands went up, and another hundred until nearly a thousand hands were lifted. A thousand clenched fists threatening death to the officers now raised in an open handed promise of life.

At this juncture arrived a delegation from the Petrograd Duma commissioned "to liquidate the civil strife with the shedding of as little blood as possible." But the Revolution was liquidating its own affairs without the shedding of any blood at all. It ignored these gentlemen, and detailed a squad to enter the building and bring the White Guards down. First came the Yunkers, and then the officers, ferreted out of their hiding places, one of them dragged out by his heels. Hustled out upon the elevated stone steps, they stood blinking in the torch-light, facing the muzzles of a thousand guns, the scorn of a thousand hearts, the grilling of a thousand pairs of eyes.

There were a few jeers, cries of *"Assassins of the Revolution!"* and then silence—the solemn silence of a court. For this was a court—the tribunal of the disinherited. The oppressed sitting in judgment on their oppressors. The new order passing sentence upon the old. The grand assizes of the Revolution.

"Guilty! All guilty!" was the verdict. Guilty as enemies of the Revolution. Guilty as retainers of the Czar and the exploiting classes. Guilty as violators of the Red Cross and the laws of war. Guilty on all counts as traitors to the workers of Russia, and to the workers of the world.

The wretched prisoners in the dock shrank before the blast and bowed their heads. Some of them would have found it easier to stand up to a volley from the guns. But the guns were there to guard them.

Five sailors shouldering rifles took their stand at the foot of the steps. Antonov seized the hand of an officer and placed it in the hand of a sailor.

"Number one," he said. "A helpless, disarmed prisoner. His life is in your hands. Guard it for the honor of the Revolution." The squad encircled the prisoner and marched thru the archway.

With a like formula the next prisoner was handed over, and the next, and the next; each one entrusted to a detachment of four or five. "The end of the rubbish," muttered an old peasant as the last officer was delivered to his escort, and the procession filed out into the Morskaya.

Near the Winter Palace infuriated mobs fell upon the Yunkers and tore them from the hands of their convoys. But the revolutionary sailors, charging the mobs, rescued the prisoners and brought them safely to the prison Fortress of Peter and Paul.

The Revolution was not everywhere powerful enough to check the savage passions of the mobs. Not always was it on time to allay the primitive blood-lusts. Unoffending citizens were assaulted by hooligans. In out-of-the-way places half-savages, calling themselves Red Guards, committed heinous crimes. At the front General Dukhonin was dragged from his carriage and torn to pieces despite the protesting commissars. Even in Petrograd some Yunkers were clubbed to death by the storming crowds; others were pitched headlong into the Neva.

The Workers' Respect for Life. The attitude of the revolutionary working-classes toward human life, however, is not reflected in these mad, sporadic deeds of the hot-blooded and the irresponsible, but in one of the first laws the Soviet made as it entered into power.

As the ruling-class the workers were now in a position to take vengeance on their former exploiters and executioners. When I saw them rise up and take the government in their own hands, and at the same time take in their grasp those who had lashed them, jailed them and betrayed them, I feared a savage outburst of revenge.

I knew that thousands of the workmen now in authority had been sent with clanking chains across the snows of Siberia. I had seen them pallid and tottering from long years in those coffins for the living—the stone sacks of Schlusselburg. I had seen the deep scars cut in their backs by the Cossacks' *nagaika* and I recalled the words of Lincoln: "If for every drop of blood drawn by the lash another shall be drawn by the sword, the judgments of the Lord are pure and righteous altogether."

But there was no dreadful blood-bath. On the contrary, the idea of reprisals seemed to have no hold on the minds of the workers. On November

A course of instruction in history and economics for those seeking admission into the Communist (Bolshevik) Party. *(See next page.)*

After joining the Communist Party every member must take regular military exercises. Also all—

Communists are expected to do emergency work without pay—called "*Saturdayings.*"

30 the Soviet passed the decree declaring the Abolition of Capital Punishment. This was not merely a humanitarian gesture. The workers turned to their enemies not only to guarantee their lives but in many cases to grant them freedom.

Many sinister figures of the old régime had been incarcerated by Kerensky in the bastion of the Peter-Paul Fortress. There we met Biletzky, the chief of the Czar's Secret Service who in his day had railroaded countless victims into these dungeons. Now the old grizzled rat was getting a taste of his own medicine. Here also was the ex-War Minister Sukhomlinov, whose intrigue with the Germans had sent tens of thousands of Russian soldiers to death in the trenches. These two arch-villains received us with the most engaging manners, proclaiming their innocence and protesting against their "inhuman persecution."

"But the Bolsheviks are more human than Kerensky," they said. "They give us the newspapers."

We visited also the ministers of the fallen Provisional Government in their cells and found them taking their misfortunes with good grace. Tereschenko, handsome as ever, received us sitting cross-legged on his cot, smoking a cigarette.

"This is not the life *de luxe*," he said in faultless English. "But the commandant is not to blame. Suddenly he had to provide for hundreds of extra prisoners and no extra rations. So we are hungry.

But we get the same as the Red Guards; tho they scowl at us they share their bread with us."

The young Yunkers we found recounting their telephone-station adventures, opening packages from friends or stretched out on mattresses playing cards.

A few days later these Yunkers were released. A second time they were paroled and a second time they broke faith with their liberators—they went South and joined the White Guard armies mobilizing against the Bolsheviks.

With like acts of treachery thousands of Whites repaid the Bolsheviks for their clemency. Over his own signature General Krasnov solemnly promised not to raise his hand against the Bolsheviks, and was released. Promptly he appeared in the Urals at the head of a Cossack army destroying the Soviets. Burtsev was liberated from Peter-Paul prison by order of the Bolsheviks. Straightway he joined the Counter-Revolutionists in Paris and became editor of a scurrilous anti-Bolshevik sheet. Thousands, who thus went forth to freedom by mercy of the Bolsheviks, were to come back later with invading armies to kill their liberators without ruth or mercy.

Surveying battalions of comrades slaughtered by the very men whom the Bolsheviks had freed, Trotzky said: "The chief crime of which we were guilty in those first days of the Revolution was excessive kindliness."

Sardonic words! But the verdict of history will be that the Russian Revolution—vastly more fundamental than the great upheaval in France in 1789—was no saturnalia of revenge. It was to all intents a "bloodless revolution."

Take the most exaggerated estimates of the shootings in Petrograd, the three days' battle in Moscow, the street-fighting in Kiev and Irkutsk, and the peasants' outbreaks in the provinces. Add up the casualties and divide it into Russia's population—not the 3,000,000 involved in the American Revolution, nor the 23,000,000 of the French Revolution, but the 160,000,000 of the Russian Revolution. The figures will show that in the four months it took the Soviet to establish and consolidate its power—from the Atlantic to the Pacific, from the White Sea on the north to the Black Sea on the south—less than one in 3,000 Russians were killed.

Sanguinary enough to be sure!

But look at it in the perspective of history. Rightly or wrongly, when the fulfillment of the national destiny of America demanded that we cut out the cancer of slavery, vast property rights were confiscated, and in doing this we did not stop until we had killed one in every 300 people. Rightly or wrongly, the peasants and workers feel it essential to cut out of Russia the cancer of Czarism, landlordism, and capitalism. Such a deep-seated and malign disease called for a major surgical operation. Yet it was performed with comparatively little letting of blood. For, like children, the nature of a great folk is to forgive and forget—not to retaliate. And vindictiveness is alien to the spirit of working-people. In those early days they strove hard to conduct a civil war in a civil manner.

In a large measure they succeeded. The death-toll of both Whites and Reds together was not equal to the casualties in a single big battle of the World War.

"But the Red Terror!" someone interjects. That was to come later when the Allied armies were to come to Russia, and under their protecting wing the Czarists and Black Hundreds were to loose upon peasants and workers the White Terror of the Counter-Revolution—a hideous orgy of butchery and lust in which helpless women and children were to be massacred in droves.

Then in defense the workers, goaded to desperation, were to strike back with the Red Terror of the Revolution. Then capital punishment was to be restored and the White conspirators were to feel the swift chastising hand of the Revolution.

There are furious charges and counter charges about Red and White Terrors. Out of the controversy four facts emerge and may be stated here.

The Red Terror was a distinctly later phase of the Revolution. It was a defensive measure, a direct reply to the White Terror of the Counter-Revolution. Both in number and fiendishness the outrages of the Reds pale before the atrocities committed by the Whites.* Had not the Allies intervened in Russia and again stirred up civil war against the Soviets, in all probability there would have been no Red Terror and the Revolution would have continued as it began—practically a "bloodless revolution."

* Appendix II. "The Train of Death" from the *American Red Cross Magazine*.

CHAPTER XI

THE WAR OF THE CLASSES

U PSTARTS, adventurers, impostors!"
Thus the bourgeoisie stigmatized the Bolsheviks, or sneered with Shatsky, "How can such dogs, such *canaille* run a government!"

The idea that the Red régime would last longer than a few hours or a few days was a joke. Again and again we were told, "The hangings will begin tomorrow." But many tomorrows passed and no Bolsheviks dangled from the lamp-posts. The bourgeoisie became alarmed as the Soviet showed no sign of falling. "It is necessary to do battle and pull it down," read the appeal of the Council of the Republic. "It is the enemy of the people and the Revolution."

The City Duma became the center for all forces mobilizing against the Soviets. It was swarming with generals, priests, intelligentsia, *chinovniks*, speculators, Knights of Saint George, Boy Scouts, French and British officers, White Guards and Cadets. Out of these elements was organized the "Committee of Salvation"—the General Staff of the Counter-Revolution.

"All of Russia is represented here," boasted the old Mayor Schreider. And so it was. "All Russia" —all except her peasants and workers, her soldiers and sailors. Coming here from proletarian Smolny was like entering another world, the world of the well-fed and well-dressed. From here the ancient order of privilege and power struck against the new order set up by the working class. From here the bourgeoisie engineered its campaign against the Soviet, using every means to discredit, cripple and destroy it.

The Bourgeois Strike and Sabotage. By one stroke the bourgeoisie sought to bring the Soviet to its knees. It proclaimed a general strike in all departments of the new government. In some ministries the white-collared workers walked out in a body. In the Foreign Office 600 officials listened to Trotzky's appeal for translators of the Peace Decree, then resigned. A big strike-chest collected from the banks and business houses corrupted the minor officials and even part of the working-class. For a time postmen refused to deliver Soviet mail, the telegraph would not despatch Soviet messages, railways would not carry troops, the telephone girls left the switchboards, huge buildings were deserted—no one was left to light the fires.*

The reply of the Bolsheviks to this general strike was to declare the positions and pension rights of all

* Appendix, p. 304.

strikers forfeit if they did not return at once. At
the same time they set to work recruiting new staffs
out of their own ranks. Men in smocks and over-
alls occupied the vacated offices. Soldiers pored over
books and figures, tongues sticking out of their
mouths from the unaccustomed mental strain. Big
sailors laboriously picked out keys on the typewriter with one finger. Workingmen at the switch-
boards in the telephone station clumsily plugged in
and out while irate subscribers screamed curses and
threats at them over the wires. They were pitifully
heavy-handed and slow. But they were in dead
earnest, and day by day their speed was increasing.
Day by day the old employes came drifting back,
and in the end the strike of the bourgeoisie was
broken.

Sabotage was the second weapon used against the
Soviets. In factories managers hid vital parts of machinery, falsified accounts, destroyed plans and
formulas and, under cover of night, shipped away
lead and flour to Germany. Officials misdirected
freight, destroyed good food under the pretext of
its being unfit for use, tied everything up in loops
of red tape.

The Bolsheviks answered with a "Warning to
all Saboteurs and Provocateurs, who have wormed
their way into Soviet Institutions." At the same
time the walls of the city were placarded with this
poster addressed *To all HONEST CITIZENS:*

ВСѢМЪ ЧЕСТНЫМЪ ГРАЖДАНАМЪ!

ВОЕННО-РЕВОЛЮЦІОННЫЙ КОМИТЕТЪ ПОСТАНОВЛЯЕТЪ:

Хищники, мародеры, спекулянты объявляются врагами народа.

Лица, виновныя въ этихъ тягчайшихъ преступленіяхъ, будутъ немедленно арестовываться по спеціальнымъ ордерамъ Военно-Революц. Комитета и отправляться въ Кронштадтскія тюрьмы впредь до преданія ихъ Военно-Революціонному суду.

Всѣмъ общественнымъ организаціямъ, всѣмъ честнымъ гражданамъ Военно-Революц. Комитетъ предлагаетъ: обо всѣхъ извѣстныхъ случаяхъ хищенія, мародерства, спекуляціи немедленно доводить до свѣдѣнія Военно-Революц. Комитета.

Борьба съ этимъ зломъ—общее дѣло всѣхъ честныхъ людей. Военно-Революц. Комитетъ ждетъ поддержки отъ тѣхъ, кому дороги интересы народа.

Въ преслѣдованіи спекулянтовъ и мародеровъ Военно-Революціонный Комитетъ будетъ безпощаденъ.

Военно-Революціонный Комитетъ.

Петроградъ.
10 ноября 1917 г.

[This poster is reproduced in English on following page.]

TO ALL HONEST CITIZENS!

THE WAR-REVOLUTIONARY COMMITTEE DECREES:

HOOLIGANS, PROFITEERS AND SPECULATORS ARE DECLARED TO BE ENEMIES OF THE PEOPLE.

PERSONS GUILTY OF THESE GRAVE CRIMES WILL BE IMMEDIATELY ARRESTED BY SPECIAL ORDER OF THE WAR-REVOLUTIONARY COMMITTEE AND WILL BE SENT TO THE KRONSTADT PRISONS TO REMAIN THERE UNTIL BROUGHT BEFORE THE WAR-REVOLUTIONARY COURT.

THE WAR-REVOLUTIONARY COMMITTEE URGES ALL PUBLIC ORGANIZATIONS AND ALL HONEST CITIZENS IMMEDIATELY TO INFORM THE WAR-REVOLUTIONARY COMMITTEE, OF ALL CASES OF THEFT ROBBERY AND SPECULATION.

THE FIGHT AGAINST THESE EVILS IS THE TASK OF ALL HONEST PEOPLE. THE WAR-REVOLUTIONARY COMMITTEE EXPECTS THE SUPPORT OF ALL THOSE WHO HAVE THE INTERESTS OF THE PEOPLE AT HEART.

IN THE PROSECUTION OF SPECULATORS AND PROFITEERS THE WAR-REVOLUTIONARY COMMITTEE WILL BE RELENTLESS.

War-Revolutionary Committee.

PETROGRAD,
NOVEMBER 23, 1917.

[*This is a reproduction in English of the Russian poster on the preceding page.*]

160

Under this threat, those speculating in the hunger of the masses took to cover. Later on, the Extraordinary Commission (*Cheka*) was created to deal with these offenders, and other enemies of the new Soviet order.

In classes where there was no enmity against the Soviet, the bourgeoisie fomented it. The sufferings of millions of cripples, orphans and wounded was made acute by closing down the Department of Public Welfare. Hospitals and asylums became foodless and fireless. Delegations on crutches and starving mothers, babies in arms, besieged the new Commissar, Madame Kollontai. But she was helpless. The safes were locked, and the officials had made off with the keys. The former Minister, Countess Panina, had made off with the funds.

The Bolshevik reply to this and similar acts was not the guillotine but the Revolutionary Tribunal. Behind a long semi-circular table in the music room of the Palace of the Grand Duke Nicholas sat the seven judges—two soldiers, two workmen, two peasants and the President, Jukov.

The first prisoner was the Countess Panina. The defense recited at length her golden deeds and charities. The young workman prosecutor Naumov replied:

"Comrades: All this is true. The woman has a good heart. But she is all wrong. She has helped the people out of her riches. But where did her riches come from? Out of the exploited people. She tried to do good with her schools, her nurses and her soup-kitchens. But if the people had the money she received out of their blood and sweat, we could have our own schools, our own nurses and our own soup-kitchens. And we could have them the way we want them, not the way she thinks we ought to have them. Her good deeds can not excuse her taking funds from the Ministry."

The verdict was guilty. She was sent to prison until the money was returned, then liberated to public censure! In the beginning light sentences like this were the order of the day. But as the class conflict grew more and more bitter the penalties imposed by the Revolutionary Tribunal grew more severe.

Money is the life-blood of all governments, and all financial institutions were in the hands of the bourgeoisie. To the City Duma and the "Committee of Salvation" the banks privately paid over fifty million rubles—to the Soviets not a single ruble. All their pleas and papers were unavailing. The bourgeoisie found great mirth in the spectacle of the Government of All-Russia going to the banks cap in hand begging for funds and not getting any.

Then one morning the Bolsheviks came to the banks guns in hand. They took the funds. Then they took the banks. By the decree for Nationalization of Banks, these centres of financial power passed into the hands of the working-class.

Alcohol, Press and Church versus the Soviets.
In their efforts to befuddle the brains of the masses the bourgeoisie saw an ally in alcohol. The city was mined with wine cellars more dangerous than powder magazines. This alcohol in the veins of the populace meant chaos in the life of the city. With this aim the cellars were opened and the mob invited in to help themselves. Bottles in hand the drunks would emerge from the cellars to fall sprawling on the snow, or rove thru the streets, shooting and looting.

To these pogroms the Bolsheviks replied with machine-guns, pouring lead into the bottles—there was no time to break them all by hand. They destroyed three million rubles' worth of vintage in the vaults of the Winter Palace, some of it there for a century. The liquor passed out of the cellars, not thru the throats of the Czar and his retainers, but thru a hose attached to a fire-engine pumping into the canals. A frightful loss. The Bolsheviks deeply regretted it, for they needed funds. But they needed order more.

"Citizens," they declared, "no violation of revolutionary order! No thefts nor brigandage! Following the example of the Paris Commune, we will destroy any looter or instigator of disorder." To meet this crisis this placard was posted:

ОБЯЗАТЕЛЬНОЕ ПОСТАНОВЛЕНІЕ.

1) Городъ Петроградъ объявленъ на осадномъ положеніи.

2) Всякія собранія, митинги, сборища и т. п. на улицахъ и площадяхъ воспрещается.

3) Попытки разгромовъ винныхъ погребовъ, складовъ, заводовъ, лавокъ, магазиновъ, частныхъ квартиръ и проч. и т. п. будутъ прекращаемы пулеметнымъ огнемъ безъ всякаго предупрежденія.

4) Домовымъ комитетамъ, швейцарамъ, дворникамъ и милиціи вмѣняется въ безусловную обязанность поддерживать самый строжайшій порядокъ въ домахъ, дворахъ и на улицахъ, причемъ ворота и подъѣзды домовъ должны запираться въ 9 час. вечера и открываться въ 7 час. утра. После 9 час. вечера выпускать только жильцовъ подъ контролемъ домовыхъ комитетовъ.

5) Виновные въ раздачѣ, продажѣ или пріобрѣтеніи всякихъ спиртныхъ напитковъ, а также въ нарушеніи пунктовъ 2-го и 4-го будутъ немедленно арестованы и подвергнуты самому тяжкому наказанію.

Петроградъ 6-го декабря, 3 часа ночи.

Комитетъ по борьбѣ съ погромами при Исполнительномъ Комитетѣ Совѣта Рабочихъ и Солдатскихъ Депутатовъ.

Типографія «Копейка», Петроградъ, Садовая ул., 6 соб. дом.

OBLIGATORY ORDINANCE

1) The city of Petrograd is declared to be in a state of siege.

2) ALL ASSEMBLIES, MEETINGS AND CONGREGATIONS ON THE STREETS AND SQUARES ARE PROHIBITED.

3) ATTEMPTS TO LOOT WINE-CELLARS, WAREHOUSES, FACTORIES, STORES, BUSINESS PREMISES, PRIVATE DWELLINGS, ETC., ETC., WILL BE STOPPED BY MACHINE-GUN FIRE WITHOUT WARNING.

4) HOUSE COMMITTEES, DOORMEN, JANITORS AND MILITIA-MEN ARE CHARGED WITH THE DUTY OF KEEPING STRICT ORDER IN ALL HOUSES, COURTYARDS AND IN THE STREETS; AND HOUSES, DOORS AND CARRIAGE-ENTRANCES MUST BE LOCKED AT 9 O'CLOCK IN THE EVENING, AND OPENED AT 7 O'CLOCK IN THE MORNING. AFTER 9 O'CLOCK IN THE EVENING ONLY TENANTS MAY LEAVE THE HOUSE, UNDER STRICT CONTROL OF THE HOUSE COMMITTEES.

5) THOSE GUILTY OF THE DISTRIBUTION, SALE OR PURCHASE OF ANY KIND OF ALCOHOLIC LIQUOR, AND ALSO THOSE GUILTY OF THE VIOLATIONS OF SECTIONS 2 AND 4, WILL BE IMMEDIATELY ARRESTED AND SUBJECTED TO THE MOST SEVERE PUNISHMENT.

PETROGRAD, 19TH OF DECEMBER, 3 O'CLOCK IN THE NIGHT.

COMMITTEE TO FIGHT AGAINST POGROMS, ATTACHED TO THE EXECUTIVE COMMITTEE OF THE SOVIET OF WORKERS AND SOLDIERS' DEPUTIES.

[*This is a reproduction in English of the Russian poster on opposite page.*]

If liquor might not poison the minds of the people, there was the press. The lie-factories ground out their daily grist of papers and posters telling of the imminent fall of the Bolsheviks; of Lenin's flight to Finland with thirty millions of gold and platinum stolen from the State Bank; of the massacres of women and children by the Reds; of German officers in command at Smolny.

The Bolsheviks replied to this by the suspension of all organs "appealing to open revolt or inciting to crime."

"The wealthy classes," they declared, "holding the lion's share of the public press seek to befuddle the brains and consciences of the people with a stream of slander and lies. . . . If the first Revolution, which overthrew the monarchy, had the right to suppress the monarchist press, then this Revolution, which has overthrown the bourgeoisie, has the right to suppress the bourgeois press."

The opposition press, however, was not wholly suppressed. Papers suspended one day came out the next under a new name. *Speech* became *Free Speech*. *The Day* appeared as *Night*, then *In The Dark Night, Midnight, Two A.M.* and so on. In picture and verse *Satire* went on merrily and mercilessly lampooning the Bolsheviks. The American Committee on Public Information carried on its propaganda unhindered, publishing the words of Samuel Gompers under the headline "Socialists Support the War." But the Bolshevik measures were effective enough to prevent wholesale lying to the masses.

The Czar had used the priests of the Greek Orthodox Church as his spiritual police making "Religion the opiate of the people." With threats of hell and promises of heaven the masses had been bludgeoned into submission to autocracy. Now the church was called to perform the same function for the bourgeoisie. By solemn proclamation the Bolsheviks were excommunicated from all its rites and services.

The Bolsheviks made no direct assault upon religion, but separated Church from State. The flow of government funds into the ecclesiastical coffers was stopped. Marriage was declared a civil institution. The monastic lands were confiscated. Parts of monasteries were turned into hospitals.

The Patriarch thundered his protests against these sacrileges but with little effect. The devotion of the masses to the Holy Church proved to be almost as mythical as their devotion to the Czar. They looked at the Church Decree giving them hell if they sided with the Bolsheviks. Then they looked at the Bolshevik Decree giving them land and factories.

"If we must choose," some said, "we choose the Bolsheviks." Others chose the Church. Many merely muttered *"Neechevo"* (it doesn't matter much), and walked in the church procession on one day and in the Bolshevik parade on the next.

Peasants, Anarchists and Germans Pitted against the Soviets.

The cities were the stronghold of the Bolsheviks. The bourgeoisie sought to play the country against them.

"Look!" they said to the peasants, "The cities work but eight hours a day, why should you work sixteen? Why deliver your grain to the cities when you get nothing in return?" * The old Executive Committee of the Peasants' Soviet flatly refused to recognize the new government at Smolny.

Over their heads, however, the Bolsheviks called a new congress of peasants. Here the old guard with Chernov made furious assaults upon the Bolsheviks. But two stubborn facts could not be downed. First: The Bolsheviks had given the peasants land—not promises. Second: The Bolsheviks were now inviting the peasants to participate in the new government.

After days of stormy debate an agreement was concluded. The peasants streamed out into the night lit with torches, the band of the Pavlovsky Regiment crashed into the Marseillaise, workmen rushed in upon the peasants clasping them in their arms and kissing them. Behind the huge peasant Soviet banner with its inscription: *"Long Live the*

* Appendix, p. 310. Soviet appeal to Peasants: "Dear Brothers."

Union of the Toiling Masses," the procession passed
thru the snow-covered streets to Smolny. Here the
formal "wedding" of the peasants with the soldiers
and workers was consummated. In exaltation an
old mujik cried out, "I came here not walking on
the ground but flying thru the air." The new government became in reality a Soviet of Workmen,
Soldier and Peasant Deputies.

In their efforts to break the Soviets the bourgeoisie struck out right and left—as far left as the
Anarchists. Hundreds of officers and monarchists
filtered into the anarchist organizations and under
the black flag became anarchists of deed.

They entered hotels and at revolver-point "requisitioned" the pocket-books of the guests. In Moscow they "nationalized" thirty-four palaces by
dumping the inmates into the streets. They found
the American Red Cross automobile of Colonel Rob-
bins standing by a curb and "socialized" it by jumping in and driving off. They justified everything by
saying: "We are the real revolutionists—more radical than the Bolsheviks."

The Bolsheviks delivered an ultimatum to the
genuine Anarchists to clean house. At the same
time they raided the "Anarchist" centers and found
great stores of provisions, jewelry and machine-guns
fresh from Germany. They restored the stolen
property to the owners and arrested all reactionaries
masquerading as ultra-revolutionists.

For help the bourgeoisie turned to their former enemies—the Germans. Again and again they told us that next week we would see the German armies marching into Moscow.

The Bolsheviks had then no Red Armies to oppose the Germans, no batteries of guns. But they had batteries of linotypes and printing-presses, which sprayed the German ranks with the deadly shrapnel of propaganda. In the *Torch* and the *People's Peace,* in all languages, flamed the appeal to the German soldiers to use their guns—not to destroy the workingmen's republic in Russia, but to set up a workingmen's republic in Germany.

In the Soviet offices John Reed and I made up an illustrated sheet. Picture No. 1 showed the German Embassy in Petrograd, a big banner on its front. Underneath this picture these sentences:

See the great banner. It is the word of a famous German. Was it Bismarck? Was it Hindenburg? No. It is the call of the immortal Karl Marx to international brotherhood—"Proletarians of all lands, unite!"

This is not merely a pretty decoration of the German Embassy. In all seriousness the Russians have raised this banner, and to you Germans they hurl back the same words that your Karl Marx gave to the whole world seventy years ago.

At last a real proletarian republic has been founded. But this republic cannot be secure until the workers of all lands conquer the power of government.

The Russian peasants, workers and soldiers will soon send a socialist as ambassador to Berlin. When will Germany send an internationalist Socialist to this building of the German embassy in Petrograd?

Picture No. 3 showed a soldier prying the Russian Imperial eagles off a palace, the crowd below burning them. Underneath these words:

On the roof of a palace, a soldier is tearing down the hateful emblem of autocracy. Below the crowd is burning the eagles. The soldier in the crowd is explaining that the overthrow of autocracy is only the first step in the march of social revolution.

It is easy to overthrow autocracy. Autocracy rests on nothing but the blind submission of soldiers. The Russian soldiers merely opened their eyes and autocracy disappeared.

These pictures, papers and leaflets were flung up into the air to be blown by favorable winds into the German trenches. They were dropped from aeroplanes and smuggled across in shoes and boxes and on prisoners returning to Germany.

All this disintegrated the German armies and made for revolution. General Hoffman said: "It was Lenin and the Bolsheviks that broke our morale and gave us defeat and the revolution you now see ruining us." Probably the propaganda was not so effective as this. But it did prevent the German troops from coming to overwhelm the Soviet. The Russian bourgeoisie began scheming for intervention by the Allies.

The Debacle of the Constituent Assembly. On January 18, 1918, at the height of the struggle between the classes the Constituent Assembly convened. It reflected an earlier phase of the Revolution—a viewpoint now discarded. It was elected from antiquated lists—lists in which one Soviet Party—the Left Socialist Revolutionists, did not appear as a party at all. The masses were indifferent to this institution coming like a ghost out of the past. But the bourgeoisie loudly acclaimed it. In reality the bourgeoisie had no zeal for the Constituent Assembly and for months had done everything to postpone or kill it. How often had I heard them say: "The Constituent Assembly—we spit upon it." Now it was their last hope, the last screen behind which they could operate, they became its ardent champions.

For the opening day a big demonstration was organized. About 15,000 officers, *chinovniks* and intelligentsia paraded thru the streets. Fur-clad ladies of leisure arrayed in scarlet colors, old monarchists carrying banners of red, large-bellied landlords lustily singing "We starved and bled in the people's cause" all tried their best to look like a revolutionary procession. But only the songs and banners were red. The marchers were largely White Guards and Black Hundreds—scarcely a peasant or worker. The masses stood aside and greeted the paraders with jeers or contemptuous silence.

The Constituent Assembly came too late. It was still-born. In the swift pace of Revolution the allegiance of the revolutionary masses had passed wholly to the Soviet. For the Soviet they had marched 500,000 strong and they were ready, not only to march for it, but to fight and die for it. The Soviet was precious to the working-classes because it was their own institution, born in their own class and admirably fitted to realize their own ends.

Every dominant class fashions the kind of state-apparatus that will best secure its power, thru which it can govern in its own interests. When kings and nobles were in power the state-apparatus thru which they functioned was the Autocracy, the Bureaucracy. When the bourgeois-capitalist classes rose to power in the 18th century they scrapped this old state-apparatus and created a new one adapted to their purposes—the Parliament, Congress.

In like manner the working-classes rising to power in Russia brought with them their own state-apparatus—the Soviet. They had tried and tested it in thousands of local Soviets. They were familiar with its workings. It was part of their daily experience. Thru it they had achieved the desires of their hearts —land, factories, and the proffers of peace. They had marched to victory with it. They had made it the government of Russia.

And now this belated Constituent Assembly refused to recognize the Soviet as the government of Russia. It refused to accept the Soviets' Declaration of the Rights of the Working and Exploited Peoples—"the Magna Charta of the Russian Revolution." *   It was as if the French Revolution refused to accept the Declaration of the Rights of Man.

Accordingly it was dissolved. In the morning of January 19, 1918, the sailor guards said they were

* Appendix VI, p. 297.

sleepy and that the remaining delegates must stop talking and go home. Thus after one session the Constituent Assembly expired, making a great furor in the Western world, but in the life of Russia hardly a ripple. It had no hold on the people. By the manner of its dying it showed that it had no right to live.

The chief mourners for the Constituent Assembly were the bourgeoisie. It was their last hope. Now it was gone their rage against the Revolution and all its works was implacable. This was quite natural. The Revolution was a catastrophe to them. It declared: "If a man does not work, neither shall he eat." "No one shall have cake until everybody has bread." It dynamited the whole basis of their lives. It took the great estates away from the landlords, the gilt-edged jobs away from the office-holders, the control of banks and factories away from the capitalists. Nobody likes to have things taken away from him. No leisure class gracefully steps down from the roof-garden and goes to work. No•privileged class voluntarily resigns any of its privileges. No class steeped in tradition discards the old and gladly embraces the new.

There are of course exceptions to this rule—in Russia some striking ones. The old Czarist general, Nikolayev, declared himself a Bolshevik and took command in the Red Army. Later captured by the Whites at Yamburg he was called upon to deny his faith. He refused. He was tortured—a red star burned upon his breast. Still he refused to recant. He was led to the scaffold and a noose placed around his neck.

"I die a Bolshevik. Long live the Soviet," he cried as he was swung out into space.

There were others like him—men whose hearts had been touched by the teachings of Tolstoy and the long line of Russian humanitarians, men who saw the iniquity of the old order and the justice of the new.

But these were exceptions. As a class the Russian bourgeoisie looked at the Revolution with horror and hate. Their only thought was to kill it. Blinded with vengeance they cast aside all codes of honor, chivalry and patriotism. They cried for foreign bayonets to strike it down. Every weapon was sanctified—even assassination. The civilized veneer dropped away. The primitive fang and claw appeared. Men of parts and culture became savages.

CHAPTER XII

BUILDING THE NEW ORDER

THE conduct of the Russian upper-classes in their efforts to regain the power of the State shows nothing new or unusual in history. The unprecedented thing is the determination of the Russian working-class to hold that power. They clung to their course with dogged tenacity, meeting thrust with counter-thrust, striking back blow for blow, steel for iron. They developed unexampled discipline and solidarity.*

It is said that the rank and file were held in line by the iron will of their leaders, that their resolution was just the reflex of the resolution of the men above. The opposite is nearer the truth.

It was the leaders who were irresolute. Three Bolshevik Commissars left their posts at a critical moment. Five others (Zinoviev, Kamanev, Milyutin, Nogin, Rykov) tendered their resignation to the Central Committee of the Bolshevik Party. Lunacharsky, believing all the tales of Moscow's destruction, cried out, "My cup is full. I am unable to endure this horror. It is impossible to work under the pressure of thoughts that drive me mad. I can bear no more. I resign."

* Appendix, p. 302: "To All Workers of Petrograd."

"Shame upon these men of little faith, who hesitate and doubt, capitulating to the cries of the bourgeoisie," cried Lenin. "Look at the masses. In them there is not a shadow of hesitation." The names of the deserters were pilloried thru Russia. Before the blast of indignation from the proletarians, the commissars scurried back to their posts never to waver again.

But they could never quite shake off the haunting fear of defeat. Even Lenin was not immune. "Ten days more and we shall have lived seventy days—as long as the Paris Commune," he exclaimed, surprised at so far escaping disaster. At times the leaders saw their venture ending in certain death.

"We did our best," said Peters dolefully one day, "but it is all over for us shortly."

"Perhaps tomorrow," said Pokrovsky, "we shall get a sleep—a long one."

These forebodings never assailed the minds of the Bolshevik rank and file. They drove ahead in full confidence and assurance, infusing their leaders above with fresh courage and determination, and inspiring the broad masses below with the will to victory.

How Many Bolsheviks in Russia? To what extent did these masses support the new government set up by the Bolsheviks? How wide a following did the Revolution find in the people? *The People's Business* (*Dielo Narodo*) said: "A revolution is a rising of

all the people. But what have we here? A handful of poor fools deceived by Lenin and Trotzky."

True, the membership of the Bolshevik Party was
a "handful" among the great populations of Russia
—not more than one or two per cent. If that was
all, the new government might well be stigmatized as
"the tyranny of an infinitesimal fraction over the
great majority." But one fact must be borne in
mind, viz.: Bolshevik sentiment is not to be gauged
by the Bolshevik Party. For every Bolshevik in the
official Bolshevik Party there were 30 to 50 Bolsheviks in the general population.

The high standard of admission, the hard duties
and drastic discipline of the Bolshevik Party, made
the masses unwilling to join it. But they voted for
it.*

In the elections to the Constituent Assembly in
Northern and Central Russia, Bolsheviks got 55 per
cent. of the vote—not 1 or 2 per cent. In Petrograd
the Bolsheviks and their allies, the Left Socialist-
Revolutionists, received 576,000 votes—more than
the 17 other parties combined.

---

* Socialist voters are always 10 to 50 times as numerous as
Socialist Party members. New York in 1920 had 12,000 Socialist
Party *members*. This election showed 176,000 Socialist Party
voters. In Vladivostok in 1918, the Bolshevik Party members
were 300. In the June election there were 12,000 Bolshevik
Party voters. This election was held under Allied auspices with
the Bolshevik papers suppressed and their leaders imprisoned,
yet more citizens voted for the Bolsheviks than for the other
16 parties combined. Yet propagandists for the Czarists Kolchak
and Denikin—like John Spargo—tried to focus all attention on
the membership, which is utterly misleading.

It is said that there are three grades of lies: "Lies, damned lies and statistics." Revolutionary statistics are particularly unreliable. For in time of revolution public opinion moves like a tidal wave. The people vote one way today. A few weeks hence they will vote quite differently.

When the Constituent Assembly was *elected* in November, 1917, about one-third were for the Bolsheviks (including their allies, the Left Socialist-Revolutionists). When the Constituent Assembly *convened* in January, 1918, possibly two-thirds were for the Bolsheviks. In the few weeks' interim the Bolshevik ideas swept from the cities into the villages, and out into the provinces. The peasants, finding that the Soviet Land Decree had actually given them the land, rallied behind the Bolshevik banners in millions.

A fair estimate of the growth of Bolshevik adherents in the adult population would go like this:

March 1917—at the fall of the Czar................. 1,000,000
July 1917—after the armed demonstration........... 5,000,000
November 1917—Constituent Assembly election (official
   returns) 9,000,000
January 1918—3rd Congress of Soviets representing....13,000,000

The Bolsheviks had not merely numbers but all the strategic positions. The big cities were Bolshevik—so were the railwaymen, the miners, the workers in basic industries. And the bayonets were overwhelmingly on their side. The Bolsheviks had the mandate of the essential forces of Russia to carry on the Revolution in the Bolshevik way.

Apathy of the Masses. It is a grave error to minimize the following the Bolsheviks had in the masses. It is an equally grave error to say that these masses were all zealots of the Revolution, all filled with a high and holy enthusiasm. On the contrary great numbers were quite indifferent. The Revolution was only "skin-deep."

One winter morning I set out in a sleigh with Charles Kuntz, a New Jersey farmer and philosopher, who had come to Russia for a scientific study of the Revolution. On finding that we were Americans, our driver, a lad of fifteen, was all excitement. "Oh, Americans!" he exclaimed. "Tell me did Buffalobill and Jessejams really live?"

We said, "Yes" and at once leaped to glory in the eyes of our driver. The exploits of these Western daredevils he knew by heart. Now this great joy—he was driving two countrymen of his heroes. He gazed long at us in big blue-eyed admiration while we tried hard to look like Buffalo Bill and Jesse James themselves.

"Oh! Ho!" he shouted. "I'll show you how to drive." He loosed the reins, cried *"B-r-r"* to his horse and with a jerk struck out into a break-neck gallop, the sleigh bounding over the ice-hummocks like a stage-coach on a Rocky Mountain road. Shouting with delight, he stood up in his box, crack-

ing his whip, the sleigh slewing fearfully from side
to side while Kuntz and I clung desperately to our
seats and begged him to stop.

We told him that Buffalo Bill at his best never
did better—but not to do it again. He plied us
with incessant questions about the West while we
tried to get him to talk about Russia. But in vain.
The Russian Revolution was in eclipse. The deeds
done in his books with glaring paper covers were so
much more blood-stirring and important than those
done in the streets of Petrograd.

Not all indifference to the Revolution was so
picturesque. The energies of multitudes were absorbed by routine, and the sheer details of finding
food and clothes. Others sordidly saw in the Revolution their chance for loot and laziness. They had
toiled like slaves, now they would loaf like lords.
The Revolution meant to them not freedom *for* work
but freedom *from* work. They lounged all day on
the corners, their sole contribution to the new order
being to spit the husks of sun-flower seeds on the
pavement. Soldiers became "State boarders," doing
nothing in return for the food, clothes and lodging
they got from the government. The nights they
spent in card playing, their days in sleeping. Instead
of drilling they became hawkers peddling rubbers,
cigarettes and gew-gaws in the streets.

There was venal criminal indifference, too, to the
interests of the Revolution. In positions deserted
by the intelligentsia, adventurers and careerists saw

their chance for plunder and glory. When John Reed and I visited the Petrograd Prefect of Police he flung his arms around us, crying: "Welcome, dear comrades. I will commandeer for you the best apartments in the city. We must sing the *Marseillaise* together. Ah! Our Magnificent Revolution," he exclaimed ecstatically. There was no doubt about his inspiration. The sources of it stood in a dozen bottles on the table. Under their influence he grew eloquent:

"Danton and Marat ruled Paris in the French Revolution. Their names have gone down in history. I rule Petrograd today. My name shall go down in history." Short-lived glory! Next day he was jailed for accepting a bribe.

Another romantic buccaneer in some way received an appointment as military commissar. His self-importance mounted with every verst that took him away from Moscow. He sent word to a local Soviet that his coming would be announced by the booming of a cannon and the delegates were forthwith to assemble. Revolver in hand he strode upon the platform and in stentorian voice read his commission to the astounded auditors, punctuating each sentence by firing a bullet into the ceiling. There was short shrift for such adventurers.

But for the broad masses the Bolsheviks had infinite tolerance. They knew that the state had stupefied their brains, the church had deformed their consciences, famine had racked their bodies, alcohol had soddened their spirits. They had been exhausted by years of war and perverted by centuries of cruelty and deceit. For these masses the Bolsheviks had patience—and education.

A New Creative Spirit. "Whatever other expenses are cut down," the Bolsheviks declared, "the expenditures on public instruction must stay high. A generous budget for education is the honor and glory of every people. Our first aim must be the struggle against ignorance."

Everywhere schools were opened—even in palaces, barracks and factories. Over them was blazoned the legend "Children are the hope of the world" (*Detye nadezhde meera*). Into them marched millions of children, some of them forty and sixty years of age—old *babas* and grey-bearded peasants. A whole nation was learning to read and write.

Alongside the revolutionary proclamations and bills for the opera, appeared on the boardings biographies of great men, screeds on health and art and science. Workmen's theatres, libraries and lecture-courses sprang up on all sides. Doors to culture hitherto tight-closed to the masses were unlocked. Peasants and workers flocked into the museums and galleries.

The Bolsheviks aimed not only at better brains but better bodies. To this end many decrees were issued, such as the eight-hour law. The right of every child to be well-born was proclaimed. The stigma of illegitimacy was removed. Each industry was to provide one maternity bed for each two hundred workwomen. For eight weeks before and eight weeks after childbirth the mother was exempted from work. A Palace of Motherhood was established in different centers. The children instead of the wealthy were given the first claim upon such "luxuries" as milk and fruit. By the housing law the rich man lost his right to ten or twenty rooms or as many dwellings. On the other hand a dozen families gained for the first time the right to fresh air, light and decent dwellings. Not only was their health better, but they gained in self-respect and dignity. The Dictatorship of the Proletariat, basing itself on the multitudes, sought to nourish multitudes of sound, clean bodies, brains and consciences. The Bolsheviks were working for the future.

Having destroyed the main foundations of the old bourgeois order, they now faced the infinitely more trying task—the construction of a new order. They had to build it anew in every department, to build it from the bottom up, to build it out of the ruins of the past, to build it while beset and bedevilled on every side.

No one can exaggerate the magnitude of the task of reorganizing a new society. Some of the obstacles I glimpsed in one department—the military. Trotzky had just flung into the face of General von Hoffman his: "You are writing with the sword on

Under the Czar this Royal Palace was for a few nobles and their lackeys; now under the Soviet it shelters hundreds of crippled and orphaned children. The former name, Czar's Village (*Tsarskoye Selo*) is changed to Children's Village (*Dyetskoye Selo*). (*See next page.*)

Play and exercise in the former Palace Park, now the Children's Colony.

Girls at work learning how a Bolshevik cow gives milk.

Boys modelling in clay. Heads are shaved to guard against the typhus louse.

The Moscow Children's Theatre. Child-actors and audience enjoying Barrie's *Peter Pan*.

"Chaos is necessary to the birth of a new star," said Nietzche. Out of Russian chaos rose the powerful Red Army—its emblem the five pointed star, its commander Trotsky.

the bodies of living nations" and had refused to
sign the First Treaty of Brest-Litovsk. The Germans then started a sudden drive on Petrograd. I
joined the Red Guards for the defense of the city.
Hearing this, Lenin suggested that I form a foreign
detachment. *Pravda* printed our "call" in such
English type as they could muster. (See reproduction of this on next page.)

About sixty men joined the detachment.
Amongst them was Charles Kuntz, heretofore a Tol-
stoyan with scruples against killing even a chicken.
Now that the Revolution was in peril, he threw over
his pacifism and took up a gun. A tremendous
change, to convert a fifty year old philosopher into
a soldier. In target practise his rifle would get
tangled in his beard, but once his bullet hit the
bull's-eye and his eyes glistened with joy.

We were a motley crowd and our fighting-strength
really amounted to little. But the spirit of it had a
good moral effect upon the Russians. It gave them
the feeling that they were not utterly alone. And
on a tiny scale it gave us an insight into the difficulties the Bolsheviks must struggle with on a colossal scale. We saw the thousand obstacles that must
be overcome before any organization could function.

British and French agents on the one hand, and
German agents on the other, tried to worm their way
into our detachment. The Whites tried to get hold
of it for counter-revolutionary purposes. Provocators stirred up jealousy and dissent. After we got

The First International Detachment of the Red Army.

Интернациональный отрядъ красной арміи.

The Section for the formation and drilling f troops of the All-Russ n College f r the Organization nd Administration of the R d Army not fies herewith that au horiza ion has been obtain d by it for the formation of a First Internation l Det chment of the Red Army to be tt ched to one of the milit ry units of Petrograd. This detachmen wi l cons st of t eigner, the g ner l langu age to be English The members are to be enrolled as volunte rs The conditions of life of he volunteers to b th same as th se of the mem ers of the Red Ar y. The persons wish ng to enroll are to pre sent themselves t the M rinsky Pa lace 3rd floor entrance V znesensky prospec , where a Burea u for the en r llment of f reigners of all nationli tes has been or an se l. It is propo sed to ttach the detachment to the Gren dier Guard Regiment (Petrogradsk ia Storon , Bolshoi Wu lova str t)

The Section geves herewith a trans lation of h C ll of the nit ators of the formation of th detachment Com ra es A er c n Soc li te Alberi wil li ms and Sam l Agurs y, who are at th head of t e Bureau for the enr lli g of vol nteers

Memb rs of College of the Section f r the Form ation an Drilling.

Отдѣлъ формированія и обученія при Всероссійской Коллегіи организаціи и упра вленія Красной Арміей объяв етъ, что имъ разрѣшено формированіе при одной изъ воинскихъ частей Петрограда, перваго Ре волюціоннаго Интернаціональнаго отряда Красной Арміи изъ иностранцевъ (разго ворный языкъ англійскій).

Запись производится на добровольческихъ началахъ. Условія жизни волонтеровъ общія съ условіями жизни красноармейцевъ. Орга низовано бюро по записи иностранцевъ раз личныхъ національностей. Отрядъ предпо ложено формировать при Гвардіи Гренадер скомъ полку (Петроградская стор., Б. Вуль фова улица).

При семъ отдѣлъ прилагаетъ переводъ воззванія иниціаторовъ формированія отря да, товарищей американскихъ соціали стовъ—Альберта Вильямсъ и Самуила Агур скаго—стоящихъ во главѣ бюро по записи волонтеровъ.

Члены: Коллегія Отдѣла Формированія и Обученія.

CALL.

In this terr ble world war demo cra cy has been threatened; the in erna to al force h ve been split a su der, nd he working classes h ve been riden into the sham les by the imp r list of all c un ries In the d rkness ther rose the Russian Revolution voking the might Hous of all man

ВОЗЗВАНІЕ!

Въ эту страшную міровую войну, всей демократіи угрожала опасность, интернаціо нальныя силы были раздроблены и рабочій классъ повсюду скованъ имперіалистами всѣхъ странъ. Изъ всеобщей тьмы выплыло заманчиво свѣтъ русской революціи, пробу ждая бѣлыя всколыхнувъ человѣчества. Са

Citizens! Comrades! Internationalists!

Russia is in prison. Even so, above the clangor of the world — war her voice cries out loudest for justice and humanity — for the poor and the oppressed.

Russia has enemies inner and outer, strong and cunning. And Russia needs not your words and pious wishes. She needs work, discipline, organisation and

guns in the hands of fearless fighters.

Do you believe in the Revolution, in the International, in the Soviet power? Then join the International Legion of the Red Army. It is formed for those speaking foreign languages and to it are coming the fighting revolutionists from around the world. Are you a free man? Then enlist at once.

Are you working in shop or office? Then give your spare time to drill, rifle practice and the military courses.

Headquarters: 2 Nijni Leesnoy Peraooluk — near the Temple of the Saviour.

Bürger! Genossen! Internationalisten!

Rußland ist im Gefängnisse. Jedoch über all den Klängen des Weltkrieges erschallt seine donnernde Stimme um Gerechtigkeit und Humanität für die Armen und Unterdrückten. Rußland ist von mächtigen Feinden belagert, inneren und äußeren. Rußland braucht nicht eure Worte und fromme Wünsche; es braucht Tat, Disziplin, Organisation, Geschütz in den Händen unerschrockener Kämpfer. Habt ihr festen Glauben an die Revolution, an die Internationale und die Sowjet-Macht? Dann schließt euch der

Internationalen Legion der Roten Armee

an. Dieselbe wird für diejenigen gebildet, die fremde Sprachen sprechen, und an sie reihen sich die revolutionären Kräfte der ganzen Welt. Bist du ein freier Mann? Dann schließe dich sogleich an. Schaffst du in Werkstätten oder Kontor? Dann widme deine freie Stunden dem Drillen, der Schießübung und dem Militzstudium.

Hauptquartier: Nischni-Ljesnoi Pereulok Nr. 2 — nahe dem Tempel des Heilands.

Citoyens! Camarades! Internationalistes!

La Russie est en captivité. Mais même captive elle domine le groupement de la guerre mondiale et on entend sa voix crier le plus haut pour la justice et l'humanité pour les pauvres et les opprimés. La Russie n'a pas seulement des ennemis extérieurs, elle en a aussi au dedans de son pays qui sont forts et rusés. La Russie n'a pas besoin de vos paroles ni de vos souhaits, elle a besoin du travail, de l'organisation et des combattants sans peur. Si vous avez de la confiance dans la Revolution, l'International et dans la puissance du Soviet enrôlez vouz dans la Legion Internationale de l'Armée Rouge.

Celle-ci est formée pour ceux qui parlent des langues étrangères, et de toutes parts du monde arrivent des combattants révolutionnaires pour la renforcer. Êtes-vous libre? Enrollez-vous alors tout de suite. Si vous travaillez dans l'usine ou dans le bureau sacrifiez votre temps libre aux exercices militaires, au tir, à la discipline militaire.

Adressez-Vous au Quartier: Nijni Lesnoy Pereulok 2 — auprès du Temple du Jésus Christ.

Граждане! Товарищи! Интернаціоналисты!

Россія въ темниц, но ея голос, заглушая шум мировой войны, провозглашает человчеству о правд и справедливости для обездоленныхъ и угнетенныхъ. У Россіи много враговъ внутренних и вншнихъ, сильных и коварныхъ. Она не нуждается в словах и пустых пожеланіяхъ. Ей нужна работа, дисциплина, организація и безстрашные бойцы.

Вруете ли вы в революцію, в Интернаціоналъ, в Совтскую власть? Если да, то немедленно присоединяйтесь в Интернаціональному Легіону Красной Арміи. Этот Легіон формируется из товарищей, говорящих на иностранных языках; в нем соберутся боевые революціонеры со всего свта.

Если вы не-занятый человкъ, присоединяйся безотлагательно. Если ты работаешь на заводъ или в конторъ, то посвяти свое свободное время тренировкъ и стрльб.

Обращаться для записи и за справками: Нижній Лсной пер., д. № 2, кв. 2—близ Храма Христа Спасителя.

Москва, 16 (3) апрля 1918 г.

Cittadini! Compagni! Internazionalisti!

Russia è in prigione. Nulladimeno sopra il clamore della guerra universale la sua voce proclama il piu alto giustizia e umanità pei poveri e soppressi. La Russia ha nemici, interiori ed esteriori, forti e cauti. E la Russia non ha bisogno delle vostre parole e dei vostri buoni auguri. Essa ha bisogno delle vostra azione disciplinata, della vostra organizzazione di fucili nelle mani di intimorosibili lottanti. Credete voi nella rivoluzione, nell'Internazionale, nella forza dei Soviet? Allora unitevi alla Legione Internazionale dell'Esercito Rosso. Esso è formato per quelli che parlano le lingue estere e vengono con ini i rivoluzionarii lottanti di tutto il mondo. Siete liberi? Allora unitevi all'istante. Lavorate nelle fabbriche oppure negli uffici? Allora dedicate il vostro tempo libero all'esercizio, alla pratica del fucile ed ai corsi militari!

Quartiere Generale: Nizuti Lesnoi Pereulco 2 — presso il Tempio de Salute.

[*This is the Moscow appeal of the International Legion as it appeared in five languages.*]

187

the men, it was almost impossible to get the equipment. Military stores were in a hopeless tangle. Rifles in one place, bullets in another; telephones, barbed-wire and sappers' tools in one vast jumble; and officers trying their best to make it more jumbled. When the sabotagers were removed, raw incompetent men took their places. We entrained two miles below Petrograd and, after a horrible ordeal in a box-car, we got up to find ourselves four miles on the other side of the city. We had lost six miles during the night and were stalled in a yard full of cursing troops, trains, broken-down engines. Exasperated commissars were shoving papers and fists into the faces of railway officers, who were frantically protesting they could do nothing.

This was a reflex of the chaos that prevailed all over Russia. To bring order out of it seemed a sheer impossibility. Yet the impossibility was being accomplished. In the welter of confusion was rising the great Red Army destined to amaze the world by its organization, discipline and effectiveness. And not only in the realm of war but in the cultural and economic fields were appearing the results of the powerful directing spirit begotten of the Revolution.

Always there were tremendous latent energies in the Russian masses. But they had never found expression. They had been locked up by the grim jailer—Autocracy. The Revolution came as their releaser, and with the pent-up fury of centuries they burst forth and smashed the old bourgeois order to pieces.

We had seen the Revolution unloose the tremendous powers of the people for destructive ends. Now we were seeing the Revolution evoke their creative powers and direct them to constructive ends. *"Order. Work. Discipline."* are the new watchwords of the Revolution.

But is this new spirit being born only in these great centres? Or is a like process at work out in the provinces and the vast populations of Russia. Presently we are to find out for ourselves. After nearly a year in the midst of the Revolution Kuntz and I are going home. Our eyes are turned to the East—toward America. Our journey is to take us thru the two continents over which Russia spreads herself, across 6,000 miles of Trans-Siberian Railway to the Pacific.

PART III

THE OUTREACH OF THE REVOLU-
TION

ACROSS SIBERIA ON THE EXPRESS

CHAPTER XIII

THE STEPPES RISE UP

IT is the end of April, 1918. Kuntz and I are saying good-bye to the Red Commune of Petrograd. The snow-flakes are falling, the night descending. Stormy, hungry old city, but dear to us, with its thousand lights and shadows of the Revolution, for nearly every street and prospekt has staged some act in the colossal revolutionary drama.

The square we gaze upon from the steps of the Nicholas Station, has been sprinkled red by the first sacrifices of the Revolution, and we have helped to sprinkle it white with a shower of Soviet posters, flung from a plunging truck at midnight. It has rumbled beneath the tread of marching columns chanting their funeral hymn, bearing away their dead; and we have heard it ring with triumphant shouts proclaiming: *"All Power to the Soviets."* It has witnessed the rush of Cossack horses thru the ranks of workingmen, felling them to the cobbles. And it has seen the return of these workers, welded together in the iron battalions of the proletariat— the invincible Red Army of Russia.

A multitude of memories bind us to the city. But

steam is up in the engine of the Trans-Siberian Express, and it does not wait on sentiment. Every week it starts on its 6,000 mile journey to the Pacific, heeding only the clanging signal-bell, whether rung by order of the Czar or by order of the Bolsheviks. On the third stroke we climb aboard and are off on our long journey to the distant East.

What will this East unfold to us? Shall we find that the spirit of the revolutionary centres carries out far toward the circumference or not?

The Émigrés' View of the Revolution. Already our fellow passengers are stretched out in their compartments, sipping tea and smoking cigarettes. In our car are about twenty landowners, speculators, war-profiteers, ex-officers in mufti, evicted officials, and three over-painted ladies—all members or retainers of the old privileged class.

Their ancient privileges are gone. But life still has its glamor. Even now, are they not engaged in the thrilling adventure known amongst their fellow-émigrés as "Escaping out of the bloody clutches of the Bolsheviks"? And before them, a few weeks hence, lies another thrilling adventure in the salons of Paris, London and Washington, recounting the terrors and perils of their escape.

That it was an escape *de luxe* in an International sleeper, with excellent beds, dining-car and porter inclusive, will be omitted from their tales. Other

details will be inserted however—little figments
about Bolshevik murders, rapes and robberies.
Every émigré must have his atrocity. At all costs
his escape must be harrowing and dramatic. Otherwise no thrill for the jaded palates of the western
democracies.

Supplied with Bolshevik passports, stamped with
a Bolshevik seal, these émigrés were driven to the
station by Bolshevik cabmen; aided by Bolshevik
porters they boarded this train, whose conductor,
brakeman and engineer belonged to the Bolshevik
faith. Riding now over a track tended by Bolshevik
laborers, guarded by Bolshevik soldiers, guided by
Bolshevik switchmen, and fed by Bolshevik waiters,
they while away their hours in cursing these selfsame Bolsheviks as bandits and cutthroats. A curious spectacle! Damning, reviling, execrating the
very ones upon whom they depend for food, shelter,
travel—for the very breath they draw. For every
member of this train-crew is a Bolshevik—all except
the porter (*provodnik*).

He had the soul of a flunkey, and the creed of a
monarchist. Tho of peasant origin, he was more
Czaristic than the Czar himself. All the émigrés he
still addressed as "my lords!" (*barin*).

"You see, my lords!" he said, "we dark people are
a lazy, shiftless lot. Give us a bottle of vodka and
we are happy. We don't need more freedom. We
need a club over us to keep us at work. We need
a Czar."

The émigrés were delighted with him. He was to them a perpetual source of comfort—a flaming light in the Bolshevik darkness.

"In this honest *mujik*," they declared, "you see the soul of the millions of Russian peasants, content to serve their master, to obey the church and love the Czar. True, a few have been misled by Bolshevik fantasies, but only a few. What have these millions of patient, plodding folks to do with that madness festering back there in Moscow and Petrograd?"

This seemed plausible. For out here it is hard even for us to sustain our interest in the Revolution at high pitch. Great concerns, political and personal, are dwarfed by the vastness of the panorama unfolding before our eyes on this, the longest railway journey in the world.

We pass over the wide stretching grain-fields of Central Russia, across the vast bridges spanning the broad rivers flowing north to the Arctic, thru the winding passes of the Urals, into the shadows of the giant virgin forest (*taiga*), almost unblazed by man, then out again upon the steppelands of Siberia.

Thru the day we watch on the horizon the peasant huts, huddled together for protection against wolves, and winds blowing from the frozen *tundras;* or take our places in the long lines that obtain hot water for tea from the tanks, buying bread and eggs and fish from the peasant women. At evening we watch the wood-burning locomotive flinging spark showers from its stack like a comet. Night after night we go to sleep with the wheels grinding beneath our car, and every morning we wake to see the track in two glistening ribbons of steel, still unrolling itself before the eastward plunging engine.

Slowly these immensities steal over us with mesmeric influence, creating the feeling the Russians call *prostor*, a sense of space and vastness. Under its spell things once mighty and imperative, become trivial and unimportant. Even the Revolution relaxes its grip upon us. May it not after all be a ferment confined to railwaymen and the industrial workers of the cities?

Back there the Revolution was an insistent fact, assailing us in eye and ear with banners and battle-cries, parades and assemblages. Out here on the Siberian steppes we see no evidence of it. We see woodsmen with axes, drivers with horses, women with baskets, a few soldiers with guns; but beyond a few tattered remnants of red flags flapping on poles there are no marks of the Revolution.

"Is the revolutionary spirit as frayed out as those faded flags?" we ask. "Are the émigrés right in summing up the aspirations of the Russian peasant as love and service to his master, his church and the Little Father? Is this after all 'Holy Russia'?"

In the midst of our ruminations—Crash! Bang! The brakes clutch the wheels, grinding and grating, sending a shiver thru the car and hurling us out of our seats. The train comes abruptly to a standstill.

Everybody stares out of the window, asking excitedly: "Washout? Cave-in? Bridge gone?" But nothing appears save the same sere, level steppeland with drifts of snow, relics of the winter.

A Bolshevik Hold-up! Suddenly from behind a snow-bank a figure shoots up, waves a signal behind him, and comes running violently towards the train. From behind a copse another form darts out and follows after. From other snow-piles and bushes and from the far horizon, more and more figures keep emerging, until the whole plain is dotted with men racing headlong toward the train. Like the ground sown with dragon-teeth, in a trice these dead waste-lands spring to life, and teem with men in arms.

"My God! Look! Look!" exclaimed one of the painted ladies. "Guns! They carry guns!" The phantasies of her imagination have materialized. Here in flesh and blood are the Bolsheviks of her tales. They have become realities, carrying in their hands guns and grenades, and on their faces a most unpleasant look. The foremost runner checks his steps, cups his hands to his mouth and bellows out to us, "Windows down."

No one argues the point. Along the whole train the windows go banging down. So do the spirits of the émigrés, finding little cheer in the faces of these oncoming men. They are a harsh, determined lot. Many of them are grimy, nearly black. All of them

have black looks for the train. By mien and gesture
they clearly indicate that their weapons have a distinct bearing upon our case.

We have no inkling of our offense. We only
know that some thunderbolt has stopped our train,
and on all sides we face a cordon of violent-talking
men. We catch wild words about "killing the bloody
tyrant" and, as the face of the florid lady appears
at the window, jeering crys of "Hey! Mrs. Rasputin!" She is certain that the ruffians are debating
whether to take us out and murder us one by one,
or destroy us *en masse* by burning or blowing up
the train.

The suspense is racking. I volunteer to investigate the situation, and start to raise a window.
When half way open, I gaze into the muzzle of a
gun thrust up into my face. A big peasant at the
other end of the gun growls, "Put the window down
quick or I'll shoot." He looks as tho he would
shoot, but my year in Russia has taught me that he
won't; that the peasant is uncivilized enough to
retain an aversion to killing a human being. So I
do not shut my window, but thrust my head out and
address the big peasant as *"Tovarish."*

"Don't you *tovarish* me, you Counter-Revolution-
ist!" he snorted back. "You drinker of the people's
blood! You monarchist, you Czarist!"

Such were the usual epithets bestowed upon the
enemies of the Revolution. But I had never heard
them rolled into one broadside and shot forth with

such malice. Hastily I produced a Soviet credential vouching for me and bearing the signature of Chicherin. But reading was not this peasant's forte. The next man, a heavy set, scowling fellow, took it and scanned it critically.

"Forged!" was his instant verdict.

I passed out a credential signed by Trotzky. "Forged!" he repeated. I followed up with a document issued by the Bolshevik Railway Commissar. The same laconic comment "Forged!" Still obdurate, was he? As a climax I would play my trump card. I produced a letter signed by Nikolai Lenin. Not only his signature, but all the letter was written out in full by Lenin's own hand. My inquisitor scrutinized it intently, while I watched to see the magic name of Lenin transform the thunder-cloud on his face into a smile. I was certain that this would settle the matter. And it did. Not in my favor, however, but against me, as I discerned by the set of his jaw. I had overplayed myself in this matter of credentials.

In his mind my case was clear. Here is a plotter up to some deviltry against the Revolution. To ingratiate himself with the Bolsheviks, he displays a grand array of Soviet documents pretending to come from even Lenin himself. This marks him as no ordinary spy. We must act at once!

He carried my sheaf of papers over to a tall man dismounting from his horse. "That's Andrey Petrovich. He will know all about these papers," declared the big peasant who had run the muzzle of his gun into my face. "He just got back from Moscow. He knows all the Bolsheviks and how they write their names. He knows the Counter-Revolutionists, and all their tricks. Those devils can't fool Andrey Petrovich."

Kuntz and I sincerely prayed that Andrey Petrovich would prove as wise as his reputation. And happily for us he did. He did know the leaders of the Bolsheviks. He knew their signatures. In a few questions he tested our knowledge. Satisfied, he shook hands with us heartily, greeted us as *tovarishe*, invited us to come outside where he would ask us a hundred questions.

"But we have a hundred questions to ask *you*," we rejoined, opening up on him forthwith. "Where did all these men suddenly spring from? Why is this train held up? What do you mean by this display of arms?"

"One question at a time," he replied, laughing. "First: These men are miners from the great coal mines less than half a mile away, and peasants from the villages. Thousands more will be along directly. Second: We grabbed up these guns and grenades fifteen minutes ago, not for display but for immediate use. Third: We held up this Trans-Siberian Express to take off of it the Czar and the Royal Family."

"Czar and Royal Family! On this train? Here?" we shouted.

"We don't know that for sure," replied Andrey Petrovich, "all we know is that about twenty minutes ago came a telegram from Omsk saying: *Release of Nicholas just effected by clique of officers. Probably escaping with staff on Express. Plan to set up Czardom at Irkutsk. Stop him dead or alive.*"

(So it was the Czar whom the crowd meant by "bloody tyrant" and the Czarina whom they were calling "Mrs. Rasputin!")

The Czar's Surprise-Party Disappointed. "We sent two men running to the villages and two to the mines, shouting the telegram," continued Andrey Petrovich. "Every man dropped his tools, snatched up his gun, and rushed for the train. A thousand here now, and they won't stop coming till night. You see how deeply we feel for our Czar! Only twenty minutes advance notice and we got this nice big reception party ready for him. He likes military displays. Well, here it is. Not in regulation style, but quite impressive, is it not?"

It was! Never have I seen such a beweaponed set of men. They were like moving arsenals. In their hands were missiles enough to blow a thousand Czars into eternity, and in their hearts and eyes vengeance enough to annihilate ten thousand.

But there seemed to be no Czar to annihilate.

"Just as I thought," Andrey Petrovich went on, "another ruse of the Counter-Revolution. That tele-

The Reception Committee which held up our train expecting to take off the Czar, recovering from their disappointment.

A Siberian mother standing by the dead body of her Bolshevik son, killed fighting against the Restoration of the Czar

gram is an act of provocators against the Soviet.
They want it to demoralize the workings of the
mines. And it will. Our men are too excited now
to do anything more today. There will be other
telegrams like this in the days to come. By crying
out: 'The Czar is escaping, the Czar is escaping,'
they think the men will get disgusted with false
alarms. Then, when we have become careless they
will try to slip the Czar through. But they don't
know our men here. For a chance to get a pot-shot
at the Czar they will turn out every day in the year."

The zest with which the searching party went thru
the cars left no doubt as to their attitude towards
the Little Father. They combed the train from end
to end, opening trunks, ransacking beds, even shift-
ing the logs on the engine tender to see if by chance
His Imperial Majesty might be hidden in the wood-
pile.

There were two white-bearded old peasants who
did a little investigating on their own account. They
would run their guns up under a sleeper, ram their
bayonets around and then withdraw them, shaking
their heads sadly. The Czar of all the Russias they
hoped to find riding the bumpers. Each time disappointed, they would hope for better luck at the next
car and repeat the prodding. But there was no Czar,
and so their bayonets did not puncture him.

But something else they did puncture—the hoary
old tradition about the deep love and devotion of

the Russian *mujik* to the Little Father. That pleasant myth could not survive the spectacle of these two devout, benign old peasants, plunging their bayonets into dark corners, and drawing them out again, aggrieved that on them were no fatal signs of the Little Father.

We Substitute for the Czar. Andrey Petrovich was a man of resources. Having no Czar for his men, he used Kuntz and me as substitutes.

"It is a strange world, *tovarishe*, full of strange surprises," he said, addressing his comrades. "We came down here to get the greatest criminal in history. Not a man here but has known pain or misery thru the Czar. But instead of finding our worst enemy, we find here our best friends. This train, instead of carrying the ideas of our autocracy, is carrying the ideas of our Revolution—and carrying them to America. Long live the Revolution! Long live our American comrades!"

There was a riot of cheer-giving, hand-shaking and picture-taking and we were off again. But not for long. Again we were halted by a storming mass. And again and again. It was in vain to protest that the Czar was not aboard. Even the documents attesting this, they waved aside as counter-revolutionary forgeries. Each crowd must reassure itself thru its own search. Thus the fastest express upon the Trans-Siberian, became the slowest.

At Marinsk, the Commissar of Transport gave a new turn to events, by despatching this telegram:

"To all Soviets:
Kuntz and Williams, General Organizers of the Red Army, are on Train Two. I ask that represen-tatives of the soviets meet with them for consulta-tion.   Sadovnikov."

The telegram was read to the crowds assembling at every station to meet the express. With their appetites and implements whetted for a Czar, suddenly two comrades were handed them. It called for a swift reversal of their emotions, but they did nobly. We rode into each station in a storm of greetings. The new detachments of the Red Army saluted, the commissars solemnly laid before us their problems, the throngs pushed forward to gaze upon us as military geniuses.

It was embarrassing, but illuminating. We got a glimpse of a new civilization in the making, the future in the act of being born. In one town the foundations had just been laid—the peasants marching over had joined the workers in one central Soviet. In another they had scarcely got to the foundations—the intelligentsia were all on strike. In many centres the new structure was well along, the Soviet schools were filled, the peasants were bringing the grain to market, the factories were turning out goods, as well as oratory. The exhibits, tho often crude and incomplete, testified to the release of real creative forces in the masses.

We pointed this out to the émigrés, but they were busy weaving fictions for the western democracies, and the facts irritated them. Some became sullen and suspicious, treating us as apostates and traitors to our class. Others fatuously returned to their usual themes: The golden days of Czardom, the "darkness" of the Russian masses, the sheer idiocy of the Bolsheviks.

CHAPTER XIV

THE RED CONVICTS OF CHERM

THE émigrés on our train had many points of conflict. But on one point they agreed: the grave danger lying ahead of us in Cherm, the great penal colony of Siberia.

"Fifteen thousand convicts in Cherm," they said. "Criminals of the worst stripe—thugs, thieves and murderers. The only way to deal with them is to put them in the mines and keep them there at the point of the gun. Even so, it is too much liberty for them. Every week there are scores of thefts and stabbings. Now most of these devils have been turned loose, and they have turned Bolshevik. It always was a hell-hole. What it is now God only knows."

It was a raw bleak morning on the first of May, when we rode into Cherm (Chermkhovo). A curtain of dust, blown up by a wind from the north, hung over the place. Curled up in our compartment half asleep, we woke to the cry, "They're coming! They're coming!" We peered thru the window. Far as we could see nothing was coming but a whirling cloud of dust. Then thru the dust we made out a glint of red, the gray of glittering steel, and vague, black masses moving forward.

Behind drawn curtains, the émigrés went frantically hiding jewels and money, or sat paralyzed with terror. Outside, the cinders crunched under the tread of the hob-nailed boots. In what mood "they?" were coming, with what lust in their blood, what weapons in their hands, no one knew. We knew only that these were the dread convicts of Cherm, "murderers, thugs and thieves"—and they were heading for the parlor-cars.

Slowly they lurched along, the wind filling their eyes with dust and soot, and wrestling with a huge blood-red banner they carried. Then came a lull in the wind, dropping the dust screen and bringing to view a motley crew.

Their clothes were black from the mines and tied up with strings, their faces grim and grimy. Some were ox-like hulks of men. Some were gnarled and knotted, warped by a thousand gales. Here were the cannibal-convicts of Tolstoy, slant-browed and brutal-jawed. Here was Dostoievsky's "House of the Dead." With limping steps, cheeks slashed and eyes gouged out they came, marked by bullet, knife and mine disaster, some cursed by an evil birth. But few, if any, were weaklings.

By a long, gruelling process the weak had been killed off. These thousands were the survivors of tens of thousands, driven out on the gray highroad to Cherm. Thru sleet and snow, winter blast and

summer blaze they had staggered along. Torture-
chambers had racked their limbs. Gendarmes'
sabers had cracked their skulls. Iron fetters had cut
their flesh. Cossacks' whips had gashed their backs,
and Cossacks' hoofs had pounded them to earth.

Like their bodies their souls, too, had been
knouted. Like a blood-hound the law had hung
on their trail, driving them into dungeons, driving
them to this dismal outpost of Siberia, driving them
off the face of the earth into its caverns, to strain
like beasts, digging the coal in the dark, and handing
it up to those who live in the light.

Now out of the mines they come marching up into
the light. Guns in hand, flying red flags of revolt,
they are loose in the highways, moving forward like
a great herd, the incarnation of brute strength. In
their path lie the warm, luxurious parlor-cars—
another universe, a million miles removed. Now it
is just a few inches away, within their grasp. Three
minutes, and they could leave this train sacked
from end to end as tho gutted by a cyclone. How
sweet for once to glut themselves! And how easy!
One swift lunge forward. One furious onset.

But their actions show neither haste nor frenzy.
Stretching their banners on the ground they range
themselves in a crescent, massed in the center, facing
the train. Now we can scan those faces. Sullen,
defiant, lined deep with hate, brutalized by toil. On
all of them the ravages of vice and terror. In all

of them an infinitude of pain and torment, the poignant sorrow of the world.

But in their eyes is a strange light—a look of exaltation. Or is it the glitter of revenge? A blow for a blow. The law has given them a thousand blows. Is it their turn now? Will they avenge the long years of bitterness?

The Comrade Convicts. A hand touches our shoulder. We turn to look into the faces of two burly miners. They tell us that they are the Commissars of Cherm. At the same time they signal the banner-bearers, and the red standards rise up before our eyes. On one in large letters is the old familiar slogan: *Proletarians, arise! You have nothing to lose but your chains.* On another: *We stretch out our hands to the miners in all lands. Greetings to our comrades throughout the world.*

"Hats off!" shouts the commissar. Awkwardly they bare their heads and stand, caps in hand. Then slowly begins the hymn of the International:

> "Arise, ye prisoners of starvation!
> Arise, ye wretched of the earth!
> For justice thunders condemnation,
> A better world's in birth.
> No more tradition's chains shall bind you;
> Arise, ye slaves! No more in thrall.
> The world shall rise on new foundations.
> You have been naught: you shall be all."

I have heard the streets of cities around the world, ringing to the "International," rising from massed

columns of the marchers. I have heard rebel students send it floating thru college halls. I have
heard the "International" on the voices of 2,000
Soviet delegates, blending with four military bands,
go rolling thru the pillars of the Tauride Palace.
But none of these singers looked the *wretched of
the earth.*" They were the sympathizers or representatives of the wretched. These miner-convicts of
Cherm were the wretched themselves, most wretched
of all. Wretched in garments and looks, and even
in voice.

With broken voices, and out of tune they sang,
but in their singing one felt the pain and protest
of the broken of all ages: the sigh of the captive,
the moan of the galley-slave lashed to the oar, the
groan of the serf stretched on the wheel, the cries
from the cross, the stake and the gibbet, the anguish
of myriads of the condemned, welling up out of the
long reaches of the past.

These convicts were in apostolic succession to
the suffering of the centuries. They were the ex-
communicate of society, mangled, crushed by its
heavy hand, and hurled down into the darkness of
this pit.

Now out of the pit rises this victory-hymn of the
vanquished. Long bludgeoned into silence, they
break into song—a song not of complaint, but of
conquest. No longer are they social outcasts, but
citizens. More than that—Makers of a New
Society!

Their limbs are numb with cold. But their hearts are on fire. Harsh and rugged faces are touched with a sunrise glow. Dull eyes grow bright. Defiant ones grow soft. In them lies the transfiguring vision of the toilers of all nations bound together in one big fraternity—The International.

"Long live the International! Long live the American workers!" they shout. Then opening their ranks, they thrust forward one of their number. He is of giant stature, a veritable Jean Valjean of a man, with a Jean Valjean of a heart.

"In the name of the miners of Cherm," he says, "we greet the comrades on this train! In the old days how different it was! Day after day, trains rolled thru here, but we dared not come near them. Some of us did wrong, we know. But many of us were brutally wronged. Had there been justice, some of us would be on this train and some on this train would be in the mines.

"But most of the passengers didn't know there were any mines. In their warm beds, they didn't know that way down below were thousands of moles, digging coal to put heat in the cars and steam in the engine. They didn't know that hundreds of us were starved to death, flogged to death or killed by falling rock. If they did know, they didn't care. To them we were dregs and outcasts. To them we were nothing at all.

"Now we are everything! We have joined the International. We fall in today with the armies of labor in all lands. We are in the vanguard of them all. We, who were slaves, have been made freest of all.

"Not our freedom alone we want, comrades, but freedom for the workers thruout the world. Unless they, too, are free, we cannot keep the freedom we have to own the mines and run them ourselves.

"Already the greedy hands of the Imperialists of the world are reaching out across the seas. Only the hands of the workers of the world can tear those clutches from our throats."

The range and insight of the man's mind was amazing. So amazed was Kuntz that his own speech in reply faltered. My hold on Russian quite collapsed. Our part in this affair, we felt, was wan and pallid. But these miners did not feel so. They came into the breach with a cheer for the International, and another for the International Orchestra.

The "Orchestra" comprised four violins played by four prisoners of war; a Czech, a Hungarian, a German and an Austrian. Captured on the eastern front, from camp to camp they had been relayed along to these convict-mines in Siberia. Thousands of miles from home! Still farther in race and breeding from these Russian masses drawn from the soil. But caste and creed and race had fallen before the Revolution. To their convict miner comrades here in this dark hole they played, as in happier days they might have played at a music festival under the garden lights of Berlin or Budapest. The flaming passion in their veins crept into the strings of their violins and out into the heart-strings of their hearers.

The whole conclave—miners, musicians and visitors, Teutons, Slavs and Americans—became one. All barriers were down as the commissars came pressing up to greet us. One huge hulking fellow, with fists like pile-drivers, took our hands into his. Twice he tried to speak and twice he choked. Unable to put his sentiments of brotherhood into words he put it into a sudden terrific grip of his hands. I can feel that grip yet.

For the honor of Cherm he was anxious that its first public function should be conducted in proper fashion. Out of the past must have flashed the memory of some occasion where the program of the day included gifts as well as speeches. Disappearing for a time, he came running back with two sticks of dynamite—the gifts of Cherm to the two Americans. We demurred. He insisted. We pointed out that a chance collision and delegates might disappear together with dynamite—a total loss to the Internationale. The crowd laughed. Like a giant child he was hurt and puzzled. Then he laughed, too.

The second violinst, a blue-eyed lad from Vienna, was always laughing. Exile had not quenched his love of fun. In honor of the American visitors he insisted upon a *Jazze-Americane*. So he called it, but never before or since have I heard so weird a melody. He played with legs and arms as well as

bow, dancing round, up and down to the great delight of the crowd.

Our love-feast at last was broken in upon by the
clanging signal-bell. One more round of hand-
clasps and we climbed aboard the train as the orchestra caught up the refrain:

> It is the final conflict,
> Let each stand in his place;
> The Internationale—
> Shall be the human race.

There was no grace or outward splendor in this
meeting. It was ugliness unrelieved—except for
one thing: the presence of a tremendous vitality.
It was a revelation of the drive of the Revolution.
Even into this sub-cellar of civilization it had pene-
trated—into these regions of the damned it had come
like a trumpet-blast, bringing down the walls of their
charnel-house. Out of it they had rushed, not with
bloodshot eyes, slavering mouths and daggers
drawn, but crying for truth and justice, with songs
of solidarity upon their lips, and on their banners
the watchwords of a new world.

The Émigrés Unmoved. All this was lost upon the émigres. Not
one ray of wonder did they let penetrate
the armor of their class-interest. Their
former fears gave way to sneers:

"There is Bolshevism for you! It makes statesmen out of jail-birds. Great sight, isn't it? Con-

victs parading the streets instead of digging in the mines. That's what we get out of Revolution."

We pointed to other things that came out of Revolution—order, restraint and good-will. But the émigrés could not see. They would not see.

"That is for the moment," they laughed. "When the excitement is over they'll go back to stealing, drinking and killing." To these émigrés it was at best a passing ecstasy that would disappear with our disappearing train.

Leaning out from the car steps we waved farewell to the hundreds of huge grimy hands waving farewell to us. Our eyes long clung to the scene. In the last glimpse we saw the men of Cherm with heads still bared to the cutting wind, the rhythmic rise and fall of the arms of "Jean Valjean," the red banner with *"Greetings to our Comrades thruout the World,"* and a score of hands still stretched out towards the train. Then the scene faded away in the dust and distance.

. . . . . .

Two years later Jo Redding came back to Detroit after working in Cherm and watching the Revolution working there. He reports its permanent effects. Thefts and murders were reduced almost to zero. Snarling animals became men. Tho just released from irons, they put themselves under the iron discipline of the Soviet armies. Lawless under the old law, they became the writers and defenders of a new law. Men who had so many wrongs of their own to brood over, now assumed the wrongs of the world. They had vast programs to release their energies upon, vast visions to light their minds.

To the rich and the privileged, to those who sit on roof-gardens or ride in parlor-cars, the Revolution is a thing of terror and horror. It is the Anti-Christ. But to the despised and disinherited, the Revolution is like the Messiah coming to "preach good tidings to the poor; to proclaim release of the captives and to set at liberty them that are bruised." No longer can Dostoievsky's convict mutter, "We are not alive, though we are living. We are not in our graves, though we are dead." In the House of the Dead, Revolution is Resurrection.

CHAPTER XV

THE VLADIVOSTOK SOVIET AND ITS LEADERS

THE limits of the Revolution—what were they? We had seen this Revolution, loosed by the city-workers, drive deeper and deeper down, taking ever lower and lower strata of the people within its grip. When it laid hold of the convicts of Cherm it reached bottom. It could go no further vertically. How far could it reach horizontally? Would it prove the same power here in these far-flung outposts on the Pacific that it was back there upon the Atlantic? Would the Revolution show the same strong pulse-beat in these extremities as it did in the heart of Russia?

In a world of Soviets we had moved across the great, slow, north-flowing rivers, the Urals, the *taiga* forests, and the steppes. Trainmen and miners had spoken of their Soviets, peasants and fishermen had greeted us with red banners in the name of theirs. We had conferred with the Soviet of Central Siberia and the Far East Soviet. This whole Amur district was dotted with Soviets. Now, as we stepped from the train at Vladivostok, we were to find a replica of the Soviet we had left at Petrograd, seven thousand miles away.

In six months the Soviet had struck its roots deep into the Russian soil, crowded out all rivals, resisted the shock of every attack, and now held undisputed sway from the Arctic Ocean on the north to the Black Sea on the south, from Narva looking upon the Atlantic all the way to Vladivostok here on its promontory looking into the Pacific.

Vladivostok is a city built on hills, with streets as steep as Alpine paths. But with an extra horse attached to the *droshky's* shafts, we rattled over the cobbles as swiftly as we did along the level wood-paved prospekts of Petrograd. The main highway, *Svetlanskaya,* lies folded up and down across the hills, flanked by the commercial houses of the French and English, the International Harvester, and the buildings of the new rulers of Russia—the Red Fleet, and the Soviet of Workmen's Deputies.

Massive fortresses frowned from all the hills around, but they were harmless as dove-cotes. In the first days of the war they had been dismantled, and the great guns shipped to the Eastern front. A defenseless city, into which extends a peculiar tongue of water called the *Golden Horn.* Here the Allied battleships, uninvited, rode at anchor. Their flags were a welcome sight to the fleeing émigrés at the end of the long Siberian journey. With a sigh of relief here they settled down. Soon, they believed, the Revolution would be over. Then they would return and take up their old life again in Russia.

A City of Refuge for the Émigrés. The city was thronged with evicted landowners, dreaming of their estates, their retinue of servants and the idle feasting of bygone days; officers telling of the former discipline, when soldiers jumped into the gutter at their presence and stood rigid in salute while beaten in the face; speculators longing for the return of the good old times of war profiteering and patrioteering, to the tune of 50, 100 and 500 per cent. Gone are all those gilded fabulous fortunes. The Revolution wrecked them along with the arbitrary power of the officers and the dreams of the landowners.

As a port of exit, Vladivostok was full of Russian émigrés coming out. As a port of entry, it was full of Allied capitalists going in. It was a key to the El Dorado beyond. With its vast unexploited natural riches and labor power, Siberia was a loadstone drawing the agents of capital from around the world. From London and Tokio, from the Paris Bourse and Wall Street, they came flocking hither, lured by dazzling prospects.

But between them and the fisheries, gold-mines, and forests they found a big barrier. They found the Soviet. The Russian workingman refused to be exploited by the Russian capitalist. At the same time he refused to allow his blood and sweat to be minted into bonanza dividends for the benefit of foreign bankers. The Soviet was the instrument of this refusal to all exploiters.

Meeting the same obstacles as the Russian bourgeoisie, the Allied exploiters had the same reaction. They lent a ready ear to the cursings and ravings of their Russian brethren, who saw the Soviet and its members as the very spawn of hell.

It was in this circle that the Allied consuls, officers, Y. M. C. A. and Intelligence men largely lived, moved and had their being. They rarely got outside of it. They were in revolutionary Russia, but out of touch with the Revolution. And quite naturally. Peasants and workers knew little French or English or how to dress well or order dinner.

Not that Allied society was without "information." Their Russian bourgeois friends and their own prejudices gave it to them. Very direct and dogmatic, it passed current in phrases like:

"The Soviet is made up mainly of ex-criminals."

"Four-fifths of the Bolsheviks are Jews."

"These Revolutionists are just ordinary robbers."

"The Red Armies are mercenary and will run at the first shot of a gun."

"The dark, ignorant masses are swayed by their leaders, and their leaders are corrupt."

"The Czar may have had his faults, but Russia needs an iron hand."

"The Soviet is tottering, and will not last longer than two weeks at the outside."

The most cursory investigation would reveal the falsehood of these phrases. One needed but to parrot them, however, to be acclaimed a man of deep insight.

The man who could add, "I don't give a damn what others say about Lenin and Trotzky, I know they are German agents," was hailed as a fellow of spirit, a true soldier of democracy.

There were some honest seekers after light. The genial commander of the Asiatic Squadron was indiscreet enough to invite me to dinner on his flagship the *Brooklyn*. The American Consul also tried hard to break thru the circle of lies. Awaiting word from Washington, however, he withheld visé to my passport. So I was marooned for seven weeks in Vladivostok.

As I grew more and more outspoken in my sympathies with the workers and peasants, the bourgeoisie grew ever more hostile towards me. Thrown now into close contact with the Soviet I had opportunity to observe and share its work, and to count many of its members as my friends.

A Few Students Aid the Soviets. First among these was Constantin Sukhanov. When the March Revolution broke out, he was a student of Natural History in the University of Petrograd. He hastened back to Vladivostok, a Menshevik. After the Kornilov adventure he became a Bolshevik, and an ardent one. He was small in stature, but great in energy. Night and day he toiled, snatching an occasional wink of sleep in a small room above the Soviet, ready at a moment's notice to spring to the saddle or the typewriter. While his face was habitually drawn tight in lines of thought, he would often explode in a contagious burst of laughter. His speech was terse, on occasion flaming. But a bare fire-brand would never have done in such a powder-magazine as Vladivostok. By skill and tact he pulled the Soviet out of many ugly positions, into which its enemies had jockeyed it.

Respected by everybody, even by his bitter political opponents, Sukhanov was chosen President of the Soviet. He was thus the tip of the spearhead that the Bolshevik movement thrust out into the Pacific and the eastern world. He found himself, at 24, facing tasks that would have taxed the resources of a veteran diplomat.

But statecraft was in his blood. His father was a functionary of the old régime, charged with the arrest of Revolutionists. Among those he had found plotting against the Czar were his own daughter, and this son Constantin. Constantin was arrested. Bitter and cynical, the father had faced his son across the table of the tribunal.

It was by grace of his Imperial Majesty, Czar Nicholas II, that the elder Sukhanov had sat in the magistrate's place, with the white, blue and red flag of the autocracy behind the dais. When we

arrived in Vladivostok the red flag of the Revolution had replaced it. Yet we found a Sukhanov sitting in the judgment seat. This time it was the
son, Constantin, now President of the Vladivostok
Soviet by grace of their Republican Majesties, the
worker, peasant, and sailor citizens of the Russian
Soviet Republic.

Curious reversal of the Revolution! Just as
the younger Sukhanov had been caught conspiring
against the rule of the Czar, now Sukhanov, the
elder, was found plotting against the rule of the
Soviet. Once more across the tribunal the two
men faced each other: father against son, Counter-
Revolutionist against Revolutionist, Monarchist
against Socialist. But this time the son was the
judge, the father the culprit. Once only was Constantin Sukhanov derelict in his revolutionary duties.
He refused to imprison his father!

Sukhanov's constant aide was the student Sebertsev. There were also three girl-students (*kursists*),
Zoya, Tanya and Zoya, respectively, secretaries of
the Bolshevik Party, the Finance Department, and
the Soviet organ, *"The Peasant and Worker";* and
respectively daughters of an officer, a priest and a
merchant. Their bourgeois life they entirely re-
nounced. They became one with the proletarians.
With proletarian incomes they thought in proletarian terms. They lived like proletarians. Their
home now was two bare rooms which they called

"the Commune." For beds they had soldier-cots, straw-pallets laid on planks instead of springs.

These students fitted the picture of the Russian student of tradition. One night, when the strain of trying to talk in the Russian language was tying my tongue and brain into knots, Sebertsev said: "We have all been to the university, we can talk in Latin!" But how many American college graduates can read even the Latin on their diplomas? These Russian students not only talked Latin, but submitted Latin verses for my approval. I made a strategic retreat upon Russian!

Leaders Out of the Rank and File. Outside of these students the members of the Vladivostok Soviet were workingmen—mechanics, longshoremen, railwaymen, etc. But they were Russian workingmen; while using the hammer, the sickle and axe, they had used their brains. For this the heavy hand of the Czar had fallen on them. Some had been jailed, others driven out as wanderers over the earth.

From exile they returned at the call of the Revolution. Utkin and Jordan came back from Australia, speaking English; Antonov from Naples, speaking Italian.

Melnikov, Nikeferov and Preminsky emerged from their prison-cells speaking French. This trio had turned their jail into a university. They had specialized in mathematics, and now were experts in calculus, plotting graphs as well as they had plotted revolution.

Seven years they were bound together in jail. Now they were free, each to go his own way. But the long hard years had forged around their hearts ties more binding than the iron chains around their limbs. They were together in death, and now in life they could not be divided. In mind, however, they were much divided, expounding their rival creeds to each other with terrific energy. Yet, however wide afield they went in theory, in action they were a unit. Melnikov's party did not then support the Soviet, but his two comrades did. So he followed them into the service of the Soviet, as Commissar of Post and Telegraph.

In the soul of Melnikov had been waged some big battle, which put furrows deep in his face, and left deep in his eyes the marks of pain. But in that face victory and a great serenity were written. His eyes sparkled, and a smile always flickered on his lips. When things grew blacker he smiled the more.

Little help the Soviet got from the intelligentsia. They declared a boycott against the Soviet until the workingmen should completely change their program. In open meeting they proclaimed a policy of sabotage.

Bitter and sarcastic was the retort shot back by a miner: "You pride yourselves on your knowledge and skill! But where did you get it? From us. At the price of our sweat and blood. In school and university you sat at your desks while we slaved in the dark of the mines and the smoke of the mills. Now we ask you to help us. And you say to us: 'Give up *your* program and take our program: then we will help you.' And we say to you: 'We will not give up our program. We shall get along without you.' "

Supreme audacity in these workingmen, tyros in government, taking over the administration of a territory large as France and rich as India, beset by hordes of scheming imperialists, challenged by a thousand tasks!

CHAPTER XVI

THE LOCAL SOVIET AT WORK

THE Vladivostok Soviet had taken power without shedding a drop of blood. That was easy. But the task now facing it was hard—terribly hard and complex.

The first problem to grapple with was the economic. The dislocation of industry thru war and Revolution, the homecoming of the soldiers, and the employers' lockouts, filled the streets with the workless. The Soviet saw the menace of these idle hands and started to open the factories. The management was placed in the hands of the working-men themselves, and credit was furnished by the Soviet.

The leaders voluntarily limited their own wages. By decree of the Central Russian Soviet the maximum salary of any Soviet official was fixed at 500 rubles a month. The Vladivostok commissars, pointing out the lower cost of living in the Far East, scaled theirs down to 300 rubles a month. After this, when anyone felt the itching desire for a fatter pay-envelope, he was liable to be asked: "Do you want

more pay than Lenin or Sukhanov?" This was un-
answerable.

Soviet Organizes
Industry.
As soon as the workmen found the
factories in their hands there came a
change in their morale. Under Kerensky the tendency was to elect
lenient foremen. Under their own government, the
Soviet, they elected foremen who put discipline into
the shop and raised production. The first time I
met Krasnoschekov, the head of the Far East
Soviet, he was pessimistic.

"For every word I say to the bourgeoisie against
their sabotage," he said, "I say ten to the workingmen against their slackness. But I believe a change
is coming."

When I saw him the end of June, 1918, he was in
happy mood. The change had come. Six factories,
he said, were producing more than ever before.

In the so-called *"American Works,"* the wheels,
frames and brakes of cars, shipped from the United
States, were assembled, and the cars sent out over
the Trans-Siberian Railway. These shops had been
hotbeds of trouble, one disturbance following on
the heels of another. The 6,000 workmen on the
payroll had been turning out but 18 cars a day.
The Soviet Committee closed the plant and reor-
ganized the shops, reducing the force to 1,800 men.
In the underframe section, instead of 1,400 there
were now 350; but by means of short-cuts intro-

duced by the workers themselves, the output of that department was increased. Altogether, the 1,800 men on the new payroll were now turning out 12 cars a day—an efficiency increase of more than 100 per cent per man.

One day I was standing with Sukhanov on the hills overlooking the shops. He was listening to the clank of cranes, and the stamp of trip-hammers ringing up from the valley.

"That seems to be sweet music to your ears," I said.

"Yes," he replied, "the old Revolutionists used to make a noise with bombs. This is the noise of the new Revolutionists, hammering out the new social order."

The strongest ally of the Soviet was the Union of Miners. It organized the unemployed into little Soviets of 50 and 100, equipped them, and sent them out to the mines along the great Amur. These enterprises were highly successful. Each man was panning out from 50 to 100 rubles of gold a day. The question of pay arose. One of the miners unearthed the slogan: "To every man the full product of his labors." It at once achieved tremendous popularity with the miners, who declared their loyalty to this basic Socialist principle. Nothing, they said, could induce them to depart from it.

The Soviet held a different view. There was a deadlock. Instead of using the historic method of settling the dispute by bombs and troops, the work-ingmen fought it out on the floor of the Soviet. The miners capitulated to the logic of the Soviet. Their wages were fixed at 15 rubles per day, with a bonus for extra production. In a short time twenty-six *poods* (there are 36 pounds in a pood) of gold were accumulated at headquarters. Against this reserve the Soviet issued paper money. The seal was a sickle and a hammer, and the design showed a peasant and a worker clasping hands, with the riches of the Far East streaming out over the world.

The Soviet fell heir to a white elephant in the shape of the *"Military Port."* This was a huge plant built for military and naval purposes—a monu-ment to the inefficiency of the old régime. It had carried on its payroll as fine a line of grafting offi-cials and favorites as ever decorated an establish-ment of the Czar. The barnacles on the ships of the Volunteer Fleet were a consequence of those on the payroll. The Soviet immediately scraped off these eminent barnacles, but retained the old man-ager as chief technician. The proletarians recog-nized the necessity of experts and not finding them in their own ranks, they were ready to pay big sal-aries for them. The working-class set out to buy brains just as the capitalists had always done.

The Committee shifted the production of the *Military Port* to implements of peace. They intro-duced a system of strict accounting. This showed that the new plows and rakes were being produced at higher cost than the same articles could be imported from abroad. They then set to work to change the machinery and speed it up. Machines and ships were brought in for repairs. When a contract was not completed at the end of the eight-hour day, the foreman would state the condition of the work and the extra hours required. The men, taking new pride in fast work, often voted to stick by the job, even if it took all night. With this went a vote of increase of pay to the foreman.

Under the old administration most of the workers lived from one to three hours' journey from the factory. The Committee started the building of new workers' quarters. Numerous devices were introduced to save time and energy. The long line of employes, waiting in turn to receive their pay envelopes, was abolished by appointing one man to receive the pay for every two hundred.

Unfortunately among the men elected was one who could resist everything but temptation. Having received the two hundred pay envelopes, he started out to distribute them. Then he thought better of it. No one knows how it happened. Some of the men said that some bourgeois devil must have whispered into the ears of this weak comrade, and driven from his mind all thought of his family, his shop, and the Revolution. At any rate he was found later beside some empty vodka bottles with his pockets empty, too. When he recovered from his happiness he was brought before the Shop Committee and charged with breach of revolutionary honor and treason to the *Military Port.*

The Grand Session of the Revolutionary Tribunal was held in the main shop, with 150 men on the jury. The verdict was "Guilty!" The jury was asked to vote on one of the three following sentences: (1) Summary dismissal. (2) Dismissal, with wages to his wife and children continued. (3) Pardon and reinstatement.

Proposition number two was carried, thus attaching a definite stigma to the culprit's dereliction, but at the same time saving his family from hardship. This did not bring back the money to the unfortunate two hundred, so the fifteen hundred voted to divide among themselves the loss of the two hundred.

In their new experiments the workingmen made many costly blunders. But their verdict upon the Soviet as a whole was that it had made good. Toward the mistakes of the Soviet they took the same attitude a man takes toward his own mistakes—a very lenient one.

Out of their experience the workers gained confidence. They found that they could organize industry; they found they could increase production, and with the Soviet daily entrenching itself in the economic field they began to fell a sense of elation. They would have been still more elated had it not been for their enemies, constantly launching fresh attacks against the Soviet.

Soviet Organizes an Army. As soon as the shops were running well, the men would have to drop tools and take up rifles; the railroads, instead of carrying food and implements, had to carry ammunition and troops. The workmen, instead of strengthening the new institutions, had to rally to defend the ground on which they stood.

Raids were continually directed against the frontiers of the workingmen's republic. As soon as the enemy broke thru the cry went up "The Socialist Fatherland is in danger!" Into every village and factory hurried the call to arms. Each formed its little detachment, and along the roads and trails they marched up into the Manchurian Mountains, singing revolutionary hymns, and folk songs of the village. Poorly equipped and poorly fed, they advanced to pit themselves against a merciless, well-equipped foe. Just as Americans today cherish the memory of the tattered barefoot troops of Washington, who left their blood-stained prints on the snows of Valley Forge, so in the future Russians will thrill to the story of those first ragged groups of Red Guards who, at the call of danger, grasped their guns and went forth to the defense of the Soviet Republic.

Beside the Red Guards were rising the units of the

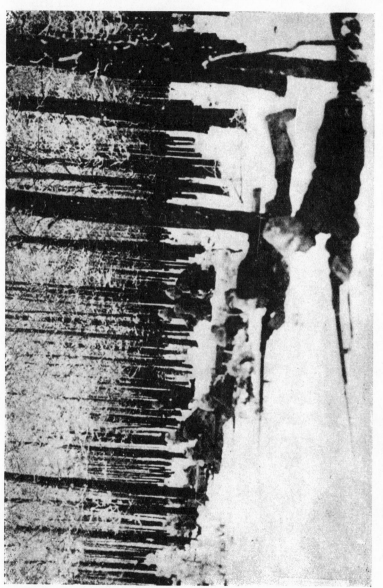

White troops moving forward in Siberia.   In the attempt to strangle the Soviets a steel ring of bayonets,   thousands of versts long, was thrown around Russia.

One of the terrible Red Guards.   I spent several days with this band of 700
peasants fighting against the Whites " For Land and Freedom."

new Red Army. It was an International Army. All peoples were represented, including platoons of Czechs and Koreans. Around the camp-fire the Koreans would say: "We will fight for you now, for your liberty: some day you will fight with us against Japan for our liberty." Among the officers were the Czech Captain Murovsky, Lenin's nephew Popov, and Abramov, who had served two years with the British.

In discipline the Red troops were inferior to the regular national armies. But they had an *élan* which the others lacked. I talked much with these peasants and workers, who for weeks had been lying out on the rain-drenched hillsides.

"Who made you come, and what keeps you here?" I asked.

"Well—millions of us dark people had to go out and die for the government of the Czar in the old days," they replied. "Surely we should be cowards if we didn't go out and fight for a government that is all our own!"

There were certain gentlemen who didn't have this view of the Soviet. Quite the opposite. They wanted the Russian peasants and workers to have a very different sort of government. In fact they themselves claimed to be the one true and only government of Russia.

In grandiose phraseology they laid claim to sovereignty over the territory extending from the Golden Horn of the Far East to the Finnish Bay in the

West, and from the White Sea in the north to the Black Sea on the south. While these gentlemen were not very modest, they were most discreet. They did not set foot upon any of their vast domains. Had they ventured to do so they would have been locked up as common criminals, by the government really functioning—the Soviet.

From the safe confines of Manchuria they issued their glowing manifestos. There all the conspiracies against the Soviet were hatched. After the defeat of Kaledin, the Counter-Revolutionists, egged on by foreign capital, put their hopes in the Cossack Semyonov. Under him were organized regiments of Hun-Huz bandits, Japanese mercenaries, and monarchists rounded up from ports down along the Chinese coast.

Semyonov declared that with an iron fist he was going to drive decency and common sense into the Bolsheviks. He announced his objective as the Urals, 4,000 miles away, then a descent upon the Muscovite plain, with Petrograd opening its gates, and the whole countryside rising up to welcome him.

Raising his standards amid great plaudits from the bourgeoisie, he crossed over into the Siberian border twice, and twice came hurtling back again. The people did rise up to meet him. Not with flowers, however, but with guns and axes and pitchforks.

The Vladivostok workers helped in this defeat of Semyonov. After five weeks they came back bronzed, tattered and foot-sore. But they came back victors. The working-class turned out to acclaim their fellow-proletarians in arms. There were flowers, speeches and a triumphal march thru the city. This victory put great elation in their hearts. But not in the hearts of the bourgeois and Allied onlookers. It was evident that in the military field the Soviet was growing stronger.

Soviet Educates the People. In the realm of culture the creative force of the Revolution succeeded in establishing a People's University, three workmen's theatres and two daily papers. The *Peasant and Worker* was the official Soviet organ. It featured an English department edited by Jerome Lifschiz, a young Russian-American. The *Red Banner*, the Communist Party organ, carried long academic articles. Neither was a masterpiece of journalism, but both were voices of the inarticulate masses, reaching out for the things of the mind and spirit.

While the Revolution was primarily a drive for land, and bread, and peace, it was more than that. I remember a session of the Vladivostok Soviet, when one of the Right was making a furious attack upon the Soviet, scoring the cutting down of food rations:

"The Bolsheviks promised you lots of things, but they didn't give them to you, did they? They promised you bread, but where is it? Where is the bread that . . . ?" The words of the speaker were drowned in a storm of whistles and hisses.

Man does not live by bread alone. Neither does the Soviet live by satisfying merely the hunger of the stomach, but the hunger of the spirit.

All men crave fellowship. "For fellowship is heaven, and lack of it is hell," said John Ball to the English peasants in the fourteenth century. The Soviet was like a great family in which the lowest man was made to feel his human worth.

All men crave power. In the Soviet, workingmen felt the joy of being arbiters of their own destiny, masters over a vast domain. A workingman is like any other human being. Having tasted power he is loth to let it go.

All men crave adventure. In the Soviet men embarked upon a supreme adventure—the quest for a new society based on justice, the building of the world anew.

All men have a spiritual passion. It needs only to be aroused. The Revolution stirred up even the dull, complacent peasant. It gave him the impulse to read and write. One day an old *mujik* appeared in the Children's School.

"Children, these hands cannot write," he said, holding them up, toilworn and calloused, "they cannot write because the only thing the Czar wanted them for was to plough." As the tears flowed down his cheeks he said, "But you, the children of a new

Russia, you can learn to write. Oh, that I might begin again as a child in our new Russia!"

Workingmen as Diplomats. The workingmen had captured the ship of state. Now they had to steer it along a labyrinthine channel, thru uncharted waters, the Allies constantly striving to sink it on the rocks.

Rebuffed by the Allied consuls, the Soviet turned to China with overtures of friendship. The Chinese had been so atrociously treated by the Czar that they could not understand any Russian government addressing them in a kindly manner. They thought it was a new species of trickery. But the Soviet backed its fair words with fair deeds. Chinese citizens were placed upon the same footing as other foreigners. Chinese boats were allowed to ply upon the rivers. The Chinese began to feel that a Russian government looked upon them not as an inferior race, to be cursed and bled, but as human beings. They sent their emissaries to the Red Army, saying:

"We know that we have no right to allow the cut-throats and adventurers of Semyonov to mobilize upon our territory. We know that the Allies have no right to make us put an embargo against you. We want our foodstuffs to go to Russian workmen and peasants."

A general conference was held in June at the frontier in Grodekovo. The Chinese were greeted in their own language by Tunganogi, a daring brilliant lad of 21, the incarnation of the spirit of young, revolutionary Russia. The delegates of these two races, representing one-third of the population of the globe, sat down together to work out the problem of living together in peace and co-operation.

It was not a Versailles Conference of old men cooped up in a gilded chamber: crafty, suspicious, duelling with words and phrases. These were young men, open-minded and open-hearted, meeting under the open sky in brotherhood. Yet it was not a welter of emotion in which reality was lost. They faced the issues squarely: the danger of swamping Russia with a yellow tide, the lower standard of coolie labor, etc. But it was all done frankly, generously, fraternally. As Krasnoschekov, chairman of the Russian delegation, said:

"The Chinese and Russian masses are true children of Nature, uncorrupted by the vices of Western civilization, unversed in diplomatic deceit and intrigue."

Yet, on this very day, while delegates from these two great child races were reaching out to one another in an effort for mutual understanding, the foreign diplomats—behind their backs—in Harbin and Vladivostok, were plotting to hurl these two peoples at each other's throats. They were planning to use Chinese troops in a raid upon Siberia, and to smash the Soviets.

PART IV

THE TRIUMPH OF THE REVOLUTION

THE SOVIETS AGAINST THE CAPITALIST WORLD

CHAPTER XVII

THE ALLIES CRUSH THE SOVIET

WHY this animus of the Allies against the Soviets? Why not regard Russia as a vast laboratory experiment?" someone once asked an American banker. "Why not let these visionaries try out their socialistic schemes? When their dream becomes a nightmare, when their Utopia collapses, you can point to it always as an example of the horrible failure of Socialism."

"Very good," was the reply, "but supposing it isn't a failure? Then where are we?"

Failure is what the Allies prayed for, and eager-eyed, they watched for Soviet collapse. But it did not come. It was precisely this that enraged the Allies. The Soviet was showing signs of success. It was creating not disorder, but order—not chaos, but organization. It was entrenching itself in the economic and military fields. In the cultural and diplomatic fields it was pressing forward. Everywhere it was consolidating its gains.

The Soviet stood straight across the pathway of the Imperialists. If it continued to grow in power their plans would be completely shattered. They could no longer hope for a free hand in the exploitation of the immense resources of Russia.*

So the crushing of the Soviet was decreed. Now, before it should become too strong and lusty, it must be smashed.

Counter-Revolution Uses the Czechs. The Czecho-Slovaks were the instrument chosen to administer the death-blow. Unwittingly they were being groomed by their French officers for this job. Regiments of these seasoned troops were strategically strung out along the Trans-Siberian line. Vladivostok held 17,000 of them armed, fed, and transported hither by grace of the Soviets.

The French said that transports were coming to take them to the Western battle-front. Week after week it was announced that the boats were on the way. But no ships came. The French had never intended to ship the Czechs away. They intended to use them here in Siberia to smash the Soviet.

The Czechs were already restless, fretting with inaction. They had a deep hereditary hatred of the Austro-Germans. The French told them that there

---

* "What we are witnessing now in Russia is the opening of a great struggle for her immeasurable raw materials."—*Russia,* the magazine of Anglo-Russian finance, May, 1918.

"In the city events are shaping more and more towards an international suzerainty over Russia modelled on the British plan in Egypt. Such an event would transform Russian bonds into the cream of the international market."—*London Financial News,* November, 1918.

were tens of thousands of Austro-Germans in the Red Army. Adroitly playing upon their patriotism, the French pictured the Soviets as friends of the Austro-Germans, and enemies of the Czechs. So they engineered friction, and got them ready for the assault upon the Soviets. The methods of attack were adapted to the place.

Here in Vladivostok surprise was deemed essential. The plan was to get the Soviet off guard, and then spring a sudden *coup*. To do this the Soviets must be hoodwinked with a show of friendship. This business was delegated to the British. Dropping their hostile front, they assumed toward the Bolsheviks an attitude of amiability.

With frank, engaging air the Consul confessed to a former antagonism to the Soviets, and the backing of Semyonov. Now that the Soviet had proved its right to live, the British would lend their aid. To begin with, they would cooperate in the importation of machinery. Following this, on Friday afternoon, June 28th, 1918, two genial officials called to present their respects to Sukhanov, bringing the information that wireless messages received on H. M. S. *Suffolk* would be daily handed to the Soviet for publication in its papers.

The editors, particularly Jerome, were jubilant. They came down to Russian Island, urging me to come up and celebrate the capitulation of the Allies. Good reason for their rapture! It had been a hard-up-hill pull, plodding thru the murk and the night.

Now suddenly the clouds break, and the sky shines blue.

Next morning at eight-thirty a thunderbolt comes out of the blue! It strikes Sukhanov, sitting in his Soviet office. It is an ultimatum in the name of the Czechs. It calls for the unconditional surrender of the Soviet. All offices are to be evacuated. All soldiers are to proceed to the High School field, and lay down their arms. The time limit is thirty minutes.

Sukhanov, rushing to Czech headquarters, begs for permission to call the Soviet together.

"Certainly, if you can do it in half an hour," coolly replies the Czech commander.

As Sukhanov turns to leave, he is placed under arrest.

All this goes on behind the scenes. The city remains in the dark. One or two commissars only have a hint of the tragedy now so imminent. On Svetlanskaya, near the Red Fleet Building, I meet Preminsky having his shoes blacked.

"Getting all shined up early in the morning," I say.

"Yes," he replies casually, lighting a cigarette. "In a few minutes I may be dangling from a lamppost, and I want to be as nice looking a corpse as possible." I stare at him wondering, quizzical.

"Our days are done for," he explained, still nonchalant and smiling, "The Czechs are taking over the city."

Even as he speaks the end of the street is filling with troops. So are the side-streets. In all quarters soldiers are moving, in boats from across the bay, in launches from the battleships. Down from the hill above and up from the piers below, like a dense fog the army of Interventionists rolls in upon the city. The open spaces are seething with soldiery, heavily armed, loaded with grenades, huge ominous-looking things. Enough explosives to pulverize the whole city!

The occupation proceeds swiftly, like clock-work, according to plan.

The Japanese seize the powder-magazine, the British the railroad station. The Americans throw a cordon around the consulate. The Chinese and others take up lesser points. The Czechs converge upon the Soviet building. They encircle it from all sides. With a loud "Hurrah,"—they rush forward, and go crashing thru the doors. The Red Flag of the Socialist Republic is pulled down, and the red, white and blue flag of autocracy is run up. Vladivostok passes into the hands of the Imperialists.

"The Soviet has fallen," a hoarse shout goes up in the street, and runs like wildfire thru the city. The patrons of the Olympia Café, rushing out into the street, burst into yells, flinging up their hats, cheering the Czechs. The Soviet and all its works is a cursed thing to them. It is fallen. But that is not enough. They would obliterate every trace of it.

Before them, wrought out in flower-beds edged with stone, is the design which spells SOVIET OF WORKMEN'S DEPUTIES. Vaulting the iron fence, they kick away the stones, stamp thru the flowers, plunging their hands deep into the soil in order to extirpate the last root and vestige of the odious symbol.

Their blood is up now. Their appetites are whetted. They want something animate to vent their rage upon.

The Bourgeois Cry for Reprisals. Spying me in the throng, they raise a great hue and cry: "Immigrant! Swine!" (*Amerikanskaya Svoloch*) they yell. "Kill him! Choke him! Hang him!" The mob of speculators converges on me, brandishing fists and cursing.

But the ring of men forming next to me makes no attempt to lay hands on me. Why, I wonder? They are partisans of the Soviet. Seeing my peril, they have wormed their way in between me and these would-be lynchers, forming a kind of protective pocket.

A low voice whispers, "Head for the Red Fleet Building. Walk, don't run." Pushed and jostled by the crowd behind, I steer my course toward the Red Fleet Building. Opposite its portal I hear the word "Run!" I slip thru the door, and escape in its labyrinths, leaving my pursuers disputing with the Czechs below.

In the front of the building I find a third story window that overlooks the city. From this vantage-point I can see and still be unseen. Up and down below me stretches Svetlanskaya, boiling now like a cauldron. This street, which twenty minutes earlier had been so placid in the shining morning sun, is now a riot of people and color and sound. Blue-jacketed Japs in white puttees, English marines with the Union Jack, khaki-clad Czechs, with green and white, marching and counter-marching, cut currents thru the eddying throng, each moment growing greater.

Thru the bourgeois quarters the glad tiding "The Soviet has fallen" spreads with magic swiftness. From boudoir, café, and parlor, in silks and smiles, they hasten forth to celebrate. Svetlanskaya becomes a grand promenade, brightly splashed with gay plumes and petticoats and parasols.

Some of the toilettes are elaborate. Fortunate ladies! Tipped off in advance they had time to adorn themselves. The officers, too, blossom out in full regalia—gold braid and epaulets, jangling spurs —and much saluting. They make escorts for the ladies, or form into marching squads. There are hundreds of them. One wonders how Vladivostok could have held so many.

And so many bourgeois! Well-kept, rotund gentlemen with avoirdupois enough to qualify as cartoons of themselves. They hail each other, faces beaming, clasping one another's hands, embracing and kissing, exclaiming "The Soviet is fallen" as tho it were an Easter greeting. Two big fat *chinovniks,* almost apoplectic with joy, try to fall upon one another's bosom, but their expansive abdomens are in the way. In their efforts to embrace, clutching at one another, they bid fair to burst themselves.

With incredible swiftness a complete change passes over this city of the proletarians. It becomes a city of the well-fed and well-groomed, their shining faces exultant, congratulating one another, praising God and the Allies, and cheering the Czechs.

Poor Czechs! These cheers embarrass and mortify them. Their heads hang in shame, meeting a Russian workingman. Some indeed refuse point-blank to go into this garroting of a workingman's government. None of them relish the job of crucifying other workmen to make a carnival for the bourgeoisie. And the bourgeoisie want more than a holiday with bands and streamers. They want a Roman holiday with blood and victims. They want vengeance and retribution on these workmen who have forgotten their station in life.

"Now, we will put them in their proper places," they exclaim. "We will put them on the lamp-posts. It's red these birds admire, is it? Very well, we shall give them all they want of their favorite color. We'll draw it from their veins!"

They urge the Czechs to violence. They want a part in it themselves. They point out the foremost

workmen and denounce them. They know where
the commissars are to be found, and lead the way
into office and workshop.

Very busy also is a crew of rat-faced, swart-faced
creatures—spies, provocators and pogromists of the
old régime. Swarming out of their holes and now
come into their own again, they seek by excesses
against the Bolsheviks to ingratiate themselves with
the bourgeoisie. Like weasels they penetrate everywhere, even into the building where I am.

Suddenly screams, curses, and the sound of pounding feet break out on the stairs above. Four men
invading the party-offices on the top-floor have laid
hold of Zoya. Single-handed she resists them, fighting back every inch of the way. By twisting her
arms, pummeling and pushing her, they drag her
down into the street and march her off to prison.
Such scenes are repeated thruout the city. Commissars and workmen are busy at their tasks in
office, shop and bank. The doors are flung open.
They are pounced upon, and dragged out into the
highway.

Thru the center of the highway a narrow lane is
opened. Thru this channel, the captives, manacled
or gripped by their captors, are prodded along by
revolver-butt, and bayonet-point. Hoots, jeers and
catcalls ring in their ears. Clenched fists are thrust
in their faces. Some are spat upon and beaten by
the mob which surges into the passageway blocking
their progress.

An extra outburst of rage breaks on the head of the Commissar of Banks. He has touched them directly in their vital center—their pocket-nerve. They yell, and hoot, and would tear him limb from limb. A white flannelled gentleman, red-faced with fury, breaks thru the Czech guards, brandishing a revolver, grabs the commissar by his arms, and stalks on beside him, howling like an Indian.

One by one the commissars are shoved along this corridor of scowling faces, derisive and hate-contorted. Their own faces by contrast are strangely serene and calm. Some are pallid, but on the whole they are dauntless, almost debonair. They are alert, terribly interested in everything. These men have tasted life. They have run its gamut, from prison-dungeons to high affairs of state. So many adventures have been theirs. What new surprise lies before them around the turning? The most thrilling of all, perhaps the final one. If so, let it come. Death has little terror for them. Long ago when they gave themselves to the Revolution, that matter was disposed of. Then they put all they had, their lives included, into its keeping.

They were conscripts of the Revolution. When it called—they came. Where it sent them—they went. What it exacted—they performed, obedient, unquestioning. Under the Czar, the Revolution had called them to the task of agitators. Under the Soviet it drafted them to the post of commissars. At the call of the Revolution they had yielded up leisure, com-

fort, health, and found joy therein. Now they were
being summoned to yield up their lives. In the
supreme sacrifice might they not find the supreme
joy?

All this was certainly written upon the face of
Melnikov. Thru this thunderstorm of foes—hiss-
ing, roaring, and howling—he came smiling thru
like a shaft of sunshine. *Svetlanskaya* means "The
Lighted Way." Always for me it will be lit with the
countenance of this workingman. About him there
was something celestial, transcendent. Climbing up
the hill, buffeted, jeered and spat upon, he was
strangely like the figure of another Workingman,
toiling thru another hostile multitude, up another hill
—long ago.

Only this was no "Via Dolorosa." It was a "Way
of Triumph," with Melnikov coming up like a con-
queror. His face was wreathed in smiles. His
sparkling eyes were still more sparkling, his features
more radiant than ever. A hoarse voice shouted
"Scoundrel! Hang him!" Melnikov only smiled.
A heavy fist struck him in the cheek. He smiled
again. It was the smile of one lifted above the base
passions of the mob, far beyond reach of its blows
and jeers. It was a smile of pity for the haters.
Could Melnikov have been aware of the power in
that smile? The silent conquests it made that day
in the hearts of his beholders? It was a magnet
drawing the hesitant and wavering, into the camp of
the Revolution. At the same time it was a sword,

wreaking havoc in the camp of the Counter-Revolutionists.

They could not abide this smile of Melnikov and the laugh of Sukhanov. They were irritated and haunted by them. The bourgeoisie would have liked to strike these young men dead in the streets. But they did not dare do it—yet. The commissars were not killed but jailed.

The Soviet Is Submerged. The Allies for the present are against any wholesale massacre of the workers. They are anxious to make intervention appear in the guise of a crusade for democracy, welcomed by all the people. Not yet has it unmasked itself as stark Czaristic reaction. Vladivostok, in the Allied plan, is to be the foothold for the spring upon Siberia. They do not want that foothold too slippery with blood. In the hinterland, in the back regions of Siberia, peasants' and workers' blood may flow in torrents. But not in this seaport town, exposed before the eyes of the world. A few Red Guards and workers are shot down in their tracks. But there is no general blood-spilling. The suddenness of the onslaught, the overwhelming masses of troops, have smothered the Soviet.

At one point only did the Soviet forces have a chance to rally. That was near the water-front, the rendezvous of the *gruzchiki,* longshoremen, stevedores, coal-heavers, loaders of ships. They were of peasant origin, huge shaggy fellows, heavy-muscled for their heavy work. The intricate problems of state and politics they did not comprehend. But one simple fact they did comprehend. Whereas once they were slaves, now they were free! From the status of beasts they had been raised to the status of men. And they knew that the Soviet had done this.

Now they see the Soviet in peril. Rushing into the nearby Red Staff Building, they bolt and bar the doors, and barricade the windows, taking their posts, rifles in hand, ready for the assault. At all costs they will hold this ground for the Soviet.

The odds against them are one hundred to one. Two hundred freight-handlers pitted against twenty thousand seasoned troops. Revolvers against machine-guns. Rifles against cannon. But on the side of this garrison of *gruzchiki* is the flame of the Revolution. It has fired the spirits of these coal-heavers, outwardly so gross and sluggish. They grow fearless, swift, and daring. All afternoon the ring of steel and flame around them grows denser and closer. They watch it undaunted, refusing every call to capitulate. And as night begins to fall, their guns are still blazing from the windows.

In the shadows a Czech crawls close up, and hurls an incendiary bomb thru a window of the building, setting it afire. The citadel of the longshoremen threatens now to become a funeral-pyre. Enveloped in flame and smoke they grope and stumble into the street, hands raised in surrender.

Some are slaughtered, some are clubbed into insensibility. The rest are marched away to prison.

Resistance is crushed. The Soviet is annihilated. The Allies congratulate themselves upon the success of the *coup*. The bourgeoisie are in transports of delight. Lights flame from the windows of the great houses and restaurants. From the cafés come snatches of song, and the throb of the orchestra. The merrymakers are laughing, dancing, cheering the Allied uniforms. From the churches breaks forth the clanging, chiming, pealing, booming music of the bells—the priests within offering up prayers for the Czar. From the decks of the battleships the bugles call across the waters of the bay. The city gives itself up to revelry and rejoicing.

But not in the workingmen's quarters. There is silence, broken only by the sobbing of women. Behind drawn curtains they are laying out their slain. From a nearby shed comes the sound of hammering. The men are joining rough planks together, making coffins for their comrade dead.

Intervention in Russia begins—the Allied armies crush the Vladivostok Soviet. The *Stars and Stripes*, the French *Tricolor*, the *Union Jack*, and the *Rising Sun* flag of Japan flying from the Czech Building.

The *Red Funeral*—the protest of the unarmed masses against Intervention. Coffins of the longshoremen slain in defense of the Soviet carried through the streets on the way to the American Consulate.

CHAPTER XVIII

THE RED FUNERAL

IT was the Fourth of July. I was standing on the Kitaiskaya looking down upon the holiday flags on the *Brooklyn*, the American battleship in Vladivostok Bay. Suddenly I heard a faraway sound. Listening, I caught the strains of the Revolutionary Hymn:

> "With hearts heavy and sad we bring our dead,
> Who shed their blood in the fight for freedom."

Looking up, I saw on the crest of the hill the first lines of some vast procession. It was the funeral of the *gruzchiki* (longshoremen) killed four days before in the siege of the Red Staff Building.

To-day the people, rising out of their grief and terror, were coming forth to bury these defenders of the fallen Soviet. Out of the workmen's quarters they streamed, jamming the street, not from curb to curb, but from wall to wall. They came billowing over the hilltop by thousands until the whole long slope was choked with the dense, slow-moving throng, keeping time to the funeral march of the revolutionists.

257

Up thru the gray and black mass of men and women ran two lines of white-bloused sailors of the Bolshevik fleet. Above their heads tossed a cloud of crimson standards with silvered cords and tassels. In the vanguard, four men carried a huge red banner with the words: *"Long Live the Soviet of Workmen's and Peasants' Deputies! Hail to the International Brotherhood of the Toilers!"*

A hundred girls in white, carrying green wreaths from forty-four unions of the city, formed a guard of honor for the dead *gruzchiki.* The coffins with the red paint still wet upon them, were borne upon the shoulders of their comrades. The music crashed out by the Red Fleet Band was lost in the volume of song that rose from the seventeen thousand singers.

Here was color and sound and motion. But there was something else, a something which compelled fear and awe. I had seen a score of the great processions of Petrograd and Moscow, peace and victory and protest and memorial parades, military and civilian, impressive as only Russians could make them.

But this was different.

From these defenseless poor, stripped of their arms, and with sorrowing songs bearing off their dead, there came a threat more menacing than that from the twelve-inch guns of the Allied Fleet, riding in the harbor below. It was impossible not to feel it. It was so simple, so spontaneous and so elemental. It came straight out of the heart of the people. It

was the people, leaderless, isolated, beaten to earth,
thrown upon its own resources, and yet, out of its
grief, rising magnificently to take command of itself.

The dissolution of the Soviet, instead of plunging the people into inactive grief and dissipating
their forces, begot a strange, unifying spirit. Seventeen thousand separate souls were welded into one.
Seventeen thousand people, singing in unison,
found themselves thinking in unison. With a common mass will and mass consciousness, they formu-
lated their decisions from their class standpoint—
the determined standpoint of the revolutionary
proletariat.

The Czechs came, offering a guard of honor. *"Ne
noozhno!"* (It is not necessary!) the people replied.
"You killed our comrades. Forty to one you fought
against them. They died for the Soviet and we are
proud of them. We thank you, but we cannot let
the guns which shot them down guard them in their
death!"

"But there may be danger for you in this city,"
said the authorities.

"Never mind," they answered. "We, too, are not
afraid of death. And what better way to die than
beside the bodies of our comrades!"

Some bourgeois societies came, presenting memorial wreaths.

"Ne noozhno," (it is not necessary), the people
answered. "Our comrades died in a struggle against
the bourgeoisie. They died fighting cleanly. We

must keep their memory clean. We thank you, but we dare not lay your wreaths upon their coffins."

The procession poured down the Aleutskaya Hill, filled the large open space at the bottom, and faced up toward the British Consulate. Nearby, on the left, was a work car with a tower for repairing electric wires. Whether it was there by design or accident I do not know. Presently it was to serve as a speaker's rostrum.

The band played a solemn dirge. The men bared their heads. The women bowed. The music ceased and there was a silence. The band played a second time. Again there was the bowing and baring of heads and again the long silence. And yet there was no speaker. It was like a huge Quaker meeting in the open air. And just as a sermon has no place in Russian public worship, so here a speech was not essential to this act of public devotion. But should some one from the people feel the impulse to speak there was the platform awaiting him. It was as if in the pause the people were generating a voice.

At last out of the crowd one came and climbed upon the high platform. He had not the gift of oratory but his frequent iteration, "They died for us. They died for us," touched others to utterance.

First came a peasant, bronzed and bearded and in peasant costume. He said: "All my life has been one of toil and fear. . . . Pain and torture and killing without end we had in the dark days of the Czar. Then the morning of the Revolution came and these terrors passed away. Workingmen and peasants were very happy and I was happy too. But suddenly in the midst of our rejoicing came this blow. Once more all is night around us. We can not believe it; but here before our eyes, dead and cold, lie our brothers and comrades who fought for the Soviet. And in the north other comrades are falling before the guns. We listen and strain to hear the sound of the peasants and workers of other lands coming to the rescue. But it is in vain. All we can hear is the sound of the guns in the north."

As he finished, against the blue sky appeared a figure in white. A woman had climbed upon the platform. At the behest of the crowd she began to speak:

"All thru the past we women have seen our men led off to the wars while we wept at home. Those who ruled told us that it was right and for our glory. Those wars were far away and we did not understand. But our men here were killed before our eyes. This we can understand. And we understand that in it there was neither right nor glory. No, it was a cruel, heartless wrong and every child born of the mothers of the working-class shall hear the story of this wrong."

Most eloquent of all was a lad of seventeen, the secretary of a league of young Socialists. "We were students and artists and such kind of people. We held ourselves aloof from the Soviet," he said. "It seemed to us foolish for workmen to govern without the wisdom of the wise. But now we know that you were right and we were wrong. From now on we shall stand with you. What you do we will do. We pledge our tongues and pens to make known the wrongs that you have suffered the length and breadth of Russia and thruout the world."

Suddenly the word went thru the throng that Constantin Sukhanov had been paroled until five o'clock and that he was coming with counsels of peace and moderation.

While some were affirming his coming and others were denying it, he himself appeared. He was quickly passed along upon the shoulders of the sailors. In a storm of cheers he climbed the ladder and came out upon the platform-top, smiling. . . .

Twice his eyes swept across that field of upturned faces filled with trust and love, awaiting the words of their young leader.

As if to avert the flood of tragedy and pathos that beat suddenly upon him from every side, he turned his head away. His eyes fell for the first time upon the red coffins of the men who had been slain in defense of his Soviet. That was too much. A shudder passed thru his frame, he threw up his hands, staggered, and would have fallen headlong into the crowd, but a friend caught him. With both hands pressed to his face, Sukhanov, in the arms of his comrades, sobbed like a child. We could see his breath come and go and the tears raining down his cheeks. The Russians are little given to tears. But that day seventeen thousand Russians sobbed with their young leader on the public square of Vladivostok.

A Pledge to the Dead. Sukhanov knew that many tears were an indulgence, and that he had a big and serious task to perform. Fifty feet behind him was the British Consulate, and fifty rods before him were the waters of the Golden Horn with the frowning guns of the Allied Fleet. He wrenched himself away from his grief and gathering himself together began his message. With an ever mounting passion of earnestness he spoke, closing with words destined to become the rallying cry for the workers in Vladivostok and the Far East:—

"Here, before the Red Staff Building where our comrade *gruzchiki* were slain, we swear by these red coffins that hold them, by their wives and children that weep for them, by the red banners which float over them, that the Soviet for which they died shall be the thing for which we live, or, if need be, like them die. Henceforth the return of the Soviet shall be the goal of all our sacrifice and devotion. To that end we shall fight with every means. The bayonets have been wrested from our hands, but when the day comes and we have no guns, we shall fight with sticks and clubs, and when these are gone, then with our bare fists and bodies. Now it is for us to fight only with our minds and spirits. Let us make them hard and strong and unyielding. The Soviet is dead. Long live the Soviet!"

The crowd caught up the closing words in a tremendous demonstration, mingled with the strains of the "International." Then that haunting *"Funeral Hymn of the Revolution"* at once so plaintive and triumphant:

"You fell in the fatal fight
   For the liberty of the people, for the honor of the people.
   You gave up your lives and everything dear to you.
   The time will come when your surrendered life will count.
   The time is near: when tyranny falls, the people arise, great
      and free.
   Farewell, brothers, you chose a noble path,
   At your grave we swear to fight, for freedom and the people's
      happiness."

A resolution was read proclaiming the restoration of the Soviet, the objective of all the future struggles of the revolutionary proletariat and peasants of the Far East. At the call for the vote seventeen thousand hands shot into the air. They were the hands which had built the cars and paved the streets, forged the iron, held the plough, and swung the hammer. All kinds of hands they were: the big, rough hands of the old *gruzchiki,* the artisans', deft and sinewy, the knotted hands of the peasants, thick with callouses, and thousands of the frailer, whiter hands of the working women. By these hands the riches of the Far East had been wrought. They were no different from the scarred, stained hands of labor anywhere in all the world. Except in this regard:

for a time they had held the power. The Government had been within their grasp. Four days ago it had been wrested from their grasp, but the feel of it was still within their hands—these hands raised now in solemn pledge to take that power again.

"The Americans Understand." A sailor striding down from the hilltop pushed thru the crowd and climbed upon the platform.

"Comrades!" he cried joyously, "we are not alone. I ask you to look away to the flags flying over there on the American battleship. You cannot see them down there where you stand. But they are there. No, comrades, we are not alone today in our grief. The Americans understand and they are with us!"

It was a mistake, of course. This was July the Fourth. Those flags had been hung out in celebration of our Day of Independence. But the crowd did not know that. To them it was like the sudden touch of a friend's hand upon a lonely traveler in a foreign land.

With enthusiasm they caught up the cry of the sailor: "The Americans are with us!" And the vast conclave of workers lifting up their coffins, wreaths and banners were once more in motion. They were going to the cemetery, but not directly. Tired as they were from long standing in the sun, they made a wide detour to reach the street that runs up the steep hill to the American Consulate. Then straight up the sharp slope they toiled in a cloud of dust, still singing as they marched, until they came before the Stars and Stripes floating from the flagstaff. And there they stopped and laid the coffins of their dead beneath the flag of America.

They stretched out their hands, crying, "Speak to us a word!" They sent delegates within to implore that word. On the day the great Republic of the West celebrated its independence, the poor and disinherited of Russia came asking sympathy and understanding in the struggle for their independence.

Afterward, I heard a Bolshevik leader bitterly resentful at this "compromise with revolutionary honor and integrity."

"How stupid of them," he said. "How inane of them! Have we not told them that all countries are alike—all imperialists? Was this not repeated to them over and over again by their leaders?"

Truly it had been. But with this demonstration of the Fourth of July the leaders had little to do. They were in prison. The affair was in the hands of, the people themselves. And, however cynical many leaders were about the professions of America, the people were not so. In the hour of their affliction, these simple trusting folk, makers of the new Social Democracy of the East, came stretching forth their hands to the old Political Democracy of the West.

They knew that President Wilson had given his assurance of help and loyalty to the "people of Russia." They reasoned: "We, the workers and peasants, the great majority here in Vladivostok, are we not the people? Today in our trouble we come to claim the promised help. Our enemies have taken away our Soviet. They have killed our comrades. We are alone and in distress and you alone of all the nations of the earth can understand." No finer tribute could they offer than to come thus, bringing their dead, with the faith that out of America would come compassion and understanding. America, their only friend and refuge.

But America did not understand. The American people did not even hear a word about it. These Russian folk do not know that the American people never heard about it. All they know is that a few weeks after that appeal came the landing of the American troops. They united with Japanese troops, marching into Siberia, shooting down peasants and workers.

And now these Russian folk say to one another: "How stupid we were to stand there in the heat and the dust stretching out our hands like beggars!"

CHAPTER XIX

EXIT

"THE Bolsheviks will be crushed like egg shells," said the wisemen as the Allies started into Siberia. The idea of serious Soviet resistance was ridiculed. The Czar's government, then Kerensky's, had tumbled like a house of cards. Why should not the Soviet government go the same way?

The American Major Thacher has pointed out, why not: The Czar's power was based on his armies; it was only necessary to disintegrate these armies and the Czar fell. The Kerensky government rested in the cabinet; it was only necessary to surround his ministers in the Winter Palace and Kerensky fell. The Soviet government, however, was rooted in thousands of local Soviets—an organism made up of countless cells; to destroy the Soviet government, every one of these separate organizations must be destroyed. And they did not relish destruction.

As the alarm was sounded thru the Far East the peasants and workers rallied against the invaders. They fought fiercely, yielding ground only inch by inch. In the two cities north of Vladivostok the Soviets had been established without the killing of a single person. In overthrowing these Soviets thousands were now killed, and not only the hospitals, but sheds and warehouses were filled with the wounded. Instead of an easy "military promenade thru Siberia" the Interventionists faced a hard bloody conflict.

The Vladivostok bourgeoisie were amazed at the stubborn resistance. Then enraged they turned on all partisans of the Soviet in fury.

I Get Arrested a Little. I had no hankering for martyrdom. So I avoided the main street and went out in disguise or under cover of night. I was an outcast. But that did not grieve me. I was concerned for the manuscript of my book on Russia. It was in the Soviet building—now headquarters of the new White government.

I decided that the only way to get it was to walk brazenly into the enemy's camp and ask for it. I did so and fell straight into the hands of the new Secret Service Chief.

"I've been looking for you. Thank you for coming," he said with mock politeness. "You will stay with us." I was a prisoner of the Counter-Revolution.

Fortunately among the Americans was an old classmate of mine, Fred Goodsell. He negotiated in my behalf and secured my release—but not my manuscript.

Now I ventured to return to my lodgings. Some

spy observing my arrival must have telephoned the Whites. I was busy arranging my papers when an automobile whirled up. Six White Guards jumped out, rushed into the room, and shoving their revolvers into my face, began yelling, "We've got you now, we've got you."

"But I've already been arrested and released," I protested.

"We're not going to arrest you, you damned swine. We're going to kill you," they shouted.

Sudden noise outside again. Another motor-car dashed up. Bang! Another crash at the door! A captain and four more men with rifles careened into the room. They were Czechs declaring they had orders for my arrest.

"But we have already arrested him," said the Whites.

"No," insisted the Czechs. "We're going to take him."

"But we've got him," persisted the Whites.

It was quite thrilling to find myself a person of such sinister importance. My gratification over it was tempered a bit by the sight of the bayonets. There were too many of them—too much readiness to use them. Instead of a captive I might soon be a corpse. Happily the Czech captain had a sense of humor.

"Your wishes in the matter?" he said turning to me with a deep bow. "Whose prisoner do you prefer to be?"

"Your prisoner—the Czechs," I replied.

With magnificent *noblesse oblige* he turned to the Whites. "Gentlemen, he is yours," he declared magnanimously.

He appeased his own soldiers by letting them loose on my papers (they were afterwards delivered to the American Consul).

The Whites hustled me into their automobile and thru the city where a few days earlier I had ridden as a guest of the Soviet, I rode now ringed with bayonets and with two revolvers pressed against my ribs—a prisoner of the Whites.

White headquarters was surrounded by an excited bourgeois mob watching the round up of Reds and hailing each victim with catcalls and cries of "give him the rope." I was pushed thru the jeering crowd into the building and by great good luck straight into the arms of Squersky, a former acquaintance. He motioned me not to recognize him and in due time secured my release. This time I came out with a document which read: *"Citizens—You are requested not to arrest the American Williams."*

Homeward Bound.   But there was little protection in this paper, for black hatred against the Soviet grew from day to day. I had the feeling of a hunted animal and in ten days lost as many pounds. "At any moment you may lose your life," said the American Vice-Consul. "Two parties have sworn to shoot you down at sight."

"I am anxious to leave but I have no money to leave with," I told him. He could see my perplexity, but he could not see that it was any concern of his.

The workingmen heard of my plight and came to my rescue. They were in hard straits but they raised a thousand rubles. The men in jail smuggled out another thousand. Now I was ready to go. But the Japanese Consul refused to visé my passport. He confronted me with a list of my crimes, chief among which were articles against intervention that I had published in the Soviet papers. The Tokio Foreign Office did not like these articles. It had cabled that in no circumstances was my presence to be allowed to pollute the sacred soil of Japan. The Chinese, however, gave me a visé and I booked on a coasting-steamer bound for Shanghai.

My last night was spent with *tovarishe* in a hiding-place in the hills. The Soviet had not been destroyed. It had gone underground. In the secret retreat the leaders yet uncaptured, gathered to plan and organize. In farewell they sang for me the hymn of the English Transport Workers, taught them by Jerome:

> "Hold the fort for we are coming!
> Union men be strong;
> Side by side we battle onward,
> Victory will come."

With these words ringing in my ears on July 11, I sailed past the Allied battleships and out into the

Pacific. I stewed in Shanghai a month before I could get passage for America. At last I got it and eight weeks after I left the Golden Horn of the Far East I sighted the Golden Gate of California.

As our steamer swung to anchor in San Francisco harbor a launch ran alongside and officers in naval uniform climbed aboard. They were members of the American Naval Intelligence sent out to welcome me to the homeland. No prodigal, returning from long rioting in a far country, could have had a warmer reception. Their solicitude for my welfare was most embarrassing. They overwhelmed me with attention, insisted on escorting me to their quarters and tending to all details of my baggage. They assured me of their profound interest in all Soviet affairs and to prove it relieved me of every pamphlet, document and note-book. Their appetite for Russian literature was insatiable. Lest one scrap of it should escape them they looked into my wallet, shoes, hat-band, even the lining of my coat. Likewise they looked into my pedigree, my past and my future. Then they passed me on to other authorities who looked into my ideas.

"Now you are a Socialist, Mr. Williams," said one of my inquisitors. "You are also an Anarchist, aren't you?"

I denied the charge.

"Well, what other beliefs do you hold?"

"Altruism, optimism and pragmatism," I told him.

He duly recorded them in his note-book. More strange and dangerous Russian doctrines being imported into America!

After three days of pleasant *camaraderie*, I was sent on to Washington.

CHAPTER XX

IT was not the revolutionists who made the Russian Revolution. This in spite of hosts of revolutionists who tried their best to make it. For a century gifted men and women of Russia had been agitated over the cruel oppression of the people. So they became agitators. Into the villages, the shops and the slums they went crying:

> "Shake to earth your chains like dew,
> Which in sleep have fallen on you.
> Ye are many, they are few."

But the people did not rise. They did not even seem to hear. Then came that supreme agitator—Hunger. Hunger, rising out of economic collapse and war, goaded the sluggish masses into action. Moving out against the old worm-eaten structure they brought it down. Elemental impersonal forces did what human agencies found impossible.

The revolutionists, however, had their part. They did not make the Revolution. But they made the Revolution a success. By their efforts they had prepared a body of men and women with minds trained to see facts, with a program to fit the facts and with fighting energy to drive it thru. There

275

were a million of them—perhaps more, possibly less. The important thing is not their number, but the fact that they were organized to act as receivers of the bankrupt, old order, as a salvage-corps of the Revolution.

At the core of this were the Communists. H. G. Wells says, "In the vast disorganization an emergency government supported by a disciplined party of perhaps 150,000 adherents—the Communist Party—took control. . . . It suppressed brigandage, established a sort of order and security in the exhausted towns and set up a crude rationing system, the only possible government . . . the only idea, the only solidarity."

For four years the Communists have had control of Russia. What are the fruits of their stewardship?

"Repressions, tyranny, violence," cry the enemies. "They have abolished free speech, free press, free assembly. They have imposed drastic military conscription and compulsory labor. They have been incompetent in government, inefficient in industry. They have subordinated the Soviets to the Communist Party. They have lowered their Communist ideals, changed and shifted their program and compromised with the capitalists."

Some of these charges are exaggerated. Many can be explained. But they cannot all be explained away. Friends of the Soviet grieve over them.

Their enemies have summoned the world to shudder and protest against them.

When I am tempted to join the wailers and the mud-slingers my mind goes back to a conversation on the docks of Vladivostok in June, 1918. Colonel Robins, of the American Red Cross, was talking to Constantin Sukhanov, President of the Soviet.

"If no help comes from the Allies, how long can the Soviet last?"

Sukhanov shook his head ruefully.

"Six weeks?" queried Robins.

"It will be hard to hold on longer," said Sukhanov.

Robins turned to me with the same question. I, too, was dubious about the outlook.

We were sympathizers. We knew the might and the vitality of the Soviet. But we saw also the tremendous obstacles it confronted. And the odds seemed against it.

Forces Ranged Against the Bolsheviks. In the first place the Soviet faced the same conditions that had overwhelmed the Czar and Kerensky governments, i. e., the dislocation of industry, the paralysis of transport, the hunger and misery of the masses.

In the second place the Soviet had to cope with a hundred new obstacles—desertion of the intelligentsia, strike of the old officials, sabotage of the technicians, excommunication by the church, the blockade by the Allies. It was cut off from the grain fields of the Ukraine, the oil fields of Baku, the coal mines of the Don, the cotton of Turkestan—fuel and food reserves were gone. "Now," said their enemies, "the bony hand of hunger will clutch the people by their throat and bring them to their senses." To prevent supply trains reaching the cities, agents of the imperialists dynamited the railway bridges and put emery into the locomotive bearings.

Here were troubles enough to break the strongest souls. But still more were coming. The capitalist press of the world was mobilized against the Bolsheviks. They were pictured as "hirelings of the Kaiser," "red-eyed fanatics," "cold-blooded assassins," "long bearded ruffians running amuck by day, carousing in the Kremlin at night," "profaners of art and culture," "despoilers of women." As a crowning infamy the "Decree for the Nationalization of Women," was forged and broadcasted thru the world. The public was called upon to transfer their hate from the Huns to the Bolsheviks.

While abroad hatred against the Bolsheviks as the new "enemies of civilization" mounted from day to day, these selfsame Bolsheviks were straining brains and sinews to rescue civilization in Russia from total collapse. Watching them at their heart-breaking, back-breaking tasks, Ransome wrote:

"No one contends that the Bolsheviks are angels. I only ask that men shall look thru the fog of libel that surrounds them and see the ideal for which these young men are struggling in the only way in which they can struggle. If they fail they will fail with clean shields and clean hearts, having striven for an ideal which will live beyond them. Even if they fail, they will none the less have written a page more daring than any other I can remember in the story of the human race. . . . When in after years men read that page they will judge your country and my country by the help or hindrance they gave to the writing of it."

This appeal was in vain.

As the monarchists of Europe combined to crush the idea loosed on the world by the French Revolution, so the capitalists of Europe and America combined to crush the idea loosed on the world by the Russian Revolution. To these famished, frozen, typhus-stricken Russians sailed no ships of good will laden with books, tools, teachers and engineers but grim ships of war and transports laden with troops and officers, guns and poison-gas. Landings were made at strategic points on the coast of Russia. Monarchists, landlords and Black Hundreds flocked to these rallying centers. New White armies were conscripted, drilled and equipped with hundreds of millions of dollars of supplies. The Interventionists started their drive on Moscow, seeking to plunge the sword into the heart of the Revolution.

Out of the East rolled the hordes of Kolchak following the trail of the Czechs across Siberia. Out of the West struck the armies of Finland, the Letts and Lithuanians. Down from the forests and snowfields of the North moved the British, French and Americans. Up from the seaports of the South plunged the tanks, aeroplanes and Death Battalions of Denikin. From all points of the compass they came. Out of the Esthonian marshes—Yudenich. Out of Poland—the veteran legions of Peltura. Out of Crimea—the cavalry of Baron Wrangel.

A million-bayonetted ring of steel closed in upon the Revolution. The Revolution staggered under the blows rained upon it, but its heart was undaunted. If it must die—it would die fighting.

The Revolution Fights for Life. Once more in the war weary villages and destitute towns throbbed the drums beating the call to arms. Once more the worn-out lathes and looms were ordered to produce uniforms and rifles. Once more the crippled railways were freighted with soldiers and cannon. Out of the almost exhausted resources of Russia the Revolution armed, uniformed and officered 5,000,000 men and the Red Armies took the field.

Only 400 miles from Moscow they hurled themselves against Kolchak and pushed his panic-stricken forces back the 4,000 miles they had advanced across Siberia. In the pine forests of the North, clad in uniforms of white, sliding thru the snow on skis, they met the Allies and pushed them back on Archangel, forcing them to ship for home across the waters of the White Sea. They stopped the headlong rush of Denikin at Tula, the smithy of Russia, "in whose red fires the red steel is welded into the bayonets of the invincible Red Army." Driven back to the Black Sea shores he escaped on a British cruiser.

Budenny's Cavalry racing day and night across the Ukrainian steppes flung themselves suddenly on the Polish flanks, turned the victorious advance of the legionaries into a disastrous retreat and harried them up to the gates of Warsaw. Wrangel was beaten and bottled up in the Crimea, and while the shock troops of the Soviet hurled themselves against his concrete forts, the main Red Army hurried across the frozen Sea of Azov and the Baron fled to Turkey. In the outskirts of Petrograd, under its very domes, Yudenich was cut to pieces, the armies of the Baltic States were beaten back behind their borders, and the Whites annihilated in Siberia. The Revolution triumphed all around the circle.

The Counter-Revolutionists were broken not only by the heavy battalions of the Soviet, but by the Idea incarnated in these armies of the Revolution.

They were armies with banners, red banners emblazoned with the watchwords of a new world. They advanced into battle singing the songs of justice and fraternity. They treated their captured enemies as misguided brothers. They fed them, bound up their wounds and sent them back to tell in their own ranks stories of Bolshevik hospitality. They bombarded the Allied Camp with questions:

"Why did you come to Russia, Allied Soldiers?" "Why should workmen of France and England murder their fellow-workers of Russia?" "Do you want to destroy our Workmen's Republic?" "Do you want to restore the Czar?" "You are fighting for the bond holders of France, the land grabbers of England, the imperialists of America. Why shed blood for them?" "Why don't you go home?" *

Red soldiers rose up to shout these questions across the trenches. Red sentries with hands uplifted rushed forward crying them out. Red aeroplanes dropped them circling down from the skies.

The allied troops pondered over these queries and were shaken. Their morale broke down. They fought half heartedly. They mutinied. The Whites in tens of thousands—whole battalions and ambulance corps—came over to the Revolution. One after another the armies of the Counter-Revolution crumpled up or melted away like snow in a Russian spring. The great steel cordon tightening around the Revolution was smashed to bits.

The Revolution was triumphant. The Soviets were saved. But with what appalling sacrifices!

Havoc Wrought by Intervention. "For three years," says Lenin, "our whole energy was devoted to the tasks of war." The wealth of the nation was poured into the army. Fields were untilled, machines untended. Lack of fuel shut down the factories. Green wood under the boilers

* Appendix IV. A Bolshevik Circular for British Soldiers.

ruined the locomotives. The retreating armies tore up railway tracks, blew up bridges and depots and fired the grain fields and the villages. The Poles not only destroyed the water-works and electric-station of Kiev, but in sheer malice dynamited the Cathedral of St. Vladimir.

The Counter-Revolutionists turned their retreat into an orgy of destruction. With torch and dynamite they laid waste the land leaving behind a black wake of ruins and ashes.

A host of other evils came out of the war—drastic censorship, arbitrary arrests, drum-head court-martials. The high handed measures charged against the Communists were to a large extent measures of war—none the less they were casualties to the ideals of the Revolution.

Then the human casualties! The death toll at the front was large. The death lists from the hospitals were appalling. Medicines, gauze and surgical instruments could not come thru the blockade. So limbs were amputated without anesthetics. Wounds were bandaged with newspapers. Gangrene and blood poisoning, typhus and cholera swept thru the armies unchecked.

The Revolution could have sustained the further loss in man-power—for Russia is vast. But it could not afford the loss in brain-power and soul-power, the wholesale massacre of its directing energizing spirits—the Communists. It was these Communists who bore the brunt of the fighting. They were formed into shock battalions. They were rushed into gaps to stiffen the wavering lines. Captured they were always killed. In the three years' war half the young Communists of Russia were slaughtered.

A mere recital of casualties means nothing, for statistics are only unemotional symbols. Let the reader recall the young men he has met in the pages of this book. They were at once dreamers and hard workers, idealists and stern realists—the flower of the Revolution, the incarnation of its dynamic spirit. It seems incredible for the Revolution to go on without them. But it does go on. For they are dead. Nearly everyone in this book is now in his grave. Here is the way some of them died:

Volodarsky—assassinated in the general plot to kill all Soviet leaders.

Neibut—executed on the Kolchak Front.

Yanishev—bayonetted by a White Guard on the Wrangel Front.

Woskov—died of typhus on the Denikin Front.

Tunganogi—shot at his desk by White Guards.

Utkin—dragged from motor car and shot.

Sukhanov—led into the woods in the early morning and clubbed to death with rifle butts.

Melnikov—taken out of prison, shot and bludgeoned.

"They were tortured, they were stoned, they were sawn asunder, they were set wandering in deserts and in mountains, in caves and in dens of the earth."

It was a cold selective killing of the keymen of the revolution, a massacre of its future builders. An incalculable loss to Russia—for these were men who could withstand the corruption of office and the poison of power. Men who could live as valorously as they died.

They went to their death in order that the Revolution might live. And it does live. Tho crippled and compromised, out of the long ordeal of famine, pestilence, blockade and war, the Russian Revolution emerges victorious.

Is the Revolution worth these sacrifices? These are its assured results:

One. It has destroyed root and branch the State apparatus of Czarism.

Two. It has transferred the great estates of the crown, the landlords and the monastic orders into the hands of the people.

Three. It has nationalized the basic industries and begun the electrification of Russia. It has fenced off Russia from the unlimited exploitation of freebooting capitalists.

Four. It has brought into the Soviets 1,000,000 workers and peasants and given them direct experience in government. It has organized 8,000,000 workers into trade unions. It has taught 40,000,000 peasants to read and write. It has opened the doors of tens of thousands of new schools, libraries and theatres and roused the masses to the wonders of science and art.

Five. It has broken the spell of the past over a great people. Their potential forces have become kinetic. Their fatalistic: "It was so, and it will be so," is changed to "It was so, but it will *not* be so."

Six. It has assured self-determination to a score of subject races formerly held in vassalage to the Russian Empire. It has given them free hand to develop their own language, literature and institutions. Persia, China, Afghanistan and other backward countries—that is "countries with great natural resources and small navies"—it has treated as equals.

Seven. It has not paid lip-service to "open diplomacy," but has made it a reality. "It has swept the secret treaties into the ash-barrel of history."

Eight. It has pioneered the way to a new society and made invaluable laboratory experiments in Socialism on a colossal scale. It has quickened the faith and increased the morale of the working-classes of the world in their battle for the new social order.

The wise men rise up to point out that these results might have been obtained in a better way. Likewise the Reformation, the Independence of America, the Abolition of Slavery might have been achieved in a more gracious, less violent manner. But history did not move that way. And only the foolish quarrel with history.

APPENDIX I

THE DEATH OF A RED REGIMENT

Interview of Mr. N. Shiffrin with the editor of a military paper of the Counter-Revolutionary army of the North. Published in the anti-Bolshevik daily *Der Tag*, September 7, 1919:

"As you know the Bolsheviks changed the names of the old regiments. The Moscow troops have 'K.L.' on their shoulder straps—the initials of Karl Liebknecht. We captured one of these regiments and they were tried. The trial at the White front is brief. Every soldier is examined, and if he admits that he is a Communist he is immediately sentenced to death by hanging or shooting. The Reds are well aware of this.

"Lieutenant K. approached the captured regiment and said: 'Those of you who are true Communists show yourselves courageous and step forward.' A painfully oppressive interval. . . . Slowly in closed ranks over half of the regiment steps forward. They are sentenced to be shot. But before being shot they must dig their own graves.

"It is twilight. The air is full of the odor of fragrant northern flowers. The green dome of the village church is seen, surrounded by sleepy poplars. Peasants, women, children and soldiers crowd on the field, huddling together like sheep in a storm.

"The condemned are told to take off their clothes. The front is poor and their uniforms are needed by the Whites. In order to save the clothes from being soiled with blood or torn by bullets the prisoners are ordered to undress before they are shot. Slowly the Communists take off their shirts, and tying their clothes together in a bundle they put them aside.

"They stand there in the field, freezing, and in the moonlight their skin appears extremely white, almost transparent. Each of them is given a pick-axe and they begin digging large common graves. The dew is falling like a mild drizzle and there is a tear in every eye. The naked Communists keep on digging. It is getting darker and darker. There is a chaos of restlessly moving limbs. It is hard to distinguish the naked from the dressed.

"At last the graves have the necessary depth. The condemned sigh from weariness. Many throw themselves on the soft wet ground and rest. It is their last repose. Only now I notice that many have bandages around their feet. They have already been wounded in the struggle.

"Lieutenant K. asks them to state their last wish. Two take thin rings off their fingers and give them to the Lieutenant. The others have no wishes to make, altho every one of them has a home, a wife, children, relatives. I ask one of them 'What made a Communist of you?'

"He replies: 'The accursed life! The world needs happiness.'

"The firing squads are holding their rifles ready to shoot. The naked Communists take their positions close to one another, forming a white wall in the moonlight. . . . There is a command, a flash and the sound of rifles. . . . The Communists are still standing erect. A second volley rings out. The bullets strike home in their hearts, thick blood streams leap into space. Some are only slightly wounded. And in the fraction of a second before the soldiers shoot again, I hear deep sickening groans. Volley follows volley. Now those who are still alive cry out: 'Ho there, take better aim!' One points to his heart, crying, 'Aim here!'

"Finally, all are dead. Some are lying near the edge of the graves, others have fallen into them. It is all over. Nothing disturbs the quiet."

II

THE TRAIN OF DEATH

This is part of the diary of Mr. Rudolph Bukely, a Red Cross worker, formerly a banker in Honolulu. It reveals the conditions

A soldier of the Red Army captured by the Whites. He confesses he is a Communist and is bound to a stake to be shot.

Some of the Bolshevik prisoners on the *Train of Death*, 2,000 of whom were shot, starved, or frozen to death.

following Allied Intervention in Siberia, and shows the atrocities of White Terrorists against Bolsheviks and even innocent people. It is abbreviated from the *American Red Cross Magazine* of April 1919 which says: "Propriety has demanded the exclusion of much that is unprintable."

"It is the eighteenth day of November, 1918. I am at Nikolsk-Ussurisk in Siberia. In the past two days I have seen enough misery to fill a life-time. I will try to set down in my own manner what I have seen.

"I have seen, through the windows of box-cars forty animals who once were human men, women and children; faces glared at me which I could not recognize as human beings. They were like beasts' faces, of a species unknown to man. Stark madness and terror stared from their eyes, and over all the unmistakable signs of death.

"I have seen the dead lying along the roadside, and fifty or sixty men fighting like dogs for pieces of bread thrown to them by the sympathetic poor people of Nikolsk. . . .

"This '*train of death*,' for by that name all Eastern Siberia now knows it, left Samara about six weeks ago in charge of Russian officers. It had on board at that time 2,100 prisoners of all sorts.

"Since that day 800 of these wretches have died from starvation, filth, and disease. There were, as near as we could count, 1,325 men, women, and children penned up in these awful cars yesterday.

"It seems a wicked thing to say, but the thought has surely come to me that to kill these people painlessly would require perhaps three dollars' worth of poison or ten dollars' worth of ammunition; and yet for weeks this train of fifty cars has been wandering, driven on from station to station, every day a few more corpses being dragged out. Many of these people have been in box-cars for five weeks in their original clothing. There are from 35 to 40 in a box-car, measuring say 25 by 11 feet, and the doors have seldom been open save to drag out the bodies of the dead, or some woman who might better be. I have climbed into these cars at night with my flashlight. I have seen men with the death rattle in their throat, half naked, with lice and vermin visible on them; others just lying in a semi-unconscious stupor; and others with the whining grin of imbeciles, holding out their hands for a few cigarettes or kopecks, chuckling with glee like apes upon being given them.

"The Russian officer in charge of the train has made inconsistent statements about the reasons why these people have been subjected to such awful deprivation and abuse. He tries to make the best story of it possible. . . . Often for days at a time there has been no one to give them even bread. Were it not for the kindness of the poor villagers who, with tears running down their cheeks, give them what little they can afford, they would be absolutely without nourishment.

"It is impossible to tell in print the story of the unfortunate women imprisoned here. They are treated better than the men. You all know why. In one car are 11 women. On the inside of the car hangs a piece of string. On it are four pairs of stockings owned by these 11 women. The floor is covered with refuse and filth. There are no means of cleaning it, neither brooms nor buckets. They have not taken off their clothing for weeks. All around the sides of the cars run two rows of planks, on which the inmates sleep at night and sit hunched up by day. If there ever is any official food for the prisoners, these women get the first pick and their physical condition is much better.

"Since we arrived a cooking car has been put on the train, with a large iron kettle, and yesterday the guards claim to have given the prisoners a little soup. One kettle for 1,325 people, and soup passed through a window a foot by a foot and a half, by means of an old rusty can! Yesterday one of the women was taken out by a Russian officer. He will return her when the train pulls out. . . . As we walked past the train, a man hailed us from one of the cars and the guards were told that there were dead inside. We insisted on the door being opened and this is what we saw:

APPENDIX 291

"Lying right across the threshold was the body of a boy. No coat, merely a thin shirt, in such tatters that his whole chest and arms were exposed; for trousers a piece of jute bag pinned around him, and no shoes or stockings. What agony that boy must have suffered in the Siberian cold before he died of filth, starvation, and exposure!

"And yet 'diplomacy' prevents us from taking charge and giving aid. But we are holding the train!

"We climbed into the car and found two other dead lying on the second tier of bunks amongst the living. Nearly every man was sunken-eyed, gaunt, and half clad. They were racked by terrible coughing. They had the stamp of death on them. If aid does not come quickly they will die. We looked into a few cars only, but at one window we saw a little girl perhaps eleven years old. Her father, she said, had been mobilized into the Red Guard. So now father, mother, and child are on that train and will die there. Dr. Rosett is one of the most beautiful characters that I have ever known. When I saw him in the car talking to these poor wretches and trying to comfort them, I could not help thinking of the Good Physician and how He, too, labored among the maimed, the halt and the blind.

". . . . It is a strange thing that they all look at you with an expression sorrowful in the extreme, but never with a trace of bitterness. Suffering seems to have destroyed in them the power to express anger. I have visited the train at least ten times and I have never as yet seen any expression of any kind pass over the faces of these poor, tortured, dumb creatures.

"I went into the hospital last night. Fourteen were lying on the filthiest straw imaginable. Three of them turned their dull eyes on me, recognized the Red Cross uniform and got upon their poor worn knees. One of them, an old man of sixty, had a silver crucifix hanging around his neck. They sobbed soundless, body-racking sobs, and said in Russian, 'May God and Jesus Christ bless you and keep you for what you have done for us.' We felt absolutely repaid for all our work of these days, during which time I have not bathed or shaved, nor had my clothes off, for I have dropped exhausted on my bed when I have finished transcribing my notes, and it was time to sleep. . . .

"There is no use disguising the fact that these people are nearly all going to die, for as soon as the train shall have pulled out the old conditions will return and there will be once more the corpses thrown out day by day."

Mr. Bukely's prophecy that the death train would still be a death train was fulfilled. It went on over the Trans-Siberian, first west then east, back and forth, driven from town to town, the authorities at each place refusing to allow the prisoners to be taken out of the train or the train to remain within its jurisdiction.

On and on, days and nights, weeks running into months, the wretched company ever dwindling as death takes its cruel and incessant toll. [*This was but one of many trains of death run by the anti-Bolshevist governments.*]

III

THE BURIAL OF YANISHEV

The Moscow *Izvestia* of July 15, 1920, says:

"On July 13 the Moscow proletariat buried Comrade Mikhail Petrovich Yanishev under the Kremlin wall. The first speaker, the Chairman of the Moscow Soviet, L. B. Kamanev said:

" 'Of the many men who gave all to the cause of the working-class, Comrade Yanishev was one of the truest. Wherever there was call for an honest, brave and energetic man, Yanishev was sent. Recently he was appointed Chairman of the Moscow Revolutionary Tribunal. He was ordered to leave that responsible post and sent to the front against Denikin. On the way to the Western front he was ordered to the defense of South Russia from the bands of Wrangel. Tho wounded in the shoulder he did not leave his place in the front lines, but continued leading his division forward until the treacherous hand of a White Guard brought him down with a bayonet. He is dead. But the cause for which Comrade Yanishev gave his life will not die. His blood was not spilt in vain. Many others will carry on the struggle and bring it to a victorious finish.'

"Comrade Likhachev spoke and the ceremony ended with a salute of three guns."

IV

A BOLSHEVIK CIRCULAR FOR BRITISH SOLDIERS

Why have you volunteered to come to Russia?

Why? Is it that you like war so much? Do you enjoy this rolling in mud and blood? Do you get satisfaction from seeing mangled bodies, and wrecked towns and villages? You claim to be the representatives of a civilized race! Is this how you propose to bring civilization into Russia?

Or is it that you feared being out of work and came to Russia as a form of employment? Were you tempted by the increased pay and extra rations? If that is so, it is strange employment for men who have just finished a war for "lasting peace."

Does it not strike you that what you are getting for your work is sheer *Blood Money?* It is the kind of work that cut-throats, blackguards, thieves and hooligans undertake to do for money. If these are the reasons for which you came, it is not much use appealing to your reason and humanity. The only argument that we can effectively use against you is the bullet and bayonet, and you will find that the Red Army will give you all you want of that. You will find your job "soft" enough when you find yourself sucked in the mud, in the marshes and forests of Northern Russia.

We cannot believe, however, that the majority of you volunteered for these reasons. Probably you were induced by the lies circulated by the capitalist press about the anarchy and terror prevailing in Russia. Probably you have been induced to believe that Bolsheviks are devils, who must be destroyed in order that the peace of the world may be secured. If that is so, we are convinced that when you learn the truth about Russia.

you too will refuse to be the executioners of the Russian people, just like the British troops you replaced in the Caucasus, and the French and foreign troops in other parts who have refused.

There is no anarchy in Russia except that which the capitalist governments of the Allies are creating by invading Russia. *You are not allaying anarchy, you are creating it. You are not bringing order in a country which is accused of disturbing the peace of the world, you are commencing a new war.*

You are simply the tools of the capitalists and landlords in your countries who have sent you here to "punish" the Russian workers and peasants for having dared to revolt against their oppressors. The Russian Soviet Republic is a Workers' and Peasants' Republic. The land and the wealth of Russia now belong to the working-people of Russia. You have been brought here to overthrow the power of the workers and restore Czarism, landlordism and capitalism. Your governments are officially supporting the Czarist officers, Kolchak and Denikin, with arms and money for the avowed purpose of restoring the old régime. And you are not merely helping, you are doing this.

Without your aid, the counter-revolution in Russia would have been suppressed long ago, the civil-war would have been ended and order restored. And the Russian people would have long ago had the opportunity of developing their agriculture and industry.

Volunteers! You are workingmen too. What interests have you in fighting for the gang of Russian counter-revolutionaries and international capitalists? As workingmen, your business should be to support your fellow-workers in those places where they succeed in taking power, for the victory of the workers in one country is a step toward the emancipation of the workers in all countries.

In fighting the Russian workers, you are *Scabbing;* your fellow-workers at home, knowing the real reason of your being sent here, are preparing for a general strike against intervention in Russia. In continuing to do the work of your government, *you are Scabbing on your fellow workers at home.*

Comrades! It is dirty work you are doing. Have the courage
to pitch it. Do not let it be said that English workingmen were
so mean and contemptible as to suppress their own fellow-workers
for the sake of a little extra money and food.

Comrades! Do not be scabs. Stand by your class in the great
world movement for the emancipation of labor.

V

YESTERDAY AND TODAY

By Maxim Gorky

Yesterday was the day of the Great Falsehood—the last day
of its power.

For ages, man has, spider-like, thread by thread, diligently
woven the strong cobweb of a cautious philistine life, impreg-
nating it more and more with falsehood and greed. Man fed
on the flesh and blood of his fellow men. The means of production were used to oppress men,—this cynical falsehood was
regarded as immutable truth.

And yesterday this road brought mankind to the madness
of the great World War. In the red glow of this nightmare
the ugly nakedness of this old falsehood was brought to light.
Now we see the old world shaken to its foundations. Its hidden
secrets are exposed, and today even the blind have opened their
eyes and see the utter ugliness of the past.

Today is the day of reckoning for the falsehood which reigned
yesterday.

The violent explosion of the people's patience has destroyed
the outworn order of life, and it cannot again be re-established
in its old forms. Not all of the outworn past is annihilated, but
it will be—tomorrow.

Today there is a great deal of horror, but it is all natural and
comprehensible. Is it not natural that people infected by the
strong poisons of the old order—alcohol and syphilis—should not
be generous? Is it not natural for people to steal,—if theft was

the fundamental law of yesterday? Is it not natural, that tens, hundreds, thousands of men should be killed, after being accustomed for years to kill them by millions? The seed of yesterday brings the fruit of today.

We should understand that in the midst of the dust and mud and chaos of today, there has already begun the great work of liberating mankind from the strong, iron cobweb of the past. It is as painful and difficult as the pangs of a new birth; but it is the death of the evil of yesterday, going through its last hours together with the man of yesterday.

It has so happened that the peoples marching to the decisive battle for the triumph of justice are led by the least experienced and weakest fighters,—by the Russians, a people of a backward land, a people worn out by its past more than any other people. Only yesterday the whole world looked upon them as semi-barbarians, and today, almost dying from hunger, they are marching toward victory or death with the ardor and courage of veterans.

Everyone who sincerely believes that the irresistible aspiration of mankind toward freedom, beauty, and a sensible life is not a vain dream, but that it is a real force which alone can create new forms of life, the lever which can move the world,—every honest man must recognize the universal significance of the activity now carried on by the earnest revolutionists of Russia.

The Revolution should be interpreted as a gigantic attempt to incorporate in life, the great ideas and watchwords created and enunciated by the teachers of mankind. Yesterday the Socialist thought of Europe pointed the way to the Russian people; today the Russian worker is striving for the triumph of European thought.

If the honest Russian revolutionists, few in number, surrounded by enemies and exhausted by starvation, shall be conquered, the consequences of this terrible calamity will fall heavily on the shoulders of all the working class of Europe.

The Russian worker is confident that his brothers in spirit will not permit the strangling of the revolution in Russia, that they will not permit the resuscitation of the order, which is expiring and which will disappear,—if the revolutionary thought of Europe will comprehend the great tasks of today.

Come and go with us towards the new life, whose creation we work for without sparing ourselves and without sparing anybody or anything. Erring and suffering, in the great joy of labor and in the burning hope of progress, we leave to the honest judgment of history all our deeds. Come with us to battle against the ancient order and to labor for the new. Forth to life's freedom and beauty!

VI

DECLARATION OF THE RIGHTS OF THE WORKING AND EXPLOITED PEOPLES

(Rejected by the Constituent Assembly, January 18, 1918. Accepted by the great Third Congress of Soviets, January 27, 1918.)

I. RUSSIA is declared a Republic of Workmen's, Soldiers' and Peasants' councils. The whole central and local authority rests with the Councils (Soviets). The Russian Soviet Republic is declared a free alliance of free nations and a federation of national republics.

II. With the object of removing the exploitation of man by man, of preventing the division of society into classes, of mercilessly suppressing all exploiters, of establishing a socialist organization of society and of securing the victory of Socialism in all lands, the Great Convention (Third All-Russian Congress) makes the following declarations:

> (a) With the object of realizing the socialization of land, all private property in the land is abolished, and the whole territory of the Republic is declared the property of the people and is without compensation handed over to the working population on the basis equal rights of utilization for all. All forests, natural wealth and water power of public value, all live and dead stock, model farms and agricultural stations, are declared national property.

(b) As a first step towards the complete transference of factories, mines, railways, and of the means of production and distribution to the possession of the Workers' and Peasants' Republic, the decrees concerning Workmen's Control and concerning the Supreme Council of Public Economy are hereby confirmed.

(c) As one of the conditions for the emancipation of the working masses from the yoke of capitalism, the transference of all banks to the possession of the Workers' and Peasants' Soviet Republic is confirmed.

(d) With the object of removing parasitical elements of society and of securing industrial organization on a public basis, the obligation of every citizen to work is recognized.

(e) In the interests of securing the full authority of the toiling masses and of removing all possibilities of a re-establishment of the power of the exploiters, the arming of the workers, the formation of a Red Army out of workmen and peasants, and the complete disarming of the propertied classes is hereby decreed.

III. With the firm intention of rescuing mankind from the claws of finance-capital and of imperialism, which have flooded the earth with blood in the most criminal of all wars, the Great Convention endorses and confirms the following acts of the Soviet Commissars:

(a) The annulling of the Secret Treaties, the organization of fraternization between the workmen and peasants of the armies now opposing each other in the field, the conclusion at all costs of a democratic peace by the workers themselves, without annexations or indemnities, on the basis of the self-determination of nations through revolutionary means.

(b) The complete break with the barbarous policy of capitalist civilization, which establishes the power of the exploiters in a few select nations at the cost of the enslavement of hundreds of millions of the toiling masses in Asia, in the Colonies and in all small countries.

(c) The recognition of the complete independence of Finland, the withdrawal of the Russian armies from Persia, and the right of self-determination for Armenia.

(d) The annulling of the loans which were concluded by the Government of the Tsar, the foreign banks and the Russian bourgeoisie, as the first blow against international bank and finance-capital.

IV. The Great Convention believes that the time is at hand for the decisive struggle with the exploiters, for whom there is now no place in the organs of government. Power must be now wholly and exclusively in the hands of the toiling masses and of their representative organs—the Soviets of Workmen's, Soldiers' and Peasants' Deputies.

Moscow, Oct. 26th, 1921—The humblest peasant may come to ask the help or advice of Kalinin, the President of the Soviet Republic, with none to bar his way.

Around him come pressing two or three score of men dressed in rough untanned sheepskin or dun-coloured cloth, that hall-mark of the Russian villagers. Some are carrying a sack of food or a bed-roll, token of the long journey they made to lay their case before Kalinin.

He greets his visitors simply and talks to one after another in the same peasant dialect as theirs.

It is hard to realise that here before one's eyes is the secret of the no small Bolshevist hold on the Russian people. More than any of his colleagues, more even than Lenin, Kalinin knows what the peasants think, what they love or hate and what they want.

However impossible it is for him to appease their grievance or satisfy their requests, he contrives somehow to send them away comforted and almost contented. For the man streams magnetism in every word and gesture.

" See, now, little mother," he says persuasively to an old woman who has travelled a thousand miles to ask Kalinin that her village be let off the food tax because the harvest is only half what was estimated, "your crop is only 500 poods instead of 1,000. Then you will pay only 25 poods instead of 55 on each hundred—that is your tax.

"More than that we cannot do, for we must feed our hungry brothers on the Volga, who have no crop at all—you would not have them starve."

The old woman shakes her head strongly and backs away with the evident feeling that somehow she has got the tax reduced 50 per cent, which will be good news for her fellow-villagers.

Next comes a young soldier who claims that as a veteran of the Polish war he should not pay a tax at all.

" But you are a man of Tula," says Kalinin, " and Tula folks, farm as well as they fight. Why I hear Tula has the best crop in Russia. Surely you won't grudge help to hungry brothers not so clever or lucky as you?"

The soldier looks sheepish but sticks stubbornly to his point.

"This is the first year I have been able to sow or reap my own harvest for seven years, Comrade Kalinin. Others reaped while I was fighting to defend them. Now let them pay the tax for me."

The President takes him up like a flash.

"What!" he cries, "Others worked to feed you while you were winning glory?"—he bends forward and touches the red star medal on the youngster's army overcoat—"well, now you, too, must give something to help those who need it."

This time he has struck home. The soldier flushes with pride and, as he shakes the President's hand with a firm grip, he mutters :

"That's only fair, comrade. I will tell the rest of the soldiers of our village what you say, and all will help."

And so it goes. An old man from Tambov and a widow from a village near Moscow get part of their tax remitted because the former is supporting a war-broken son, and the latter, five fatherless little children. And the peasants go back to Russia's myriad villages with a message of good tidings from Kalinin, the new Little Father of the people.

WALTER DURANTY, correspondent, in the *New York Times,* Oct. 29th, 1921.

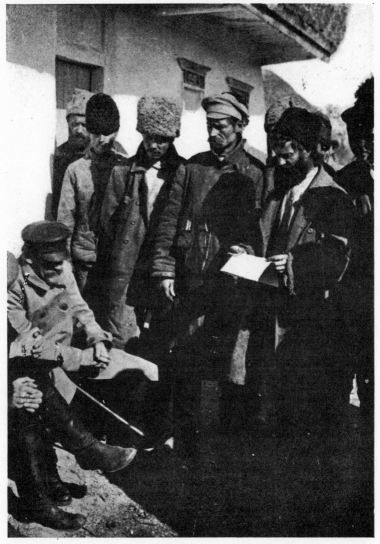

The President of the Soviet Republic is Kalinin—not Lenin. Kalinin is here
seated in front of a village hut conferring with the peasants.

VII

PLACARDS AND POSTERS

Machine-guns played their part in the Revolution. But a bigger part was played by the printing-presses. The Soviet waged a mighty battle with ink as well as lead. Every crisis, every important event, produced its corresponding placard or poster. They were pasted on walls and *kiosks*—one on top of the other—in some places 20 and 30 deep. Arranged in order, they would tell a complete story: *The History of the Revolution in Posters from the Walls of Petrograd and Moscow.*

Six of these posters appear in the foregoing text. Five more are printed in the following pages. (On the left hand page, a facsimile of the original Russian; on the right hand page, in English.)

1. To ALL WORKERS OF PETROGRAD (page 303). An appeal to celebrate the success of the November Revolution—not by strikes and demonstrations, but by quietness and work.

2. THE COMMISSION ON PUBLIC EDUCATION (page 305). The Bolsheviks had the majority in the newly elected Petrograd Duma. They sought to arouse public sentiment in protest against the teachers' strike.

3. PRAVDA (*Truth*) (page 307). Two half-pages of the official Bolshevik newspaper, calling the people to arms against the Germans and Japanese. In issue *No. 33, February 23,* the price is 25 kopecks. In issue *No. 45,* two weeks later, the price is 30 kopecks. The two issues show likewise the change of name in the Party. Note also the double number in the date line, *"23 (10) February."* By Soviet decree the old Julian calendar— 13 days behind the rest of the world—was replaced by the Gregorian calendar.

4. FROM THE SAMARA FEDERATION OF ANARCHISTS (page 309). In order to blacken the Anarchists, it was said that they had declared for the Nationalization of Women. Infuriated at this slander, they put out this hot repudiation. The so-called *"Decree for the Nationalization of Women,"* of course, had no existence anywhere in Russia. Even the most extreme groups never considered the idea. It was a monstrous canard invented by the enemies of the Revolution.

5. THE CRY FOR BREAD (page 311). This is an appeal of the cities to the peasants of the Ukraine and the Volga in 1918. Now it is this Volga region that is stricken with drouth—the worst since 1873. These peasants in turn are appealing for bread.

301

Ко всѣмъ рабочимъ
ПЕТРОГРАДА!

Товарищи! Революція побѣждаетъ—революція побѣдила. Вся власть перешла къ нашимъ Совѣтамъ. Первыя недѣли самыя трудныя. Надо раздавить до конца сломленную уже реакцію, надо обезпечить полное торжество нашимъ стремленіямъ. Рабочій классъ долженъ, обязанъ проявить въ эти дни **величайшую выдержку и выносливость,** чтобы облегчить Новому Народному Правительству Совѣтовъ выполненіе всѣхъ задачъ. На этихъ же дняхъ будутъ изданы новые законы по рабочему вопросу и въ томъ числѣ одинъ изъ самыхъ первыхъ законъ о рабочемъ контролѣ надъ производствомъ и объ регулированіи промышленности.

Забастовки и выступленія рабочихъ массъ въ Петроградѣ теперь только вредятъ.

Мы просимъ васъ немедленно прекратить всѣ экономическія и политическія забастовки, всѣмъ стать на работу и производить ее въ полномъ порядкѣ. Работа на заводахъ и во всѣхъ предпріятіяхъ необходима новому правительству Совѣтовъ, потому что всякое разстройство работъ создастъ для насъ новыя затрудненія, которыхъ и безъ того довольно. Всѣ къ своему мѣсту.

Лучшее средство поддержать новое правительство Совѣтовъ въ эти дни— исполняя свое дѣло.

Да здравствуетъ твердая выдержка пролетаріата! Да здравствуетъ революція!

Петроградскій Совѣтъ Р. и С. Д.
Петроградскій Совѣтъ Профессіональныхъ Союзовъ.
Центральный Совѣтъ Фабрично-Заводскихъ Комитетовъ.

Типографія «Копейка», Петроградъ, Садовая ул. д. соб. домъ.

To All Workers
OF PETROGRAD!

Comrades! The Revolution is winning, the Revolution has won. All the power has passed over to our Soviets. The first weeks are the most difficult ones. The broken reaction must be finally crushed, a full triumph must be secured for our endeavors. The working-class ought to —must—show in these days

THE GREATEST FIRMNESS AND ENDURANCE

in order to facilitate the execution of all the aims of the new People's Government of Soviets. In the next few days, decrees on the Labor question will be issued. Among the very first will be the decree on Worker's Control over the production and regulation of industry.

STRIKES AND DEMONSTRATIONS OF THE WORKER MASSES IN PETROGRAD NOW CAN ONLY DO HARM.

We ask you to stop immediately all economic and political strikes, to take up your work, and do it in perfect order. The work in factories and all industries is necessary for the new Government of Soviets, because any interruption of this work will only create new difficulties, and we have enough as it is. All to your places.

The best way to support the new Government of Soviets in these days—is by doing your job.

LONG LIVE THE IRON TENACITY OF THE PROLETARIAT! LONG LIVE THE REVOLUTION!

Petrograd Soviet of W. & S. D.
Petrograd Council of Trade Unions.
Central Council of Factory-Shop Committees.

(This is the translation of the Russian text on opposite page.)

303

Отъ Комиссіи по Народному Образованію при Центральной Городской Думѣ.

Товарищи рабочіе и работницы

За нѣсколько дней до праздника была объявлена забастовка учащими городскихъ училищъ. Учащія оказались на сторонѣ буржуазіи противъ рабочаго и крестьянскаго Правительства.

Товарищи, организуйте родительскіе комитеты и выносите резолюціи противъ забастовки учащихъ. Обращайтесь въ районные Совѣты Рабочихъ и Солдатскихъ Депутатовъ, профессіональные союзы, фабрично-заводскіе и партійные комитеты съ предложеніемъ устраивать митинги протеста. Устраивайте собственными силами елки и развлеченія для дѣтей. требуйте возобновленія занятій послѣ праздника въ срокъ, который укажетъ Центральная Дума.

Товарищи, укрѣпляйте свои позиціи въ дѣлѣ народнаго образованія, настаивайте на контролѣ пролетарскихъ организацій надъ школой.

Комиссія по Народному Образованію
при Центральной Городской Думѣ.

From the Commission on Public Education of the Central City Duma.

Comrade workingmen and workingwomen!

A few days before the holidays, a strike has been declared by the teachers of the public schools. The teachers are siding with the burgeoisie against the Workers' and Peasants' Government.

Comrades, organize Parents' Committees and pass resolutions against the strike of the teachers. Propose to the District Soviets of Workers' and Soldiers' Deputies, the Trade Unions, the Factory-Shop and Party Committees, to organize protest meetings. Arrange with your own resources Christmas trees and entertainments for the children, and demand the opening of the schools, after the holidays at the date which will be set by the Central Duma.

Comrades, strengthen your position in public education, insist on the control of the proletarian organizations over the schools.

> Commission on Public Education
> of the Central City Duma.

(This is the translation of the Rnssian text on opposite page.)

Россійская Соціаль-Демократическая Рабочая Партія.

Цѣна 28 коп.

ПРАВДА

ЦЕНТРАЛЬНЫЙ ОРГАНЪ Р. С.-Д. Р. П.

Пролетаріи всѣхъ странъ, соединяйтесь!

№ 33 (269), Суббота. ЕЖЕДНЕВНАЯ ГАЗЕТА. 23 (10) февраля 1918 г.

Нѣмецкіе генералы организовали ударные батальоны и врасплохъ, безъ предупрежденія, напали на нашу армію, мирно приступившую къ демобилизаціи.

Но уже сопротивленіе организуется. Оно ростетъ и будетъ рости съ каждымъ днемъ. Всѣ наши силы отдадимъ на отпоръ германскимъ бѣлогвардейцамъ!

Ибо они идутъ, чтобъ вернуть помѣщикамъ отобранныя крестьянами земли. Они идутъ, чтобъ возстановить хозяйскія права и хозяйскій произволъ на фабрикахъ и заводахъ. Они идутъ, чтобъ вернуть бывшимъ помѣщикамъ и хозяевамъ Романовымъ — тронъ, земли и милліарды.

Рабочіе, крестьяне, солдаты! На защиту совѣтской республики! Всѣ, не медля, въ ряды Красной арміи соціализма!

Россійская Коммунистическая Партія (большевиковъ).

Цѣна 30 коп.

ПРАВДА

ЦЕНТРАЛЬНЫЙ ОРГАНЪ КОММУНИСТИЧЕСКОЙ ПАРТІИ (большевиковъ).

Пролетаріи всѣхъ странъ, соединяйтесь!

№ 43 (271), Суббота. ЕЖЕДНЕВНАЯ ГАЗЕТА. 9 марта (24 февраля) 1918 г.

Русскіе контръ-революціонеры, съ княземъ Львовымъ во главѣ, создали на Дальнемъ Востокѣ новое правительство.

Предатели вступили въ союзъ съ японскими имперіалистами, чтобы закабалить страну.

Помѣщики и капиталисты изъ-за возстановленія своей власти надъ рабочими и крестьянами продаютъ Японіи Дальній Востокъ.

Къ оружію, рабочіе и крестьяне! Вставайте всѣ, какъ одинъ человѣкъ, на борьбу за великую революцію!

Всѣ на защиту соціалистическаго отечества!

КЪ ОРУЖІЮ!

Russian Social-Democratic Labor Party.

Price 25 kopecks.
on railroad stations 30 kop.

Workers of all Countries Unite!

TRUTH

CENTRAL ORGAN OF THE R. S.—D. L. P.

Editorial and Main Offices. Petrograd,
Ivanovskaya No. 14

Callers on business
with the editor re-
ceived daily. except holidays from 12 to 1 P. M
and from 7 to 8 P. M.

Office is open daily, except
holidays from 10 A.M. to 4 P.M.
Subscriptions:
From March 1st (new calendar)
6 roubles per month.
10 percent. discount on bundle
orders of not less than 10 copies.
75 kop. charge of change of
address.

Telephone
Editorial Offices } 177-18
400-23
524-86

Subscriptions are accepted
from the 1st to the 1st of the
following month.
Telephone 437-55

No. 33 (259) Saturday   DAILY PAPER   23 (10) February, 1918

German generals organized shock battalions and without warning attacked our army which was peacefully beginning to demobilize.

But resistance is already being organized. It grows and will continue to grow daily. We shall exert all our strength to drive out the German White Guards!

For they come to restore to the landlords the peasants' land. They come to restore the employers' rights and the employers' arbitrary rule over the mills and the factories. They come to restore the Romanovs who are both landlords and employers— their throne, their estates and their billions.

Workers, Peasants and Soldiers! To the Defense of the Soviet Republic! All, to the ranks of the Red Army of Socialists!

Russian Communist Party (Bolshevik).

Price 30 kopecks.
at railroad stations 35 kop.

Workers of all Countries Unite!

TRUTH

CENTRAL ORGAN OF THE COMMUNIST
PARTY (BOLSHEVIK).

Editorial and Main Offices. Petrograd,
Ivanovskaya No. 14

Callers on business
with the editor re-
ceived daily, except holidays from 12 to 1 P. M
and from 7 to 8 P. M

Office is open daily, except
holidays from 10 A.M. to 4 P.M.
Subscriptions:
From March 1st (new calendar)
6 roubles per month.
10 percent. discount on bundle
orders of not less than 10 copies.
75 kop. charge of change of
address

Telephone
Editorial Offices } 177-18
400 23
524-86

Subscriptions are accepted
from the 1st to the 1st of the
following month.
Telephone 437-53

No. 45 (271) Saturday   DAILY PAPER   March 9 (Feb. 24) 1918

Russian counter-revolutionists, with prince Lvov at the head, have formed a new government in the Far East.

The Traitors have allied themselves with Japanese Imperialists in order to enslave the country.

The landlords and capitalists in order to restore their rule over the workers and peasants are selling the Far East to Japan.

To arms, workers and peasants! Arise all as one man and fight for the great revolution!

All to the defense of the socialist fatherland!

TO ARMS!

(This is the translation of the Russian text on opposite page.)

307

ОТ САМАРСКОЙ ФЕДЕРАЦИИ АНАРХИСТОВ

ПО ПОВОДУ „ДЕКРЕТА".

Враг безсилен. Враг падает ниже и ниже. И в своем падении кощунствует. И в своем падении клевещет. И пускается на самыя отвратительныя провокационныя меры.

Враг угнетенных — он жаждет господства, и страшнее всех для него анархисты, поднявшие знамя явной свободы.

И враг распространяет злостную клевету, что свобода эта простирается до насилия женщин. От нашего имени распространяет он своими грязными руками «Декрет о социализации женщин».

Какая грубая, нелепая провокация!

Веками, везде и повсюду анархисты борются со всякими декретами и законами всяких властей, — так могут ли они сами выпускать декреты?

Враги всякаго насилия, — могут ли анархисты требовать или даже допускать принудительнаго отчуждения женщин?

Сколько же найдется таких буридановых ослов, что поверят этой провокации, что запрягут себя в стан этих гадюк шипящих?

Нет и нет! Стремясь натравить на нас безсознательныя массы, враг не разсчитал и обнажил только свою грязную душенку.

Увы! — он еще не узнал всей остроты нашего оружия — так узнает!

Смерть провокаторам! Безпощадная смерть! На месте — без колебаний — всеми средствами и всяким оружием!

И всякий, кто — тайно или явно — будет поддерживать эту клевету, прикидываясь одураченным ягненком, — будет объявлен соучастником этой темной банды, будет объявлен провокатором. И постигнет их участь одна.

И всякий, кто — с нами или не с нами — но честно живет и борется, будет помогать нам в расправе, будет сам мстить этим ядовитым гадам подымающейся реакции.

Для расправы огня хватит у нас!

И все средства будут хороши!

Самарская Федерація Анархистов.

FROM THE SAMARA FEDERATION OF ANARCHISTS

ⴰⴰⴰⴰ

IN VIEW OF THE "DECREE"

The enemy is impotent. The enemy is sinking ever lower and lower. And in his fall he blasphemes. In his fall he slings mud at us. He stoops to the most hideous provocatory measures.

The enemy of the oppressed—he thirsts for domination. He fears the Anarchists who have raised high the banner of freedom.

The enemy is spreading malicious calumny, insinuating that our freedom includes violence and rape. In our name he is spreading with his own soiled hands the "Decree about the Nationalization of Women."

What crude, absurd provocation!

For ages, everywhere, the Anarchists have fought against all kinds of decrees and laws no matter by what authorities these were set up. How then can they themselves issue decrees?

Enemies of all violence, how can the Anarchists demand or even allow force in the treatment of women?

How many such asses will be found who will be ready to believe the provocateurs and who will appear in the camp of these serpents?

No, never! In his attempt to set against us the ignorant masses, the enemy did not calculate correctly and only exposed his own filthy soul.

Alas! he does not yet know the power of our weapon—but he will know it!

Death to the provocateurs! No mercy for them! On the spot—without hesitation—by all means, with any weapon!

And everyone, who—secretly or openly—supports this calumny, by pretending that he is an innocent lamb who has been duped by someone, will be considered an accomplice of this black band, as a provocateur. And they will meet the same fate.

Everyone—whether he be with us or not—but who lives honestly and struggles for his living, will help us dispense justice, and will himself mete out vengeance to these venomous reptiles of reaction.

We have enough fire for this purpose!

And all means will be fair!

Samara Federation of Anarchists.

(*This is the translation of the Russian text on opposite page.*)

309

Для успѣшной борьбы с надвигающеюся опасностью нѣмецкаго рабства и буржуазной кабалы необходимо весь сѣвер России НЕМЕДЛЕННО обезпечить ХЛѢБОМ!

Ко всему крестьянству хлѣбородных областей и губерний

БРАТЬЯ КРЕСТЬЯНЕ!

Дорогіе братья! Криком души мы, боевые революціонеры, обращаемся к Вам с этим призывом. Опомнитесь отъявленно! Бьет послѣдній час нашей рѣшительной битвы. Окончательно рѣшается вопрос: о закрѣпленіи передачи трудящимся земли без выкупа, фабрик, заводов и банков.

Шлите нам хлѣба, чтобы мы не были изнурены голодом и имѣли бы возможность крѣпко держать в своих руках винтовку против разбойников міра.

СОЦИАЛИСТИЧЕСКОЕ ОТЕЧЕСТВО В ОПАСНОСТИ

Хлѣба! Хлѣба! Хлѣба!

Ссыпайте хлѣб въ пустующіе элеваторы, в амбары и ссыпные пункты близ станцій желѣзных дорог и пристаней судоходных рѣк.

Наши желѣзныя дороги разрушены [...] продолжаются на них невѣроятным в сказочным безпорядкам. Трусы, мародеры и спекулянты, натянувши на плечи солдатскія шинели, чинят насилія на станціях желѣзных дорог и останавливают правильное движеніе поѣздов.

Сознательные и вѣрные революціи солдаты, крестьяне, и рабочіе! Мы призываем вас, оказывать содѣйствіе всѣм тѣм, кто охраняет наши желѣзныя дороги и препятствует хулиганам вмѣшиваться во внутренній распорядок их. Разрушеніем желѣзных дорог всѣ эти отбросы увѣнчат нашему защитнику врат—нѣмецкой буржуазіи и поэтому они—нѣ враги.

Хлѣба! Хлѣба! Хлѣба! Хлѣба!

To win the fight against the threatening danger of German slavery and bourgeois serfdom it is necessary to supply IMMEDIATELY all northern Russia with bread.

To the peasants of all the bread-producing districts and provinces

BROTHER PEASANTS!

Dear brothers: From the depths of our souls we, fighting revolutionists, appeal to you. ANSWER THE CALL! The last hour of the decisive battle strikes. This is the question at stake.

LAND TO THE TOILERS WITHOUT COMPENSATION, THE FACTORIES, SHOPS AND BANKS. Send us bread, that we may not be broken by hunger and that we may be able to hold up our bayonets against the cut-throats of the world.

THE SOCIALISTS FATHERLAND IS IN DANGER!

Bread!   Bread!   Bread!

Bring your bread to the empty elevators and granaries, to the shipping-points on railways and the wharves of navigable rivers.

Our railroads have broken down on account of unprecedented disorders. Cowards, marauders and speculators having put on soldiers' uniforms are doing violence at the railway stations and are thus hindering the regular movement of trains. True and class-conscious soldiers, peasants and workers of the Revolution! We appeal to you to aid those guarding our railways, and to stop the hooligans from further violence. All these destroyers of the railways are helping our bitter enemy—the German bourgeoise, and are therefore—without the law.

Bread!   Bread!   Bread!   Bread!

311

(This is the translation of the Russian text on opposite page.)